A RORSCHACH STUDY
OF CHILD DEVELOPMENT

A Rorschach Study
of Child Development

By NETTIE H. LEDWITH

Chief Psychologist
Pittsburgh Child Guidance Center

UNIVERSITY OF PITTSBURGH PRESS

Library of Congress Catalog Card Number: 60-8307

© 1960, University of Pittsburgh Press

Printed in the United States of America

PREFACE

THIS IS A BOOK which has been many years in the making. Only when one contemplates the years of data gathering, the years of trial of the data against clinical material, the years during which others than the author worked the basic normative data into their individual-istic Rorschach interpretive techniques, does one recognize the real imagination, the steadfastness of purpose, and monumental energy which went into this book.

There is no question that there is a very real need for this book. The basic Rorschach data gathered and previously published by Dr. Ledwith in following as many children as she did through prelatency, latency, and into the teenage period would stand on its own. (*Rorschach Responses of Elementary School Children,* Pittsburgh, 1959.) No one else has published as much material of this kind. Especially for one who has spent all of his efforts in dealing with adult Ror-schach material and always been puzzled by Rorschachs of younger children, the values which were laid out by Dr. Ledwith have served as a real anchor when a child's Rorschach came under consideration.

But these figures, useful as they are, perhaps would be only con-sulted by experts and by specialists. With the publication of this present volume many other workers are presented with a gold mine for dynamic understanding of the growth of children. That the Ror-schach material is the cohesive element which binds this material is obvious. But with the adding of information from other clinical sources and the adding of interview material an example is presented of the constant interplay which must go on between the recognition of the meaning of the Rorschachs and the other kinds of data which are available.

We grasp all the material better as we understand the children better; as the picture of the children come into clearer focus, we penetrate deeper into the more subtle meanings of the Rorschach protocols.

The writer of this Preface is of the opinion that the individual interpretive efforts of the various psychologists represented here are excellent. Perhaps he would disagree with details in the interpretations of some of the individual protocols. Certainly, his total approach would not be as some of the individual interpreters made it.

But it is in this very fact that much of real value lies. Individuals put their personal stamp on Rorschach interpretations. Some short-sighted "methodologists" have been critical of the technique for this reason. This collection shows not only the value of the individualistic approach, but clearly demonstrates very basic interpretive agreements in a disparate group of interpreters. Even for one who has always had faith in Rorschach's original experiment the concurrence of so much of the blind interpretation with the other known facts is at times startling. That stability of this kind shows through the individual styles represented demonstrates again the investigative potential of this tool.

The methodology pursued in presentation of the material seems to represent an almost ideal teaching approach. The raw data are given and are there for any student to work out his own solution of the problem. They are there for teachers to follow with him. In each instance, there is an admirably documented approach of another person to his solution of the material. Not only are his findings given, but the method arriving at these is given. For both teacher and student there is real learning potential in this.

Finally, documented clinical details are supplied to check interpretations. To my knowledge there is no other source book which permits this kind of student-teacher work. And certainly the ordinary individual protocols gathered in clinics do not offer the learning potential which is here represented. For here both isolated individual values and groupings and constellations of values can be followed through years of either stability or change.

Altogether Dr. Ledwith is to be congratulated for this work. That she had able collaborators and students is true. But her foresight, her devotion and especially personal qualities which drew these collaborators to work with her are apparent in every section of this book.

L. W. Earley, M.D.

Pittsburgh,
May 13, 1960.

ACKNOWLEDGMENTS

IT IS IMPOSSIBLE to acknowledge each individual source of help and encouragement that made possible the writing of this report on an investigation that extended through twelve years.

Appreciation is accorded many groups and individuals, foremost among whom are the members of the Staff and Board of Directors of the Pittsburgh Child Guidance Center, for their continued help and support through the years. Much credit for the successful outcome of the study should be given the principals, teachers, and parents of the children studied, without whose cooperation the personality pictures that appear in the following pages would be less complete. To the children themselves I want to express my gratitude for their continuous interest and enthusiasm. I have learned during the course of our association to think of them not as "subjects," but as friends and co-workers, and regret that they must remain anonymous.

Special recognition and appreciation go to the following people, whose ideas and efforts have helped to vitalize the subject matter of this book:

1. Mrs. Helen Harsha Cummings, a psychiatric social worker experienced in child guidance work, who, on visits to the homes of the children, interviewed their parents in regard to each child's background and development.

2. The following psychologists: Drs. S. Thomas Cummings, Pearl Butler Diana, Robert Drechsler, Roy Hamlin, David Lazovik, Harry Saslow, and Ed Speth, and Miss Dorothy Bender, whose "blind" interpretations of the children's Rorschachs have added convincing evidence to the validity of the personality pictures. Thanks as well as apologies go to a number of other psychologists whose interpretations could not be used because of lack of space.

3. Among the many psychologists who gave generously of their time and effort, Dr. Mary I. Elwood from the Pittsburgh Public

Schools deserves especial thanks for her continued constructive interest and her many important contributions to the study.

4. Dr. Joseph Cramer and Dr. Earl Loomis, psychiatrists, who interviewed individual children, making an evaluation of each child's personality structure.

5. The following psychiatrists: Drs. William Finzer, Ruth Kane, Tarlton Morrow, Naomi Ragins, John Reinhart, Marvin Shapiro, William Tobin, and Karla Walter, whose formulations of the dynamics of the personality development of individual children serve further to validate the effectiveness of the Rorschach in reflecting personality patterns.

My last but not least debt of gratitude is to Mrs. Katharine Zimmerman, whose untiring efforts in typing and retyping the manuscript and in taking care of routine matters, have made the preparation of this book a less tedious task than it might have been otherwise.

N. H. L.

December, 1959.

CONTENTS

PART I

New Gains Through Research on Personality Development

PART II

Eleven Representative Cases

PART III

Technical Aids to Clinicians and Researchers

New Gains

Through Research on

Personality Development

I : OVERVIEW

MORE THAN A DECADE AGO, in the testing of emotionally disturbed children at the Pittsburgh Child Guidance Center, it became apparent that we needed a technique whereby we could add more depth to the personality pictures of the children with whom we were dealing. An investigation of a variety of personality tests, including several projective techniques, resulted in the conviction that the Rorschach test offered the greatest potential for achieving the desired third dimension that I had previously found lacking in the test battery we routinely employed.

At that time, the Rorschach had been used widely and successfully with adults for more than twenty years. There were numerous reports in the literature on the use of the test with different types of people; there were discussions of how personality factors were revealed and personality structure determined by the responses given to this series of ten ink blots; there were, in addition, indications of the kinds of responses that could be expected from so-called "normal" adults. In need of just such information about children, I looked to the literature for help in interpreting the Rorschach responses of the disturbed children with whom I was working. I had hoped to find how normal children respond at different age levels; instead, I found that no such information had been published. Rather, there were indications that the establishment of these norms was considered of little importance. Challenged by this situation, and convinced of the value to be gained from these data, I decided to discover for myself what could be expected in the Rorschach protocols of normally functioning children.

Twelve years and many hundreds of Rorschachs later, I found myself with a wealth of data about 138 children who were studied longitudinally during the ages of six through eleven years. The original sample consisted of 160 six-year-olds chosen from thirty different school populations considered representative of the popula-

3

tion of Pittsburgh and surrounding Allegheny County. Every effort was made to stratify the sample of schools so that a fair representation of all socio-economic levels within the city and county would be selected.[1] The individual children—80 boys and 80 girls—were selected on the basis of chronological age, with six years and eight months arbitrarily chosen as the optimal age for first contact. This sample of children was representative of normally functioning children in the sense that they were in regular school attendance and had not been referred to any agency or institution because of emotional maladjustment.

Beyond the yearly Rorschach protocols, as much other data as possible were obtained about each child. Each year, one additional individual psychological test was administered: at year 6, the Revised Stanford-Binet Examination, Form L; at 7, the Goodenough Draw-a-Man test; at year 8, the Monroe Diagnostic Reading Examination; at year 9, the Grace Arthur Performance Test; at 10, the Wechsler Intelligence Scale for Children; and, at 11 years of age, the Human Figure Drawings. Added to this, there were psychiatric interviews, social histories taken at home, interviews with parents and teachers, follow-up interviews during adolescence, and, in a few cases, psychological testing of parents.

The objective findings or "norms" resulting from an intensive analysis of these data are published elsewhere [1] and have provided the answer to my original inquiries as to how normally functioning children respond to the Rorschach cards at different age levels. These "norms," however, can only hint at some of the valuable information gained from the material obtained during the study. All of the data described in the paragraph above are not available for every one of the 138 children retained in the sample, but the great variety of information about each child constitutes a rather extensive case history of each. While the norms (resulting from pooling the information on all the subjects at each age level) give weight to the aspects of personality development that "normal" children of a given age have in common, they obscure the very interesting and unique elements obvious in the individual cases. Each complete history provides a developmental portrait of the individual child: in each case, there are periods of acceleration and regression, periods of relative calm or relative stress, based upon the idiosyncratic environmental or consti-

[1] For further information see: *Rorschach Responses of Elementary School Children*, Nettie H. Ledwith, University of Pittsburgh Press, 1959.

tutional factors with which the child was forced to cope at that particular time. The emergence of various defense mechanisms can be noted as they arise. These, too, have unique qualities based on the particular need situation of the individual as well as upon how well they serve the ego as a means of resolving conflicts. Sometimes we see them drop out again when the stressful situation changes or if they prove to be unsuccessful mechanisms for helping the child.

In essence, what these case histories provide, when studied individually and in their entirety, is an excellent opportunity to view personality development at a depthful level, progressively—from year to year, as it emerges in complex interaction with the many elements present in the individual's life. Rather than the usual necessity of piecing together what "must have been," retrospectively, from the data we acquire on already-established patterns of behavior observed in older subjects, we have the objective data on hand as they occur, and can view the effects of various factors first-hand rather than in the subjectively weighted memory of the adult. Interestingly, the individual importance of events as against their objective significance can be observed. By this, I mean that in these progressive portraits, we often see environmental stresses taken in stride by the child despite our prediction that they will prove too much to deal with; or, we see seemingly minor difficulties casting long shadows over the entire future picture of the child as he matures. Here are experimentally collected data, obtained from each subject individually, which allows us to measure the relative weights of various factors connected with personality development. From a study of these cases, we may be able to predict, with much greater accuracy, the future adjustment of a given individual.

This last point is an important scientific stride. Until now, much fault has been found with the study of personality on the basis of its retrospective nature. That is, the variable is given great weight once we see the results and trace back to the cause. We do not know how significant it is until it is strong enough, seemingly, to influence the future course of the individual's adjustment. Worse still, than this science in reverse approach, we are forced to weigh the variable without accurate measures of it in the population as a whole—our data being based on the few clinical patients whom we are able to study intensively. This longitudinal study of a large normal sample is an unusual and invaluable opportunity to study these variables progressively, extensively, and at first hand. As we read through each case, such factors as rejecting homes, divided families, and strong disciplinary measures are seen in a clearer light as to their significance. We get an indication that, perhaps, the complex interaction of certain key variables is necessary to sow the seeds of adult personality difficulties, whereas, formerly, we were naive in assuming that certain key factors alone were sufficient.

One variable emerges as worthy of much greater attention than it has been given until now. It is interesting to note in these case histories the importance that vocational aims have in either magnifying or resolving adjustment difficulties. We have long been interested in the observed similarities among members of the same occupation or individuals with similar interests and ambitions; vocational guidance test batteries include interests tests in which the basic concept is that the client's interests should match those of successful individuals in the given field. Yet, knowing the importance of enjoying one's work as instrumental in bringing success, we have very little scientific evidence as to how these interests are generated or how we can experimentally control them.

To attack the problem from another point of view, Freudian theory has indicated that the displacement of energy into acceptable cultural goals, i.e., sublimation, is responsible for the achievements of mankind. Sublimation, as the ego's means of satisfying both inner needs and outer pressures, is the key to adequate adjustment. Here, again, the importance of vocational aims and the general ambitions of the individual are given first importance, theoretically, in aiding his fullest creative self-expression. They may be the resolving factor for his conflicts. On the other hand, if the individual is "displaced" personality-wise, in what he strives for as goals, these goals do not provide the outlets adequate to relieve the conflicts already generated and connected to his conscious pursuits.

The interests and goals, then, of the individual are depthfully involved with the other facets of the individual and are complexly determined by many environmental and constitutional factors intricately attached to the ego itself. They are of great importance in aiding or hindering the individual's total adjustment. Yet, very little has been done to study intensively the way in which sublimations emerge in the developing personality or to study the factors denying the individual this means of conflict-resolution. The progressive case histories gathered in our study throw much light on the problem. Verification of the importance of adequate cultural goals as well as data giving depth to our heretofore vague concepts of why common interests yield more probability of success (and, therefore, an additional satisfaction) is evident as one reads through each individual story. We get an intensive look at the individual needs and individual social pressures that must be dealt with in arriving at these future life-courses. We also can note and investigate the development of malad-justments—discrepancies among needs, abilities, and goals. This important aspect of the adult's real and fantasy life with its relation-ship to the ego has long demanded more attention. "What does he want?" and "Why?", as well as "How can we alter his needs or de-sires so that they are more in keeping with what is attainable?" are questions of fundamental importance in psychotherapy. Here we seem to have much empirical data that may answer these questions and improve our techniques for handling this problem.

One more fundamental concept of personality theory has been widely evident in clinical reports but only rather vaguely extended as to its existence and importance in the population as a whole. This is the extent to which the defense mechanisms are utilized by the indi-vidual. Again, in psychotherapy, breaking them down because of their obvious inadequacy in adjustment is an established technique; and subsequent re-establishment of firmer props to support the ego is an essential of the therapy process. We recognize that the enlight-ened use of displacement, identification, and so forth, is always nec-essary to adequate cultural adjustment of the individual, but we attempt to remove his repressions as basic causal factors for his anxi-ety and inadequate defenses. Theoretically at least, the less repression the greater the adequacy of adjustment. Substantiation of this princi-ple, since it is such a guidepost to present therapeutic techniques, de-pends on our investigating and measuring the limits of the principle. Does optimal adjustment, regardless of whether it exists in any given individual or not, entail no repression whatsoever? And does the most distorted individual contain the most repression? To what ex-tent are projection, reaction formation, etc. utilized by those whom we look upon as "normal" in the sense that they function adequately in society and manage, to a considerable degree, to give expression to their fullest potentialities? To give needed scientific status to our present theories and improve our present probability of success in psychotherapy, the answers to these questions, and techniques for more adequate measurement devices are necessary. Until now, despite the fact that many therapists will agree to the necessity of examining our basic principles experimentally, very little of scientific value has been done in this direction. One important reason for this has been our lack of "normal" subjects whom we can subject to the long-term depth analysis of their personality structure—a necessity if we are to establish more rigid criterion measures. Another has been our necessarily scanty and retrospective information on the development of this structure. These 138 individual portraits of developing egos studied over a long period of time and in depth give us the rare but necessary opportunity we have been hoping for. These case histories provide much invaluable information for theorists and therapists alike.

The general comments above are just part of what can be gained from a study of some of these longitudinal data. The uniqueness of each individual, the great variety that the personality patterns assume, and the individual variations in rate of development from age to age must be studied case by case. Beyond the contributions to developmental psychology and personality theory, much of value to the child therapist emerges. One significant element is the fact that, within this non-clinical sample, there are many instances where a child is at one age accelerated and at another retarded in relation to the norms of psychosexual development. This should suggest to the therapist dealing with children that repeated testings are necessary, with periods of time intervening between them, to estimate adequately the abnormally immature development or pathological regression in a given instance. In addition, a better estimate of the effects of therapy can be obtained by him once he has acquired more developmental information on the expected growth with age in a large population of children not treated clinically. He may also note that the emergence of certain neurotic defenses does not necessarily imply their perpetuation, even where guidance does not intervene. What factors are necessary for their dropping out "naturally"? Are there clues the therapist can discover for aiding their disappearance where his help is necessary? Extracting the pertinent variables from case histories of adaptive development can add speed and accuracy to his work with patients who have not been able to accomplish this without his help.

Thus we see, that what started out as a means of adding scope to a preliminary test battery at the clinic, has yielded much broader information than we had hoped. Our immediate goal was realized and the norms have already been of great value to us in child guidance work. But to put aside the data at this point would mean wasting much more important information, essential to the very bases upon which our clinical work is established. It is for our benefit that an analysis of the content of each case is persuasively indicated; it is also greatly to the benefit of all those interested in developmental psychology or adult therapy. Even our techniques and what we have learned along the way in terms of research procedure may implement future, much-needed research. This book is written with the hope of aiding those working in the fields now as well as stimulating new and further research in this important area.

II : THE RORSCHACH AS A
RESEARCH TOOL

IN THE BEGINNING of Chapter I, we mentioned several other kinds of data besides the Rorschach protocols that were collected from each child. These other data—as extensive as possible in each case—have been quite commonly collected not only by psychologists but also, to a certain extent, by educational researchers working with children. Roughly, it cover the topic of 1) family history and biographical data, 2) objective growth data—health, etc., 3) school history—I.Q., achievement tests, and teachers' reports, and 4) reports from the child himself, about his interests, problems, family relationships, and anything else personally significant to him. Educational and psychological journals are replete with both longitudinal and normative data on these subjects. Even the observational reports of clinicians based on sampling the behavior of children under either free or experimentally structured circumstances have been published. Why is it then that we had only rather sterile personality pictures of "normal" children—two-dimensional photographs rather than depthful portraits of structured, integrated individuals?

The answer, of course, seems to lie in the previous lack of projective personality technique systematically added to the other measurement devices used. Quite apparently, the Rorschach serves the function of giving structure and depth to the other observations in the present study. In the case histories of Part II, the role of the Rorschach is clearly revealed as essential in giving our data a richness and dynamic quality heretofore lacking in developmental reports. While the other variables observed and measured are necessary in attaining a total picture of the individual, the Rorschach seems to tie them together in their *weighted* significance to the individual. It also seems to point up the way in which all factors, constitutional and environmental, that impinge upon the person interact and are incorporated by the ego in

10

such a way that the observed behavior appears integrated and pur- posive. By adding this depth tool to our research battery, we seem to have greatly increased the level of predictive significance we have strived for in the past.

The Rorschach protocols of these children seemed to point up their individuality right from the beginning. With the gathering of the first data at age six, it was clear that the group was not just an abstract sample of boys and girls giving Rorschach protocols to be analyzed according to age, sex, and intelligence levels; rather, it consisted of distinctly individual persons showing a large variety of patterns and many variations in rate and stage of personality development. As the study continued from year to year, the protocols revealed the answers to such questions as: 1) What type of personality structure does the child have? 2) What is the predominant stage of the child's current psychosexual development? 3) What are the sources of his anxiety? 4) How does the child deal with his anxiety? 5) What sort of peer relationships does he have? 6) How does he feel toward parental figures? 7) What is the *potential* level of his intelligence? and 8) How near this level is the child functioning? These empirical data, used in conjunction with the other information about the child, seem to hold the key to the understanding of all our observations and their integration into one recognizable individual person.

One may question the basis for our judgment of the Rorschach re- sults. What means of validation for our interpretations did we use? It is, of course, true that a level of inference beyond the actual verbal statements made about each card is integral to the use of this projec- tive technique. In order to validate empirically the Rorschach interpre- tations, interviews with parents and teachers were used and the verbal data from these reports were compared to our results. Additionally, clinical observations by psychiatrists as well as the other psychological test data we had available were used for comparison. As one may ob- serve in studying the cases reported here, this material bears out and is consistent with the "blind" interpretations of the Rorschach ana- lysts. Follow-up interviews with the subjects several years after the termination of the study provide evidence of the predictive validity of the interpreters' comments on the direction the subjects' behaviors will take in the future. The accuracy with which the interpretations of skilled clinicians tend to reflect both the present behavior, attitudes, and general developmental stage through which each child is passing (as well as the future predicted course of development) is weighty evidence of the Rorschach's effectiveness.

The technique of "blind" interpretation is one which has its greatest use in research where the reliability and validity of the Rorschach itself is to be investigated. These interpretations in this study are "blind" in the sense that the clinicians making them knew only the sex and Binet I.Q. of the child whose protocols they were interpreting. Other than these two facts, the Rorschach protocols stood alone as the sources of information about the personality structure of each individual; and the accuracy of the clinicians' observations can be attributed only to the combined effects of the test as an accurate measurement device and the skill of the clinician in using it. In an attempt to control this second variable, only interpreters with two or more years experience with children's Rorschachs were used. It seems scientifically clear, therefore, that our results provide validating evidence for the Rorschach itself.

Since several clinicians were used to cover the large number of protocols needing interpretation from 138 subjects, each was asked to cover certain key areas of interpretation so that consistency from case to case could be maintained. These specified areas were: personality structure, source of anxiety, defenses against anxiety, peer relationships, attitude toward parents, identification, and prognosis for future development. These areas also provide uniform and consistent points of reference for comparing the Rorschach interpretation with other data about each child.

While clinicians themselves differ as to the method they prefer to use in interpreting the Rorschach, the technique of strictly "blind" interpretation such as was used in this study seems to have its greatest utility in improving the interpretive skill of the clinician (by allowing him minimal cues beyond the protocol upon which to base his inferences) or in experimentation which centers about the reliability or validity of the Rorschach test itself. Under clinical circumstances, where all possible aids to personality assessment are warranted in order to deal effectively with the problem at hand, it would seem advisable to combine the results of all tests and observations so that cross-inferences can be drawn. In the cases that follow, you will note that this has been done in order that the fullest possible portraits of each subject be presented.

The value of the Rorschach is evident. In each case, at the very least, it substantiates and gives added weight to certain "clinical observations" made on the basis of the other data. At most, it points up features not obvious from the other data, but significant to the total picture. It is worth considering that part of its effectiveness lies in the fact that *more* objectivity is possible where it is included as a source of information about the subject. Strange as this statement may seem at first glance, its significance is clarified by noting that, by the use of the Rorschach, we get below the social overlay that is an inherent part of all our other sources of information about the individual. Distortions that are difficult to assess adequately are inherent in the verbal information from all other sources because of the effects of past learning upon the informer; here, with the Rorschach, we are given the opportunity to remove this "protective" layer and can glimpse the pertinent variables in the perspective they seem to hold relative to the observed behaviors of the individual. The Rorschach test, as the added ingredient to the investigation of personality development, has given us a "wholeness" to the picture and an ability to add scientific control and prediction to personality study.

III : AN INTRODUCTION TO
THE CHILDREN

OUR TWOFOLD PURPOSE in writing this book is, first, to provide a learning device for those interested in an intensive study of the development of personality, and, second, to stimulate research further into the areas that are pointed up in these cases as being potentially fruitful to researchers in human behavior. While the two preceding chapters have attempted to provide a synthesis of some of our major findings and hypotheses stimulated by all the material gathered in the study, it is necessary to present the actual data collected in order to substantiate our general comments and provide the richness for the reader which we have said is evident to us as we study the cases one by one.

Limitations of space make it virtually impossible to present all 138 cases, and the choice of a few as representative was a difficult one to make. Each child in the study showed unique and interesting variations in his developmental process which captured our attention and would be of interest value to the reader. However, in concurrence with the generally accepted hypothesis that native endowment and environmental conditions are two important factors that interact with each other, albeit in a myriad of devious ways, toward the development of personality traits, an attempt was made to select children differing from one another in the physical and mental attributes that are considered hereditary, and also differing in environmental experiences of socio-economic, racial, religious, or cultural nature. With this idea in mind, differences in physique, physical appearance, in intellectual status and other characteristics that are generally accepted as hereditary were taken into consideration; and such environmental factors as relationship between parents, size of family, ordinal position in family, race, religion, socio-economic and educational status of family, type of school attended by the child—were likewise

14

considered. In this way a variety of combinations of the two general factors, heredity and environment, was included within the group of children with whom the reader will soon become acquainted. The end result of the great variety of hereditary and environmental factors is individualization; and it is the development of the individuality or idiosyncratic aspects of each child which is a major theme of this book. The Rorschach is one way of pointing out and emphasizing this within the framework of factors common to all human beings.

Eleven children—six girls and five boys—are presented in Part II of this book. In each case, as much material as possible is included about each child so that the portraits can be as complete as possible. Each Rorschach protocol as well as the "blind" interpretation of it is presented as a means of allowing the reader to see the actual bases upon which personality assessment and prognosis were made. This, and all other information about the child are interwoven developmentally year by year during the collection of the data. Follow-up reports are given so that we can evaluate the validity of the interpreters' predictions. We have also tried to emphasize certain interesting points for speculation as to their individual importance in the given case as they present themselves. The reader is invited to add his own, based on his study of these children.

Part II is divided into eleven chapters, with the available information on a given child and interpretive comments based on this constituting each chapter. In order that the reader may have a means of appreciating the diversification of hereditary and environmental variables that these cases represent, a short introduction to each child is included here.

The first case to be presented is that of *Larry,* a healthy, attractive, intelligent boy, reared in a middle-class home where considerable thought was given his development. One of the subtle but important factors to be noted because of its influence on his personality development is the effect that a strong mother figure has had on this male child.

Patty is a girl of barely average intelligence whose early years were fraught with instability in the home situation and with the need for her to assume a great deal of responsibility within the family. Neither the lack of a comfortable family income nor the lack of watchful planning on the part of parents seems to have prevented Patty from achieving a personality structure that might well be envied by many children of greater intellectual endowment, and living in seemingly more favorable environmental conditions.

Phillip, whose case history is given in the third chapter, is a boy whose tragic physical liabilities present at birth and continually increasing, are, therefore, necessarily major factors of influence on the structure of his personality. His terrific, although perhaps unconscious, struggles to effect a fair, but adequate, adjustment afford us an opportunity to study a child who must accommodate experiences that few children are required to face.

Adele is an only child of upper middle class parents whose own immaturities and adjustive problems greatly influence her development. Perhaps her greatest aids to potential stability for herself have been her own high intelligence and the fact that these parents, so involved in their own emotional needs, have allowed her a good deal of freedom to make use of her resources.

From this case of an only child, the reader proceeds to a study of *Edgar,* one of four children born to a well-to-do family. Here, where it is difficult to discriminate strong adverse factors from the case material obtained. the Rorschach protocols provide the basis upon which Edgar's later manifestations of poor adjustment can be detected early and be more clearly understood. It is through these protocols as well, that we are best able to hypothesize the environmental circumstances leading to his difficulties.

Molly, a Negro child of very low intelligence, is an amazing example of a person whose present contentment seems startling in the light of the many difficult barriers she must cross. Her native endowments and home environment leave much to be desired, but she has achieved her limited ambitions and appears, by this device, to have resolved many of her early problems.

Allan is a boy whose potentially high intelligence functions at an increasingly low level as he progresses through the many difficult environmental circumstances that confront him, and for which he is given little emotional support. His overtly quiet appearance belies the extent of the anxiety displayed in his Rorschach responses as this boy develops through the years.

Eileen, like Allan, lacks the emotional support of an accepting mother; and the way in which she arrives at the path that she is presently pursuing is intricately involved with her personalized needs as manifested in her Rorschachs. She never resolves her strong dependency needs, but for the present, she seems to have found a source of strength through which she can utilize her potentialities.

In the next chapter, the reader is introduced to *Danny,* a boy of average intelligence whose early problems centered mainly around a frustrated mother who planned his every move in an effort to realize her own former ambitions through him. Fortunately, there are increasing indications through the years that he has been able to resolve many of the conflicts set up by this circumstance.

When the obvious assets and liabilities for a good personality adjustment are carefully balanced, *Anna* is, no doubt, "in the red." This child was reared from the age of six in an institution for dependent children, but the adjustment she has made speaks well for her innate characteristics, as well as for her early family relationships, both of which evidently have helped to see her through many unhappy situations.

The final case to be presented, stands out as the most detailed and comprehensive. *Amy* is a child of unusually high intelligence who has been studied intensively since birth. The wealth of interesting data on her early years is much more extensive than is generally found anywhere in the literature, as are the yearly reports obtained along with the Rorschach protocols.

The individuality of each child based on the interaction of various hereditary and environmental factors becomes evident when the case studies are surveyed. The important part that the Rorschach data have had in reflecting the personality development and individuality of these children is an outstanding characteristic of Part II and cannot be overestimated.

PART : II ————————————————

Eleven

Representative

Cases

IV : LARRY

THE STORY OF LARRY'S LIFE and background during his preschool years has been obtained mostly from his mother. Both his parents are professional people with successful careers, one in the field of education, the other in science. Mother gave up her college teaching position at marriage and has since devoted herself to her home and children. She subtly, perhaps unconsciously, presents herself as the more understanding of the two parents, and one gets the impression in talking with her that she is also the more controlling of the two. Father seems to be less outgoing than she; even his interests outside of work are of an introverted nature, such as a collection of early American glass. Both parents were in their middle thirties when they married and Larry was born when the mother was thirty-seven years old. He has a sister five years younger than he.

There were no pregnancy or delivery difficulties reported and Larry was breastfed for his first nine months, with gradual weaning to the cup. He is described in infancy as "just too good," "a jolly, giggly baby, who did very little crying, appearing happy and content." He was responsive to attention but apparently made no protests when this was withdrawn. Mother expressed revulsion of "dirty pants" and, therefore, began toilet training at five months of age, "before he could sit up." She estimated that he was dry day and night by about fourteen months. There was no regression after control.

By the time Larry walked alone, at fourteen months, he was already saying many words. He was a "happy-go-lucky child, never bothered too much by anything." His mother described him as greeting all new situations with a great amount of enthusiasm. Beginning in preschool years, he has spent every summer on a farm in another state where the parents formerly lived. In the early years, his parents accompanied him and the activity on the farm provided great enter-

21

tainment for him throughout his childhood. He continued a close feeling of friendship for the older couple who own the farm.

At home during the winter months, Larry was never any trouble. He was able to amuse himself and got along well with the other children in the neighborhood. He indicated no undue reaction at the birth of his sister.

It was shortly after her birth that he entered kindergarten in the same private school that he attended throughout his elementary school experience. He greeted this experience with his usual enthusiasm and interest, and got along well with both children and teachers there. Larry made the same easy transition to first grade the following year.

Our first contact with Larry came when he was six and a half years old and had been in the first grade for two or three months. At that time, he was a handsome blond boy, tall for his age, unusually talkative and using an extensive vocabulary. The teacher reported that he "learns quickly, but one idea may start him thinking or talking along another line, and then his mind wanders far from the thing at hand. He is a happy child in the schoolroom, laughing much, enthusiastic and often bursting into talk. He is full of fun and trickery. He loves to play tricks on the other boys, but sometimes his tricks are a little beyond their understanding. Just so, his conversation is often beyond the understanding of his contemporaries." His teacher had the impression of a little boy with a good mind who had been much with grownups and subjected to a technical conversation. "Yet in play, he is just a normal boy who loves the companionship of other boys. He is a leader, even to plotting against rival leaders for supremacy in school activities."

In the testing situation, Larry was interested, cooperative, and even enthusiastic. It was felt, however, that the anxiety factors noted clinically, as well as in the test material, tended to impair his functioning. Even so, the intelligence test results indicated very superior intelligence. Larry's drawings at this time portrayed two houses—one a tall, garish structure with an almost bare tree on one side. This house was where "people were visiting in the daytime." On the other side of the paper was a gaily-colored house surrounded by a black background where "they came home to their house in the dark." People were not pictured.

His Rorschach responses at this time were as follows:

Larry's Rorschach Protocol at the Six Year Level

Performance	Inquiry
I 8" 1. A big piece of rock that somebody has made a face out of— a kind of face—cat's face.	1. (Why rock?) Because it's black and has lots of out-pieces that stick out overhanging.
2. Men's faces are sticking from ears.	2. Mouth, chin—wears his cap like me with forepiece up. Q. Looks like a mountain climber.
45"	
II 7" 1. It looks like Mickey Mouse.	1. Feet, face, ears stick up. Q. He's running toward me.
2. A little bit of red sun showing.	2. Under here and it's red.
18"	
III 3" 1. Two monkeys or two possums sitting on a little rock and they are playing something. Don't you see how it's made?	1. Rock is black. Monkey is black. This is a table and they're eating.
30" Their face and feet.	a. Red sun is showing.
IV 3" 1. Face. (Lower D.)	1. Eyes, nose, neck. Q. Animal.
8"	a. Backbone of some animal I saw at the museum.
V 4" 1. An insect.	1. That's a bird—it has things here—wings, feet. Q. In the sky —the sky really should be blue.
8"	
VI 2" 1. Insect sitting on top —and	1. And the bone goes right here. Q. Flying in the air.
17" 2. They dug it out of the rock.	
VII 3" 1. Two monkeys sitting on top of	1. Little caps up here, tail, legs, go right down there.
2. A rock	
1. (Contd.) Looking at each other, playing	
18" some kind of game.	
VIII 8" 1. Looks like two bears —let me see, two camels or lions walking	
31" 2. Up the mountain.	

Performance	*Inquiry*
IX 6″ 1. Oh, it looks like a cave. 12″	1. Right in there—it looks like the bear cave in the Carnegie Museum.
X That the last one? 7″ 1. Some bones. 12″	1. Some bones of an enormous fish —has so many parts and hitched together in so many different ways.

The following "blind" interpretation of Larry's first Rorschach was made by the same child psychologist who interpreted the five succeeding ones:

"Intelligence seems to be at work in this six and a half year old boy, as shown by the organizational activity, differential approach to his environment, as well as the degree and accuracy of reality bound perception. There is a sensitivity to the environment, perhaps resulting from a realistic encounter with the burdens of acculturation experienced in school. This appears to have a tempering effect upon the usually egocentric pattern of relationships characteristic of this age. Accompanying this feature in the child's development is a capacity to give expression in a rather comfortable fashion to his impulses. Possibly, this might even be expressed in a rather independent self-assured fashion. While relating well to his peers, he is apt to want to lead.

"A masculine identification appears with a certain awe or healthy respect for male authority. A defensive struggle is not too active and the usual degree of repression seems to be quite successful. In face of threat, there is a slight tendency to isolate, but judgment is not adversely affected. Threat appears to stem from father, and with the cave responses and bone responses as content, might suggest that an oedipal situation is the possible source of anxiety."

What the interpreter did not know, of course, was that the father is a geologist and that this fact is further verification of Larry's attempt, in the use of such content as rocks, stones, and caves to identify with his father. That some resolution of the oedipal conflict has been made at this age and that Larry is not beset by undue rivalry with his younger sister is attested to by his masculine identification, his enjoyment of peer relationships, and his ability to take initiative and compete for leadership. His evident anxiety, which is interpreted as stemming from an oedipal situation, may have additional sources. For example, his drawings of the austere "daytime house" and the gaily colorful but black surrounded "come-home-in-the-dark-to house" suggest a "businesslike" or "visiting like" reality relationship with mother which is in conflict with his wish for more warmth and perhaps more freedom to regress, the latter being seen in the black background as dangerous or unacceptable. Larry's response to Card VII gives further indication of the mother-son relationship at this time—"monkeys playing a game."

The presence of only two populars in the record of such a bright child, indicating less conformity in thinking than is usually present at this age, is another suggestion of Larry's less than adequate functioning. Although Larry's anxiety persists, fluctuates in intensity, and is mildly jeopardizing at various times, it is generally compatible with growth and the boy is able to handle it with non-pathological defenses.

A year later, when seen at age seven and a half in the same school setting, Larry had changed little in appearance. He greeted the examiner cordially and was both interested and cooperative during the testing period. At this time, his second grade teacher saw him as outgoing, active, and slightly advanced in his school achievement. Larry expressed his feelings about school as, "It's fun after you really get started in school—it wasn't much fun in the first grade." His talkativeness was not as pronounced as the year before, but there was a tendency for him to stutter.

His drawing of a man comprised a poorly-shaped trunk, with a hat above, but not connected to the head. Arms were closely adjacent to the trunk, with hands and five fingers carefully drawn. Legs, in the proper position but not joined to the trunk, ended in large, boat-like feet, both pointed in the same direction. The facial features, as well as body structure, gave the general appearance of a clown. The suggestion of insecurity seen in the details of this poorly executed drawing, Larry's stuttering, and his desire to stay with the examiner in an accepting one-to-one relationship, together are suggestive of conflict in the dependent-independent area. There was, however, no indication of this anxiety having a noticeably crippling effect on his functioning. His Rorschach responses were as follows:

Larry's Rorschach Protocol at the Seven Year Level

Performance	*Inquiry*
I 12″ 1. It's a formation of rock.	1. Out in the mountains. Color of rock and rough like rock and formed like rock—like the mouth of a cave.
22″	

Performance	*Inquiry*
II 16″	Well, it looks like a . . . a . . .	
	1. Mouth of a cave. (Stutters—told of living in a cave. Told of his father's work).	1. Right in there.
III 6″	1. Formation of rock or something that is carved in rock.	1. Statutes—they are men cooking or something. They are sitting down.
15″		
IV 8″	Umm.	
	1. That kinda looks like a sort of a face carved out of rock.	1. Eyes. (Stutters). Mouth closed. Like a saber-toothed tiger. (S). Teeth. I haven't found any nose —it's probably in here. I don't know whether you'll have me next year. This school is expensive.
16″		
V 4″	1. That looks like a butterfly.	1. That's the easy one. Q. Flying in the air. Here are his feet and here's little hairs growing off his head and here are his wings.
9″		
VI 6″	1. Formation of rock— no, I mean some kind of a skin opened up. For instance, I'll say a tiger skin. I don't know much about that.	1. These are his whiskers and these are shaped like his feet. Q. Shaping of it.
28″		
VII 14″	1. That looks like some rock just about to fall down—it's had so much wear.	1. Q. See how little that is? Q. It's so thin all over.
26″	How do you make this?	
VIII 7″	1. Looks like some kind of skeleton of somebody.	1. Like for his bones and here are his ribs.
	2. Last year I remember saying these look like two animals climbing	2. Yes, they look like animals but the legs are so short. Animals couldn't walk on that.
	3. Up the hill.	
	2. (contd.) They would be like that if one foot wasn't so short.	
56″		
IX	It's fun when you get started in school. It	

Performance	Inquiry
wasn't much fun in first grade.	
22″ I don't know.	
I can't find out anything that that would look like.	I just don't know that one.
X 4″ 1. That looks like a whole lot of insects	a. There are two spiders.
	b. And some bugs.
20″ 2. Over some blood.	

The "blind" interpretation of this second Rorschach is reprinted verbatim:

"At the age of seven and a half, Larry appears considerably more anxious than on the previous examination. His defenses, in addition to increased repression, include isolation, denial and reaction formation. However, this occurs without an appreciable effect on his perceptual accuracy or reality contact. The over-all effect is one of constriction with some regression in terms of his relationships, perhaps being a little more demanding.

"The increased concern with the insides of caves and the perseveration of rock responses, which earlier had faces in them, suggest that the increase in anxiety may be due to an oedipal conflict becoming more severe. The fears of castration implicit in such a conflict now appear and have an oral tinge to them. There is ever so slight a possibility that a certain degree of caution or suspiciousness may also be operative in this boy's behavior at the present time."

Larry's constriction noted in the interpretation tended to give him a superficially less anxious clinical appearance than the Rorschach indicated. His somewhat brittle defenses are broken through with the stuttering, which appeared twice in the Rorschach—both times in connection with the father figure. His hostility toward and resulting fear of father are real sources of anxiety. At the same time, he sees mother "falling down" in her support of him, so that another source of anxiety is the lack of emotional sustenance which he needs so badly at this time. It would appear from the record that his productive efforts are still falling short of this potential and that much of his psychic energy is going into the defense against these anxiety-producing situations. Since he was so well able to deny these conflicts to himself, and thus to hide them from others, only the Rorschach could have pin-pointed them at this time.

It was about this time that Larry became aware that he was attending the private school at a real sacrifice to the parents. The parents were emphasizing the fact that his continuation in this school depended upon a good school performance. Evidently there was pressure from the teacher as well. It was not until the following year, however, when Larry could look back in retrospect to his second grade experience, that he was able to express a dislike of this teacher: "If you're one of the good ones and made even a little mistake, she tried to make you feel bad."

Thus, a certain sense of insecurity and consequent anxiety arises from the feeling that security, rewards and acceptance require continuous high-level production and assumption of responsibilities. Becoming more uneasy about his performance and adequacy, and feeling unable to turn to his parents for comfort, he has resorted to stuttering and clings to the examiner whom he sees as a kindly, accepting adult.

A year later, at the age of eight and a half, Larry was again delighted to see the examiner and expressed his pleasure about the things he was asked to do. He was eager to talk on this occasion and the tendency to stutter, while still noticeable, was not as pronounced as the year before. He mentioned his enjoyment of reading, saying that he had read to his little sister so much that he had memorized the stories. He seemed quite comfortable in the achievement test situation and demonstrated that he was more than a year advanced in his school achievement.

There was no enthusiasm noted in his response to the Rorschach cards, however. In fact, there were a few overt signs of boredom and dislike during this performance, despite the fact that he was polite and cooperative.

Larry's Rorschach Protocol at the Eight Year Level

Performance	*Inquiry*
I Sighs. "Well."	1. 1. Mouth, teeth, ears and here's
30" 1. Looks something like the skull of a cat. (Looks at examiner).	his nose and this is just some shaggy fur.
2. I see those two little things but I don't know what that would be—some kind of a little animal.	2. (upper d)

Performance	*Inquiry*
3. These could be a man's head.	3. (side d)
75″ That's all I can see.	

II 15″   Look.

1. Looks like two bears with their noses together and I wouldn't know what that red part would be—maybe they could be fighting and

2. The red stuff would be blood—that's all I could see.

(Looks on back of card).

That's eleven. Oh, no, that's Roman numer-
41″   als.

1. Noses are together. These red spots are where they are bleeding—some is coming out of their heads.

III 10″ 1. That could be some barbers washing their hands or just plain men washing their hands. (Looks out the window while examiner completes record-
40″   ing).

1. Trousers, necks, tight necks, heads and here's the wash basin, and what made me think of barbers was because their wash basins are in the middle of shops and one on one side and one on another.

IV 7″ 1. I would say this was a piece of rock, though I would say that for all of them because that is what they all look like.

2. The middle part looks something like the in-side of a person's
31″   body.

1. High and mountains of rock—have lots like hangover.

2. Right in here—like jut-outs and things like that.

V 2″ 1. A bat. Looks like a dragon fly or any thing like that.

I guess this is the easiest one.

I would say a butter-fly or bat.

Looks like he's been

1. Up in the air. He's flying. Been in a fight. Wings are torn.

Performance	*Inquiry*
34″	in a fight—his wings are sort of shaggy.	
VI 6″	(Laughs).	1. There's his legs. Has quite a nose and has whiskers, I think, and his face is quite a bit wider than his nose.
	1. That looks something like a fox with all his whiskers. It's a rug. He's lying on the floor with insides out —head isn't cut off. Laying on the floor in	
39″	front of fire.	
VII	This one is a hard one.	
	1. Looks like some people dancing on	1. Both girls.
30″	2. A rock.	
VIII 10″	(Smiles). Ummm.	1. Maybe fox.
	1. That looks like some bears walking up something very colorful and steep and two animals that are red are walking up	
	2. Mountains, if there are any that colorful.	
IX	(Blows as if he doesn't like it, but)	
22″	1. Well, this looks like it's on green grass. There's been a fight.	a. That could be under the sea —lots of seaweed. What gave me that impression is this in here (middle).
	2. There's a little red blood left over here and on this side it's been out in the open	
40″	and it's yellow.	
X 5″	1. Well, it looks like a lot of insects and that's all it looks like.	1. In a flower garden.
	2. Two spiders.	2. (P)
	3. Two beetles.	3. (upper gray)
	4. Two tomato worms.	4. They're green and long.
	5. Flowers, yellowish	
30″	and red and blue.	

The following is the psychologist's "blind" interpretation of this record:

"At the age of eight and a half years, ambivalent feelings, especially in relationship to mother, are now suggested in the Rorschach protocol. This is most apparent from the content. Aggression comes into play where caves were seen on the previous Rorschachs. There is a mixture of sexual urges and aggressive urges involved in his close interpersonal relationships, which, while they make him anxious, the aggressive feelings now are more openly expressed. He appears to accept himself more spontaneously. If he has siblings, perhaps he is more aggressive towards them. Accompanying a more open expression of his feelings has come a clearer representation of his fears of castration. Defense by repressive measures appears quite adequate and not constrictive. The use of more primitive defenses of isolation and denial do not appear as frequently as in former years. Energy is more readily available for dealing with the environment, including attention to intellectual pursuits."

Larry's Rorschach responses at this age are certainly more productive than on previous occasions, as noted in the increase in number of responses and an increase in good form. More conformity of thinking is noted in the increase of populars. That the "blind" interpretation has connected his "cave" responses with the mother figure is understandable, but it would seem in Larry's case that the aggressive hostile feelings noted in connection with these responses are directed against father. If anything, there appears to be a slight improvement in his relationship to mother.

There were a number of indications in Larry's behavior around this period that he was much more mature than a year ago. That family relationships have become more positive and less anxiety-provoking was manifested in his seeming acceptance of family standards and values. The high level of achievement expected from parents and teachers seems to have been accepted as his own expectation, and is employing his wholehearted energies. Here his excellent capacities serve him well. A less able child might find the burden too great and become discouraged and distressed as a result of failing to earn the acceptance and rewards which undoubtedly attend the intellectual and social achievement which he is now experiencing.

By nine and a half years of age, Larry had grown into a tall, almost adolescent-appearing blond boy—most agreeably polite and pleasant. He asked intelligent questions about the research project and seemed genuinely interested in the answers. Despite obvious restlessness which made it difficult for him to remain seated throughout the testing hour, he achieved as high a rating on the Grace Arthur performance material as he had achieved on the more verbal Binet examination at age six and a half. There is no doubt but that Larry is a very intelligent boy, functioning well—although not up to capacity—in both verbal and performance areas. He appeared somewhat bored with the Rorschach cards but was cooperative and even persistent in giving responses to each card.

Larry's Rorschach Protocol at the Nine Year Level

		Performance	Inquiry
I	9″	Uh, ah.	
		1. These look like birds with (d) funny notches on top of their head.	1. Bird's head.
		2. Altogether it looks like a cat with ears bent back—bent to the side. Cat looks kinda rocky color. The cat or its head has two little bumps that look like	2. (WS) Grayish black.
		3. Two little animals. Look like dogs.	3. (d) Just the head.
	78″	4. Two little bumps that like mountains.	4. (d).
II	8″	1. That looks something like an explosion, the bottom part. (D)	1. Stuff flying up in the air.
		2. The top part looks like a woman sticking her feet up and she has red socks.	2. Just the feet.
		3. The rest looks a little like ant-eaters but more like bears with noses together.	3. Bears.
	73″	4. Looks like the entrance to a cave. I guess that's about all.	4. Right in here.
III	7″	(Laughs)	
		1. This reminds me of	

Performance   *Inquiry*

two poss . . . no,
coons in suits. They
are bowing to each
other and are wash-
ing their hands at
46″ 2. Two separate bowls.

IV 4″ 1. That looks something
like an octopus and it
—let's see. Here's the
top part of head.

         2. Looks like bones in   2. Marking in there (at first forgot
the front here (rubs   where he saw it).
his chest).
Your chest bones.

         3. Something that looks   3. (dd at bottom). Just little feet.
like pig's feet down
there.

  64″   I guess that's all.

V 2″ 1. Looks like a dragon   1. A dragon fly in the air.
fly with ripped wings   Q. Flying.
and it looks like a bat
too. It has very
ragged wings. And
that's about all of
31″   that.

       (Stretches).
(Getting tired?) Yes.

VI 2″ 1. That looks like a fox   1. He didn't have any tail.
skin and a . . . and
a wolf's skin—more
like a wolf than a
fox. It's got very
big whiskers—thick
whiskers and thick
41″   fur.

VII 9″   (Stretches again).

        1. Looks like a cave en- 1. Nothing in here and this looks
trance that's been dy-   rocky like and small.
namited.

        2. And this looks some- 2. (Lower d).
thing like the main
part of your back-
bone.

Performance   *Inquiry*

3. Something like little
   people with a dog's
   head standing
4. On a cliff.
3. (Contd.) They are
   women and they have
   great long dresses—
   and have little tails
   too and horns on
62″   their heads.

VIII 7″ 1. Those look like bears
           climbing up.
        2. And looks something   2. This part here.
           like the inside part of
           your body—backbone
           and chest.
           Is there really any
           real answer to them?
           (Listens to outside
   50″   noises).

IX 8″ 1. That part there looks   1. The center line.
         like the side of the
         body—the backbone
         really.
      2. This looks something   2. Green and has little places like
         like a valley here with   water (S).
      3. Little water.
      4. This reminds of the   4. Wavy and red.
         Red Sea—this place
         here.
   45″   There, I guess that's
         all.

X 2″ 1. That looks like a big
        basket of bugs all
        crawling around.
     2. Tomato worms.   2. Green and wriggly-looking and
                                   looks like they are climbing.
     3. Spiders and   3. Here and here.
     4. Some beetles and   4. (Gray) Climbing a tree.
     5. Then there's some
        blood there and let's
        see—(tch tch tch).
     4. (Contd.) And the
        beetles are climbing a
     6. Tree.
     3. (Contd.) And the

Performance	*Inquiry*

   spiders are clinging to
   blood.

2. (Contd.) And tomato
   worms are climbing
   up

7. A little stalk.

The "blind" interpretation of this protocol is as follows:

"At the age of nine and a half, Larry continues to utilize adequate energy in the pursuit of intellectual activity, perceiving his environment accurately and dealing with it rather practically. However, he does not appear to be as comfortable as he was in the previous year, his fantasies being more disturbing to him, to a large extent, because of the heightened ambivalence which he feels toward his mother. Perhaps Larry has repressed the fears of castration in relationship to father even more than the previous year. As a result of this, he may be relating, relatively speaking, better to father than to mother, toward whom he now feels some hostility and sees as a source of threat possibly of a castration variety in some oral terms.

"Larry's inability to give more than one good human movement response is unusual for a nine and a half year old of his intelligence. A similar decrease in or reluctance to give as many popular responses as the year before suggests a regressing from the previous high level of functioning. In looking for a cause, one sees in the Rorschach indications of an aggressive upsurging of feelings, which appear to be sexual in nature. For example, the explosion of Card II has a sexual connotation when the second response is considered with it. A similar explosion response on the mother card offers a further suggestion that these sexually aggressive feelings are connected with mother, whom he sees with "horn and tail." Neither the mother nor the father figure, who is seen as an "octopus" seem to present any helpful or succoring attitude toward him. Despite these disturbing fantasies and concomitant fears of castration noted in other responses, Larry is still able to present a fairly conforming appearance in his interpersonal relationships. Only a child of his intelligence and ego strength could continue to face the pressures which he is experiencing both from within and without. That he must at times react to these pressures in sudden bursts of anger or defiance could be expected from his Rorschach at this time. Feeling unjustly imposed upon by parents but afraid to react directly, he might tend to project his anger upon peers or others toward whom he can more easily express hostility."

It was around this time that Larry again became concerned about parents' budgetary problems. His little sister was approaching kindergarten age and parents felt they could not afford private school for both children. Although mother did not make this relationship when she told about Larry's coaxing parents to permit him to have a paper route, it seems fairly obvious that he was trying in this manner to help out in family finances. Mother thought him a little young for such a routine job, but believed in retrospect that this experience taught him many things. For the first time he had to "handle people himself." She considered this as Larry's initiation in independent functioning, since he did not have a protective adult on hand to intercede on his behalf when small crises arose. Simultaneous with the paper route, Larry also had an egg route, delivering weekly to neighborhood families. The money earned from these endeavors was budgeted by Larry, at the suggestion of parents. He listed three areas where he wanted his money to go: 1) spending money; 2) additions to his coin and stamp collection, which was considered an investment; and 3) savings account. He divided his earnings into equal parts. This was the beginning of Larry's demonstration of ability to handle money maturely. The restlessness noted clinically and the anxiety seen in the Rorschach at the nine and a half year level are no doubt related in part to his precocious attempt to help solve his problem by sharing thus in the family responsibilities.

Larry was continuing to get along well with his peers. At this time, he had many friends. The only area of concern within his peer relationships that had been noticed by parents and his counselor related to Larry's intense feelings about a "sense of fairness." Mother believed that this existed to an unhealthy extreme. If Larry was treated unfairly by anyone, he became "furious." Usually even-tempered and functioning calmly, Larry could become "infuriated when someone's unfairness shows him to a disadvantage." He actually had to be involved in the situation to become angered, although he verbalized dislike in observing someone else being unfairly treated. Mother said that he had always been more than adequate in fights "with his tongue and brain." She explained further that he had a knack of knowing what to say to irk other children or to whip them verbally. It is possible that Larry at this time was displacing onto his classmates the anger he felt toward his parents and sibling for the excessive demands he seemed to feel they were making on him.

At ten and a half years of age, Larry had grown taller and thinner and was quite mature in behavior. Though shabbily dressed in worn jeans and torn tennis shoes, his manners were charming and he seemed most comfortable in the test situation. He again asked intelligent, sincere questions about the research project. To my inquiry about school, he said that he had made the honor roll and was president of his class. To this he quickly added, "But it's not all good, being president—sometimes you get in bad with the boys." While pleasant and cooperative, Larry had difficulty in concentrating on the test material. A wide scatter of scores on the Wechsler Intelligence Scale for Children and the disparity between the performance and verbal ratings suggests an unevenness in functioning that is no doubt related to anxiety. While the performance rating on this test was only high average, the verbal scale was high enough to raise the full-scale I.Q. to a level that indicated that Larry's over-all functioning, although depressed, is still at the superior level. He was dutifully cooperative in giving his responses to the Rorschach cards.

Larry's Rorschach Protocol at the Ten Year Level

Performance	*Inquiry*
I 14" 1. That reminds me of a great big grinny cat.	1. Ears, eyes.
2. This reminds me of a crow's head right here. (d)	2. Beak, not any of the rest.
V3. That looks like a sugar bowl this way.	3. Legs and handle and there's the top. (W).
42" Guess that's all.	
II 7" 1. This bottom part looks like something exploding.	1. All the red popping.
2. This looks like old woman's,—a person's red shoes with socks and sticking up like this.	2. Just the shoes.
3. This looks like two bears with noses together.	3. (P)
4. This hole here looks like a big cave.	4. Opening and looks like you are looking down on something and how jagged.
42"	
III 5" 1. These look like waiters washing their hands	1. Have pants and tie.
2. In a basin here.	

Performance	*Inquiry*
V3. These two things look like two natives sit- 32″ ting on a thing here.	3. Just chest and head.
IV 5″ 1. This looks like the head of an octopus here.	1. (Dr. at top).
2. This looks like the in-sides of an animal.	2. Way it is here—here's legs and veins there. (lower D)
3. This looks like a rug —a bear skin rug or 36″ something like that.	3. (W)
V 5″ 1. Looks like a big bat here or an insect. 25″	1. In the air. Q. Flying. Q. Head reminds you of something like that. Q. Just insect to me.
VI 8″ 1. This looks like two skins hung up on	1. (W)
2. A pole.	
3. A fox skin stretched out like that with the 31″ head on it.	3. Q. Looks like the place where the backbone is.
VII 1. Looks like the open-in a cave.	1. In here.
2. Looks sorta like two little dogs standing on	2. Here and here.
3. This rock here.	3. Sorta like rocks.
4. This reminds me of a 34″ butterfly's wings.	4. (Lower D). Just the wings.
VIII 8″ Ah . . .	
<1. Looks like there's some sort of an ani-mal	1. The way they are divided.
2. Standing on a rock and	
1. (Contd.) This is his reflection in the water here.	
3. This reminds me of the insides of a per- 32″ son or animal.	3. Red stuff and that looks like bones—red, yellow and green. Q. Blue, that's dry.
IX 6″ 1. This looks like some underwater growth or seaweed and things.	1. (All except red). Underwater green.
2. This reminds me of the face of an under- 40″ water squid.	2. (Same portion).

Performance	Inquiry
X 8″ 1. I think these two things look like spiders.	1. Climbing on something (blue).
2. This looks like two tomato worms.	2. Coming out of eyes. Q. Greenish.
3. This part here looks like the bank of a river (red) with a	3. Looking down on it. Q. From an airplane.
4. Little bridge (blue) going across here.	
5. This looks like two crabs, trying to lift up	5. Here and here.
41″ 6. A pole.	6. (upper D).

The psychologist gave the following "blind" interpretation of the above Rorschach:

"At the age of ten and a half, relationships appear even more difficult than the previous year, perhaps because he had experienced the eruption of some pre-puberty changes with masturbation concerns being included. He seems to be dealing with the anxiety over this by putting distance in his interpersonal relationships, and withdrawing, becoming a bit more introspective. Superficially, he might appear clinically as calmer than the previous year. While he continues to react to the many facets of his environment, he has less energy available for intellectual pursuits and is capable of greater error in judgment, even doing some sloppy thinking. In such an over-all picture of struggle and defense through the years, this temporary "looseness" in thinking might be viewed as regression in the service of the ego.

"Despite Larry's inability to apply himself at an optimal or even desirable level because of intermittently overpowering anxiety, his adoption of introspective techniques at this time has given him some insight into his conflicts in relation to parents. He appears to have gained more understanding and empathy with father, as noted in the texture response to Card IV. This he has achieved despite the fact that he still feels resentful of father's all-encompassing attitude and demanding characteristics. His antagonism toward mother is even stronger, but his ambivalence and confusion in regard to her make him less able to express his anger toward her. Because of his inability to understand her as well as father, he fears her, and thus no such flare-ups as occur between him and father would occur in connection with mother."

During an interview at this time, Larry was able to talk about some of his concerns. Family finances were worrying him. "I'm afraid you won't find me here next year, because this school is so expensive," he stated at the end of the interview. When I inquired about his paper and egg routes, he said that they kept him pretty busy but did not prevent him from participating in school athletics or being on the school teams. Larry's principal and teachers were high in their praise of him because of his superior intelligence, his interest in extra-curricular activities, especially athletics, and his responsible attitude toward his business ventures. It was evident that they were not aware of any anxiety that Larry might be experiencing at this time. Mother, on the other hand, reported some "touchy" family relationships. Larry and father quarrel frequently over the adequacy with which Larry performed tasks assigned to him by father. Mother felt caught up in the middle of these frictions and had tried to appease Larry who complained that father is a perfectionist and "always knows everything." In these disagreements, mother saw Larry's sense of humor as a desirable asset. "It sometimes serves as a balance wheel in family quarrels." Mother admitted that she too has her disagreements with Larry, but despite his evident annoyance with her, Larry was "never rude." It would appear that much of Larry's conflictual feeling centered around the demands for independent action made on him by both his parents and himself. One wonders how and where his dependent needs were gratified at this time. It seems that his conflict with father has been more open and thus more comfortably recognized and resolved, while the conflict with mother has probably been quite subtle and hence more threatening, less tangible and less worked through.

Little is known about how and where Larry obtained his sexual information. He asked few questions and mother answered these factually with little elaboration. It was felt that she was not comfortable in talking about this area of development, and it is possible that she could have transmitted this discomfort to Larry. Father was of less help than mother in this regard. One wonders how the boy handled his feelings in regard to the masturbatory tendencies and castration fears noted through the years in his Rorschach responses. They have undoubtedly been subjected to the same repression as have many other of the anxiety provoking situations.

When next seen at eleven and a half years of age, Larry was a tall, lanky boy, adolescent in appearance, personable and again quite talkative. He spoke with enthusiasm of his first man teacher—in fact, he was thrilled with the whole sixth grade program, adding, "You really have to get good grades to stay in this school." He asked more questions about the research project and again expressed his pleasure in being included in it. He was polite and cooperative in the test situation but showed little enthusiasm.

In his human figure drawings, the only difference between the male and the female figures were: 1) the shape of the face—the woman's face being rounder than the man's; 2) the extension of the hairline to cover the ears of the woman; 3) the absence of feet on the male figure. Each figure, which filled an entire page, consisted of: a square trunk with a belt separating it from asymmetrical thick legs; long, thin arms with round balls for hands. Facial features included eyes close together at the top of the face, beetle brows, a long phallic nose, and an opened mouth holding a drooping cigarette from which smoke was coming. As Larry drew the male figure, he talked about his male teacher, adding, "But Mr. Jones doesn't smoke." He laughed as he realized he was making the female figure with trousers and said, "She's a mannish woman."

Larry's approach to the Rorschach cards at this time was serious and businesslike. Following are his responses:

Larry's Rorschach Protocol at the Eleven Year Level

Performance	*Inquiry*
I 16″ Well, umm.	
V1. I see two faces on each side and looks like they are sticking out arms and pointing to something and looks like they haven't combed their hair for quite a while.	1. Big man with a very fat face —something like a genie or . . .
V2. Looks like a face of some sort.	2. Looks like here are his two eyes and here's his nose and he has his mouth closed in here and opened at the corners. Q. Could be a man.
∧3. And these look like big birds like and a crow with . . . (upper side D).	3. Looks like he's sitting somewhere. Q. Just his head.
V4. And this up here looks something like a man like Paul Revere like	4. See mostly the hat. Just outline of face coming down.

Performance	*Inquiry*
the Revolutionary time. Has a hat on and looks like he's looking way up somewhere (Lower side d).	
5. Looks something like a cat (WS).	5. It looks like it's been laughing or grinning at something.
6. Looks something like a map of some type having four small lakes.	6. WS.
2'1″ I guess that's about all.	

II 7″ V1. This part here looks like a big explosion—like an atomic explosion.	1. The way it's coming up—so many pieces are spraying up —well, it's in the young stage and just exploded and one-fourth of a second and just comes up. Q. Color
V2. Looks like two dogs with big red noses kissing each other.	2. Just the head and part of body next to the head. Q. Might be a police dog. (Twisting around—I said, "You are tired."—he admitted it saying he didn't sleep much last night—he had a cold).
V3. Women's feet here with red galoshes and white socks.	3. Just the feet.
4. This here looks like a man (d).	4. Just his head. (Excused himself to blow his nose). Not even his neck. He seems to be laughing at something or being very gay and he might be yelling at somebody or getting mad at them.
5. This looks like two elves putting their front knees together and where they put them together is a sort of explosion—blood coming out.	5. (Same as dogs).
6. This looks like some man with a big lower jaw that's talking— with a big long nose	6. (side d).

Performance	Inquiry
and other side looks the same.	
7. Looks like you're in a cave and you're looking into the open and there's a big crevice at the mouth of the cave.	7. (S)

1'50"

III 11"

Performance	Inquiry
1. Looks like there's a wash basin here	1. One on each side.
2. And two butlers or very distinguished men that wait on people are washing their hands and	2. (P)
3. Here is a butterfly here and	3. Red and has a sort of square body. Q. Flying.
4. This looks like somebody has some sort of —looks like somebody is bleeding and blood is dripping down.	4. (Doesn't see the person). Q. It's red and it's spread out.
5. Looks like a mouth of a big head with one eye and he doesn't have a chin. Mouth that closes sidewise and jagged teeth.	5. Big creature that eats meat. (Lower D)
6. Jack-O-Lanterns without any teeth.	6. (Same as 4).
V7. Looks like two Negro kings who are sitting on a throne back to back and are kicking one of their legs up above their head— looks like the heads are stuck together— no, resting on a cushion that is supported between their heads.	7. (W) All the black and gray.

2'17"

IV 9"

Performance	Inquiry
1. This looks like a big fish coming out from under a rock.	1. Got its mouth open.
2. This looks something like two camels' heads back to back.	2. Have head cocked and not sleeping—right up and alert.

Performance	*Inquiry*
3. And then there's down in here a pig had been butchered. They've taken all his hide. Hooves and legs are spread out on the ground.	3. Not a very pleasant subject. (Lower D).
<4. This looks like a dog with hardly any jaw— and it's laughing.	4. (Side d).
5. This looks something like an octopus only its eyes are practically separated. They are coming out the side of his head.	5. WS.
6. This looks like a wolf with legs crossed looking down at something.	6. Arms in like this and legs are. (Upper d).

102″

V 8″ 1. This looks something like a crocodile here opening its jaw.	1. (Side d).
<2. This looks like a big eagle with long, slender jaws that's making a big squawk or something.	2. Just see the head—half of head. (Lower d).
3. This looks like a bat or butterfly. I guess that's about all on that one.	3. Butterfly, because a butterfly has those do-hickies. Q. Flying.

56″

VI 10″ 1. This looks something like a rhinoceros with a horn out off out here.	1. Looking straight ahead— standing still. (side d)
2. Looks like ledges with two birds sitting on the very edge.	1. (Same as 1).
3. Looks like the skin of a fox or a wolf spread out with the inside out and haven't taken off the head yet.	3. Cut up the middle and you didn't see that when you spread the other side. (W)
4. And a . . . this up here looks something like a butterfly.	4. Flying.

	Performance	*Inquiry*

<5. This looks like a cave coming in here with sharp spines coming out of it—looks like the mouth of a cave.

79"

5. Spines like pointed pieces of rock or stick. Q. The way it goes back in and gray makes it look like a rock. (bottom S and de)

VII 11"   1. This looks like two elephants with real skinny necks and they only have one leg each and all the back is gone except a little bit up next to the head.

1. Could be dancing but I don't think so—they could be.

2. This looks like a huge bat or butterfly with big wings and little wee body.

2. Flying. (Lower D).

3. And these look like oh, sort of two little girls with big thick feathers sticking up out of their head and little tails.

83"   I guess that's all.

3. Here and here.

VIII 15" V1. This looks sorta like the insides of an animal and two sorta

1. Different colored and has this place where the backbone is right up here.

2. Coyote-looking animals climbing from rock to rock.

2. Not big enough for wolves.

3. This part looks like a big animal that's white and has horns coming out and has a big horn and his eyes right next to the horn.

3. Just looking straight ahead —looks as if he might be mad. (Inner D).

4. And something else like an octopus with two long arms coming out and its eyes are right next up to its head and there's one that is long and slender and it's right out near the skin and there's another part that's farther in.

4. No special way. (Upper gray D).

Performance	*Inquiry*
>5. Dog with yellow hair —sort of a yellow wig on. (Side d).	5. See his little white eyes. Looks something like a St. Bernard—got great big full face and eye makes him look sad and nose is big, flat and pinkish red. Makes me think of a St. Bernard.
V6. Something that looks something like a screech owl—a long, slender nose and eyes away back in his head. I guess that's about all 150″ on that one.	6. He looks angry. (dr).
IX 10″ 1. This looks like two funny sorta men with great big stomachs and long noses and coming up out of the	1. Just ordinary men.
2. Ocean and laughing at each other.	2. Looks like greenish water.
3. This looks something like an elk. No, a bear and its eyes are great big round things—they are out of proportion.	3. Just his head. Q. He could be trying to get some place awful fast. (green area)
4. This looks like a little man climbing up over a big ridge from a canyon. He has a long nose.	4. (red).
5. Here's a man with a big green nose, eyes are long and narrow and come to a point like but are up and down and not across like ours.	5. Might be peeping through a hole or something. Q. Foxy sly. (dr).
V6. Man climbing up over a green cliff and has a huge pink hat on and	6. (Same as 4 upside down).
7. Looks like two men have just been out in space and are making a dive for these rocks 2′6″ here.	7. (Upper d).

Performance	Inquiry

X 6″ 1. This looks like there's a whole lot of groups of insects like you would use for fishing.

1. Just crawling and so many —all over green and brown and yellow and blue and orange.

2. A rabbit head down here.

2. (P)

V3. And two little beetles with crowns on their heads are carrying

3. These are legs and these are crowns and see the face. (dr—lower green).

4. Big green poles.

4. Carrying the rabbit.

5. Crabs here are having an argument.

5. (upper gray).

6. Two little wee octopuses are having a fight and are about to hit each other

7. With a club.

7. This green here.

8. Little yellow island.

9. Little brown bugs are jumping from the little yellow island to

10. A big red island.

11. Trapeze actors are hanging from rocks and holding hands.

11. (inner blue)

V12. Two sea horses with two necks and two heads and only one body.

12. (lower green)

13. A wolf with a long steel tube for a nose and eyes are setting way back in his head.

13. (top D)

<14. Looks like there's some kind of creatures with two great big mouths and food comes into the long slender pipe.

14. Two heads and getting food.

160″   That is the body.

The above protocol was interpreted by the psychologist as follows:

"Apparently, at eleven and a half years, puberty changes have affected this boy considerably. There is a marked increase in the degree to which he is experiencing an upsurge of impulses. He seems to have become quite anxious over these changes and has reacted with an obvious verboseness and, in a sense, pseudo-productivity in view of the restricted theme of much of his content. With his marked anatomy concern, and the degree of aggression expressed in the content of the Rorschach, as well as his tendency to internalize things, it is quite possible that should he develop a symptom, it might be of the GI variety. On the other hand, it is equally possible, and perhaps more probable, that once the tensions of this period decrease, this boy shall develop quite effective patterns of defense, permitting him to deal very effectively with his environment.

"His approach at the present time is somewhat scattered under the threats he is experiencing and we see quite a few inefficiencies in his perceptual judgment. However, this again might best be viewed as temporary regression in service to the ego. He seems to have considerable recoverability and shows no over-all pattern of disorganization. While he might be showing considerable introversive tendencies and, with this, perhaps giving his parents a difficult time, he nevertheless maintains a relationship to people in his environment, though again at the present time he is perhaps somewhat egocentrically oriented in his interpersonal relationships."

In addition to, or perhaps in lieu of, what the "blind" interpretation suggests, one can sense in this increase of anatomy responses and phallic symbols, considerable body preoccupation that may have little manifestation in psychosomatic symptoms. Such responses have been present in varying degrees throughout Larry's six Rorschachs and, while undoubtedly suggestive of bodily preoccupation, may be a thin cover-up for sexual curiosity and sexual urges that he has tried to repress, and which now are too much for him to deal with in this way. In this record, there are also a number of "back to back" responses, which suggest a homosexual orientation. He continues to work on his relationship to the opposite sex, as he lives with a mother about whom he has been ambivalent through the years, sometimes antagonistic toward, and oftentimes confused about, and to whom, in this record and in his drawing, he is ascribing masculine qualities. Larry has never felt a sense of having his dependent needs adequately met by her. Instead, he has always felt a need to achieve premature independence in order to please her. He is, at present, unprepared for a heterosexual stage of development. Why should he be interested in the opposite sex since he has little of the comfort one might expect in such a relationship? Even his women teachers have exacted the same high standards as mother.

This record at eleven and a half years of age is filled with men's faces in various positions and activities, with considerable emphasis on noses. Since encountering men teachers in his academic programs, he has developed "crush" tendencies which have not been superseded by or even supplemented with an interest in girls. His drawings at this age which distinguish so inadequately between the two sexes are further indications of this lack or repression of heterosexual interest. One would suspect that he may be reacting toward his sister as toward other female figures by giving her a rough time in an unconscious attempt to deny interest in all females.

The interpreter goes on to say, "It is expected, however, that Larry will develop into a well-organized and quite adequate individual. His defenses appear to be sufficiently strong that he will be able to make an adequate adjustment to his environment. He may have in his personality makeup certain features resembling the obsessive compulsive style of personality, although he does not appear to be headed toward a neurosis of this variety."

When Larry was asked at eleven and a half years of age what he worried about, he remarked, "About getting good grades—I won't stay here if I don't"—and about his paper route "when it isn't going good." When asked about the things that make him angry, he said that such things as "when people do underhand things in football" or "when someone is always telling me what to do or where to go" or "when my boss is real late bringing the papers." He also described how he handled this anger on the spot. For example, if a boy pushed him in the face when they were playing football, he would do it right back to him. This led him to talk about his sister, who he thought was getting to be a pest. In fact, he had to "biff her one" every once in a while. Then she would run to mother and they would both get in trouble. It would seem that Larry's sensitivity to "fairness" and his recent tendency toward physical expression of anger are related to the wavering self-certainty of early adolescence. There was reluctance to compete or be tested because of this uncertainty and the fear of finding himself inadequate or vulnerable.

Larry talked spontaneously about his summers on a farm "upstate," describing how hard he worked and how much fun the experience was. He sometimes enjoyed playing Little League baseball during the summer months, but there was little time for this sport because of the farm work. Larry thought he got more pleasure from this work than from anything he had ever done, and, for that reason, might even decide to be a farmer. This choice of farming as a vocation would seem to have been multi-determined and possibly transient. It would seem to have represented a fulfillment of the need for acceptance, support, and freedom which characterized his farm summers. It supplied a need to be different from parents and to assert and establish an identity of his own. It also helped him to apply and integrate his newfound physical strength. In fact, Larry's intense devotion to his yearly farm experience is interesting and might be viewed as a "regression in service of the ego" analogous to the pattern seen several times in response to the Rorschach cards. Here, with all-giving adults and in relative isolation from peers, perhaps he supplemented and replenished his stores of unqualified love and acceptance and dependency gratifications, retreated from the school year's strivings, consolidated maturational gains, and at the same time experienced new masteries and different energy investment possibilities.

Larry accepted an invitation to come in for further interviews at the ages of thirteen and fourteen. Additional Rorschachs were given and he also had a psychiatric evaluation by an experienced child psychiatrist. Another psychiatrist, in reviewing the wealth of information about this boy's growth and development, as well as the results of the psychological tests and the interpretation of the Rorschachs, summarized her impressions of Larry by saying: "Larry is, at this time, a well-compensated adolescent. He has capacities for sublimatory, rather than compulsive activity, for enriching interpersonal experience, for perceiving and expressing his own feelings, for empathizing with the feelings of others, possessing responsibility and taking leadership. His outlook for future health, happiness and maturation is good."

Seen again at age seventeen, Larry was at that time a senior in the same private school with plans for college. He was tall, slender, handsome and appeared to be the ideal stereotype of a well-functioning teenager. The bruises and abrasions on his arms were explained as due to a recent soccer match in which he played goalie for his team. He gave the impression of being outgoing, mature and sensitive to the feelings of others. In his interview, he expressed his usual interest in the Rorschach study and believed that the findings should be helpful in understanding children. Since his current choice of vocation was that of a teacher in a private boys' school, he hoped to be able to use the book himself some day.

The riddle that confronts us here with Larry is one of psychological health, and not one of sickness. A mentally healthy person can be more of an enigma than one who presents symptoms of mental illness, for it is frequently easier to explain the etiology of sickness

than that of health. As with Larry, each of the successfully functioning children of this study had many points of weakness. As a
psychologist, I was sometimes a little doubtful as to whether these
children with the seemingly best accommodating power would
make the final grade. Even as I perceive my doubts, I was equally
aware, in reviewing their Rorschachs and development through the
years, that they have always maintained a safe margin. The struggle
of these "healthy" children can be clearly seen in their Rorschach
responses; and, yet, in each instance, they always come out "on top"
—indeed, in each Rorschach through the years, they were continually
on top. This has been true of Larry since he gave his first Rorschach
at the age of six.

V : PATTY

WHILE STABLE HOME CONDITIONS and high intelligence seemed to play important roles in the personality development of some children in this study, neither of these factors is all-important or even indispensable in the growth of a well-functioning, even happy individual. The case history of Patty points this up clearly.

Patty is a girl of average intelligence, whose mother, with a long history of psychosomatic complaints and dependency on her own mother, has never been a source of strength for her, and whose somewhat ineffectual father has spent very little time in the home. A younger brother, for whose supervision Patty was given responsibility very early in her life, is the other member of this family.

Patty was born during the first year of her parents' marriage when mother was twenty-five and father twenty-six years of age. Before marriage mother had done housework and father had changed jobs frequently. Father's employment record continued to be unstable after marriage and the couple moved ten times during their first year together.

Despite this unsettled state of affairs, mother remembers her pregnancy with Patty as uneventful and the hospital delivery as normal. A small baby weighing not quite six pounds, Patty was breastfed for nearly a year and was then weaned to a cup without difficulty. Mother recalls that she was a good baby, never giving her any trouble. At the time of Patty's birth, father and mother were living with maternal grandmother in their first even semi-permanent home, and the baby had much attention from grandmother and aunts. She walked before she was a year old and, because of her small stature and attractiveness, "looked like a walking doll."

When Patty was two years old her brother was born. Mother was in ill health during this pregnancy. A Caesarean section was followed shortly by a hysterectomy, and both resulted in a long convalescence period for mother. During mother's hospitalization, the children were cared for by the grandmother; but the separation from mother did not seem to cause any anxiety in Patty.

Shortly after Patty's third birthday, father, who had been deferred up to this time because of age and dependents, went reluctantly into military service. Mother, who had been annoyed by his failure to hold a job and his lack of responsibility toward her and the children, reported the situation to his draft board. As a result, father was drafted; and mother took pride in the fact that it was she who had "put him in."

The family had been on relief before father went into service, and it was through the help of the relief agency that mother and children moved into a housing project shortly after father was drafted. When Patty was four years old, she was enrolled in the local kindergarten.

Although Patty was smaller and somewhat less mature than the other children, she enjoyed school and got along well with her peers. She attended kindergarten for two years and it was during this period that she had all of her illnesses. These began with a broken leg which necessitated a cast to the knee; following in close succession, she had chicken pox, measles, and whooping cough. It was only a short time after this that she had a tonsillectomy.

During her convalescence from these numerous illnesses, Patty's eyes crossed and she wore glasses for a short time. When she had regained her former good health, no further need for them was indicated. However, it was also during this period of kindergarten experience that mother became concerned about a speech difficulty connected with Patty's enunciation. It was a sort of infantile lisp that cleared partially as she grew up. This seemed to be only part of a generally dependent stage of development which Patty was going through at that time. With father out of the home and mother preoccupied with her own health and the care of Patty's little brother, Patty was expected early in life to assume a more mature role than it was possible for her to maintain consistently.

Since her father was absent from the home, Patty was prevented from a natural development and handling of oedipal feelings at the ages when they generally arise. Even after his discharge from the army, he was only at home for a month before going to work in a neighboring state. His family did not move with him since mother claimed that he had never been able to provide for them and she was not going to give up the only permanent home she and the children had ever known. This was the beginning of a separation of the family unit, in which father came home only on weekends and for his two-week vacation each year. However, Patty became devoted to him and began to visit him for short intervals during her summer vacations.

Patty recognized that her family life was different from that of other children, but tried to be loyal to each parent. Although her mother prided herself on never saying anything derogatory about father, she requested that Patty check his mail when she went to visit him so that she could report to mother about any women who might be writing to him.

The strain of this anxiety-producing situation was not without its toll on Patty. She was not able to show her distress, however, except in relation to her brother, toward whom she adopted a "bossy" role in which she often berated him for his misbehavior. She sometimes reported to mother the situations in which he embarrassed her, but would also frequently attack him physically on such occasions.

It was in the early stages of such relationships to the different family members that Patty's first Rorschach was obtained. She was in the second semester of first grade in one of the city schools. A very pretty little blond girl with gray, expressive eyes and curly hair, she smiled frequently in the test situation and was spontaneous in a quiet, almost prim, manner. She used her hands to emphasize what she was saying and it was evident that she was on her best behavior, trying to appear more adult than she really was. A slight infantile lisp was noticeable at this time.

Patty's first grade teacher saw her as a pleasant, conforming child who did average work and got along well with her peers. The child was obviously pleased at being singled out for testing, and related easily to the examiner. Her performance on the Binet test was even, and she achieved an average intelligence rating, indicating that she was functioning as well as could be expected in her classroom work.

Patty's responses to the Rorschach cards were as follows:

Patty's Rorschach Protocol at the Six Year Level

	Performance	*Inquiry*
I	(Holds it at arm's length).	
17″	1. Looks like a ghost to me.	1. Eyes. If he didn't have this he wouldn't be a ghost. (Puts hand over S and says) Then it looks like a false face.
	V2. This way it looks	2. Looks like a leg here and a

Performance	*Inquiry*

<table>
<tr><td colspan="2">like an elephant.
(D)</td><td>leg here. This looks like his eyes and this looks like his nose. They're not big—they're little. This looks like his nose.</td></tr>
</table>

50″

II	10″	1. This looks like a statue and	1. All this looks like the statue. Q. I don't know.
		<2. This is a fire and the statue is getting fired up.	2. This stuffs looks like fire (Points to red areas). I saw fire that color.
III	7″	1. This looks like a bow.	1. Bows is round like that.
		2. This looks like a brownie, and this l o o k s l i k e a whitey.	2. All this looks like a brownie —no mouth, hand. Whitey is like this. a. This looks like a violin. Hickey out here (dd on red).
		3. This looks like a frog with a bow on its back. Don't it look like it to you?	3. Here's his legs, body, eyes. Bow is pink and he is black and gray. (WS) I like this.
	60″	ΛThis way it don't.	
IV	7″VΛ1.	This looks like a cow getting burned up.	1. This looks like burn and this looks like burn.
	VΛ	This way it looks like a . . .	
	ΛVΛ	This way it looks like a cow.	
	ΛV2.	This way it looks like a horse.	2. (Can't locate horse). I thought these were designs. They don't look like designs, do they?
	60″		
V		This is fun.	
	3″ Λ1.	This looks like a butterfly. W.	1. Hickeys that go up here—his wings all this.
	V2.	This way it looks like a grasshopper. W	2. A flying grasshopper. I catch —they spit juice.
	17″		
VI	ΛVΛ 4″ 1.	This way it looks like a pussy cat and W.	1. There are the whiskers— that's something on her neck and all this is pussy cat.
	V2.	This way it looks like a baby dog.	2. Mouth and something in mouth—and all this is dog. Q. He is eating it.
	20″		

Performance	*Inquiry*
VII I like this.	
3″ Λ1. This looks like a house getting fired up. dW	1. All this is fire and this is the chimney and this is the door. (d-w)
V2. This way it looks like a grasshopper getting fired up.	2. (Denies grasshopper).
	a. Ah, it looks like a puppy —ears, paw; he's opening his mouth (D).
	I lost my glasses and if I don't get them soon I'll
20″	have cross eyes.
VIII That's pretty.	
5″ Λ1. This way it looks like a pretty design. W.	1. This does look like a design.
V This way it looks like a funny de-	a. Looks like a bear—looks like a bear climbing up rocks and this way looks like an elephant climbing
20″ sign.	down rocks.
IX 6″ V1. That looks like this is a stick and all this is ice cream—looks like ice cream is falling off. This looks like ice cream is get-	1. Pink green. This is ice cream and this is ice cream and this is the fire firing it up.
30″ ting fired up.	
X 6″ 1. Ooh, that looks like a spider.	1. Here is the spider. (P)
V2. This way it looks like a telepole getting all fired up. Does it look like	2. Here is the telepole (D) and all this is the fire firing it up.
20″ that to you?	
"My brother would cry if he had to do this— it's too hard for him. Mother said she was glad I didn't fail. You're writing and I'm doing work. I like this room and these cards."	

The "blind" interpretation of this Rorschach, made by a psychologist who knew only the sex and Binet I.Q. of the child, is given verbatim:

"Patty, at six years and eight months of age, appeared to be a very responsive little girl. Her test responses suggested that she attempted to appear mature, but her pose was thin disguise for quite infantile aspects.

"She appeared to be constantly concerned with home relationships. She seemed to have a strongly erotic attachment to both her mother and father. She probably was rather uneasy in her relationship with both, but she savored the excitement inherent in this. The situation was particularly evident in the titillation connected with her resistance to her mother, which the child seemed to engage in rather like a game. Certainly she seemed to feel there was greater understanding between her and the mother, and probably considerable similarity in the two. One might infer from her response that the mother displayed a rather sharp temper on occasion, in contrast to a more placid father.

"Patty herself seemed to display her emotions readily, and at times the immediate connection between feeling and situation might not be obvious to the observer. Her overt behavior might stem from internal stimuli as well as from external. She would like to appear grownup and very proper, but she actually exercised relatively little restraint in most of her reactions.

"She seemed to wish to dominate any situation, but her essentially phallic identification was somewhat tentative. Her spontaneous remarks gave the specific information that she felt very rivalrous toward a younger brother and competed directly with him, apparently with the purpose of securing all her mother's attention for herself. She seemed to be so deeply involved in her family relationships that peer contacts outside the home would probably be quite peripheral. Competition with other children, slight negativism when she felt relatively secure, and generally rather immature behavior for her age might characterize her dealings with other people."

This "blind" interpretation points up most of the areas of Patty's life about which there was historical information, and gives additional insight into her feelings about her unusual family relationships. The anxieties that she was trying so hard to repress or deny consciously show up clearly in the Rorschach protocol.

Despite Patty's concern about her home situation, she did not protest when mother told her that father had never taken care of them and that it was better to live the way they were living. She never pressed her mother to join father, but continued her close relationship with him and looked forward to his visits home as well as to her summer visits with him. Father never failed to remember birthdays and special holidays, and always supplied allowances to the children.

Patty had few playmates in the neighborhood during her early school years; she preferred to play inside with her dolls or to help mother with the housework. During this phase of Patty's life, her mother had many physical complaints and began to delegate an increasing number of responsibilities to Patty in regard to her brother. Such pressures as mother seemed to be putting on Patty, while anxiety-provoking, as noted in both the Rorschach record and her behavior, were pressures within her capacity to endure. It was fortunate that Patty's school achievement was of secondary concern to mother at this time, since she was barely able to manage her academic work from one grade to the next.

In the fall of the year when she was seven years and eight months old, Patty gave her second Rorschach protocol. Her summer had been spent visiting her father, taking care of brother, and assuming some of the home-making responsibilities. She had changed little in appearance since the year before, but her smile had an anxious quality about it and her efforts to please the examiner seemed forced and exaggerated. Patty's teacher considered her hyperactive, constantly bidding for attention and easily distracted in the classroom. She was achieving at a barely average level and her teacher thought her capable of better work. According to the teacher, "Patty found it necessary to go as many as three times to the lavatory in a single morning or afternoon session." It seemed evident that Patty was expressing her anxieties over her family relationship through poor schoolwork and restlessness.

There was a superficial quality to her cooperation in the test situation—as if her thoughts were elsewhere. The first test, a drawing of a man, reflected her average intelligence, as well as giving indications of feelings of insecurity and instability. Castration anxiety was also suggested by the drawing. Perhaps she sensed that her brother, with a penis, had more security and, in many ways, fared much better than she without one.

Following is Patty's Rorschach protocol at the seven year level:

Patty's Rorschach Protocol at the Seven Year Level

		Performance	Inquiry
I	9″ 15″	1. A cat.	1. Eyes, mouth, ears, face—two little bumps on top—chin.

II   15″   1. Looks like half of a butterfly. This part (black) looks like his wings. This here looks like little part of his head. Looks like two big 50″ bumps.

1. Inside (S) with wings—tail.
a. Things that climbed up on top of him—worms (upper red).
Q. Looks like he's flying around.

III   4″   1. This here looks like a ribbon.
2. This here looks like a skeleton.
V 3. Looks like a frog with a ribbon on it.
V 4. Two heads of a man with a neck 35″ (outer red).

1. Like daddy wears—a tie.
2. Legs, sides, eyes, nose, mouth.
3. Two hands, nose, big eyes, body, with ribbon.
4. Skeleton man.

IV   V10″   V1. Looks like a dog with his shoes on. 18″

1. Tail, eyes, head, shoes—looks like a dog that put his father's shoes on.

V   5″   V1. Looks like a butterfly. 7″

1. Flying in the air.

VI   5″   VΛ1. These here things look like whiskers. Looks like a big thing that looks like a kitty—has whiskers and no tail—four legs. 45″

1. Cat. There's his two paws. I have a cat. And there are two paws and there are his whiskers, nose and mouth.

VII   17″   V1. Looks like a lady with no head. 20″

1. Legs, arms. Here's her head with eyes and nose and body is in here (S).

VIII   7″   VΛ1. These here look like lions.
2. This here looks like a hill with two lions 24″ climbing up on it.

1. Here is the lions and here is the mountain, and this is the top.

Performance	Inquiry
IX 5″ 1. Looks like a different kind of butterfly.	1. I didn't say a butterfly. a. It looks like a waterfall with a red bottom. This (green) looks like . . . a hill with water coming out and over to squirt the grass down here.
10″	
X 4″ 1. This looks like what comes out of a chicken—the wishing bone.	
2. Things that come out of the water (outer blue).	2. With long legs and thing that snaps things.
3. This one looks like pliers.	3. (Lower green).
4. Ribbon (Inner blue).	4. That you tie in a double bow.

5. Hills (red).	5. Big stones that's going to go down.
	   a. Turtles in water (brown).
	   b. Part of the inside of a horse—nose, eyes—he's

40″	dead (upper D).

The "blind" interpretation by the same psychologist shows the reflection of Patty's development during the year following her first Rorschach.

"Patty has changed a great deal from the spontaneous, slightly erratic, not too happy little girl of last year. One is immediately impressed by the degree of conformity and by the systematic approach used in this record. Her behavior is no doubt rather regimented, and she is far more reticent to express feeling than she had been at earlier ages.

"Much more hostility toward mother is being experienced, but any demonstration of this would have to be covert, as she is probably denying such feelings at a conscious level. The father has apparently become more acceptable to her and is now perceived as a warmer, more admirable person than her mother. The fact that penis envy is present in this record is probably directly connected with the change in her perception of her parents.

"Along with the loss of freedom in her responses, new evidence of tension and mild anxiety has appeared. However, she has become more aware of her environment, and places considerable importance upon her relationship with others. She is working, with success, no doubt, at getting along with others, since a good bit of her overt behavior has become practical and adaptive with fewer self-determined outbursts."

There were some indications that Patty was going through a delayed oedipal reaction. Since father was absent from her life during her fourth and fifth years, such a relationship might well have been delayed. In addition, there was the hostility toward mother because of the amount of responsibility which mother placed upon her. This hostility to mother was evidently carried over to her second grade teacher, who quite obviously disliked the child in return. It was with this teacher that Patty presented her least conforming behavior.

During the following year, Patty was expected to accept an increasing amount of responsibility for household tasks and for her brother's supervision. Fortunately, however, Patty was away from home for several weeks during the summer—at camp and also visiting her father. She enjoyed the camp very much and got along well with both counselors and peers. This was the beginning of yearly camp experiences which mother arranged for both children as soon as they were of eligible age.

When Patty was seen for testing in the fall, at the age of eight years and eight months, she was still quite small for her age but seemed much more mature than the year before. She looked very pretty and was conforming but quietly spontaneous in the test situation. She mentioned liking her new teacher, implying without saying so that this was in contrast to her feelings about the second grade teacher. Her favorite subject was arithmetic, but she stated that she was beginning to like reading and spelling, two subjects in which she had not done well the year before.

Testing at this time indicated that Patty was achieving slightly below the third grade level in reading and spelling. She was aware of this and was determined to bring these subjects up to grade. Her appraisal of her progress in arithmetic was equally realistic; in this test, she rated adequately for her third grade placement.

Patty made every effort on this occasion to impress the examiner with superfluous "Thank you's," "Pardon me's" and other social amenities. It was evident from her conversation that she was still concerned about the family situation, but she never asked mother questions about the parents' separation or about the possibility of their rejoining father. When she talked about father, it was always as if he were an immediate member of the household.

Her Rorschach responses at the eight year level were as follows:

Patty's Rorschach Protocol at the Eight Year Level

Performance	*Inquiry*
I 3″ 1. Looks like a "punkin".	1. Ears on punkin, little whiskers, and here are eyes, nose, and teeth sticked together and here are wings.
2. These here two things— look like deers with antlers. 16″	2. Horn and nose of deer.
II 4″ 1. Looks like two cats sticking their tongue out to one another.	1. There are two little heads— neck, ears and long head. (upper red)
2. This here can look like a butterfly. 14″	2. All of it.
III 7″ 1. This here looks like a frog with a	1. Feet, stomach, bow and here's his nose and eyes.
2. Tie on his back.	2. (P)
3. These here little things look like dwarfs with big long hats and sticking tongue out with hand up. 31″	3. (Upper red).
IV 5″ 1. These look like feet of a man—looks like doggie put feet on like a man and he's smelling along. 20″	1. Eyes, nose, and smelling along on ground and this is the tail and the tail is sticking up in the air.
V 3″ 1. It looks like a butterfly. 7″	1. Here's the tail and here's the wings and here's the face and here's the two things on his paws. Q. Sitting on something.
VI 5″ 1. Looks like a cat and he's going "awow" and his things are hanging out whiskers are hanging out. 15″	1. He must be on the wall— can't see back legs or tail. Looks like he's "yoo-hooing" on a wall.
VII 5″ 1. Well, it looks like two little puppies and they are begging for things with little paws like that	1. Here and here and

Performance   *Inquiry*

(dem.) and they are
opening their mouth to
each other saying some-
thing and ears are stick-
ing up. They are stand-
ing on

2. A butterfly.   2. Down here is the butterfly.

VIII 5″ 1. This looks like a moun-   1. Here is the mountain and—
             tain—a real pretty moun-   has pink, orange and blue.
             tain right here and
         2. This here looks like wa-   2. Here's where the water is
             ter dripping down and   coming down.
         3. This looks like two pink   3. (P)
             bears walking up the
      27″   mountain.

IX 10″ 1. This looks like a-a-some   1. Looks like dough—round and
             mush here (red).   furry.
         2. And two dogs here   2. Eyes, ears, tail and face—
             (green).   one paw itching his ear.
         3. And some witches with   3. She looks like she's there
             funny ugly noses up   looking at one another.
             here.

X   7″ 1. This looks like two skele-   1. Skeletons of crabs when they
             tons with one horn—   are dead. (upper D)
             they are blowing up in
             the air.
         2. These here little things   2. Animals. (brown)
             are walking up here
         3. Here are two ugly peo-   3. Nose, eyes, top of lips here
             ple with   and bottom lip here. (red)
         4. A ribbon in their mouth.   4. A bow. (inner blue)
         5. Little green grass.   5. Upper green.
         6. These are—I forget what   6. Mouth and legs. (outer blue)
             they are—you see them
             in windows—people eat
      50″   them.

The "blind" interpretation of this Rorschach protocol by the same
psychologist is as follows:

"Patty's record at eight years and eight months displayed more obviously some of the compulsive tendencies glimpsed the preceding
year. She apparently used the technique of repressing hostility but
utilizing energy in well systematized methods of accomplishing things

which result in praise and recognition. Her use of these defenses seemed effective and she appeared to be rather well adjusted and to have found a satisfactory way of getting along with any problems.

"She appeared to accept both her mother and father rather well as companions and perhaps to feel, at times, a bit older and wiser than they. There was a friendlier, more accepting attitude generally prevailing throughout this record.

"A new strength was apparent in a greatly enriched fantasy life. Although she was quite chary of overt emotional expression, her capacity to achieve in an emotionally uncharged situation was very satisfactory. Whenever placed in a strongly stimulating or demanding situation, however, she might be expected to exhibit distinctly oral regressive behavior.

"Her psychosexual identification seemed still to be somewhat phallic and she might well be rather tomboyish at times. All of her behavior though, would be well within accepted bounds for her age group, and she seemed to have found a way to get along with just about everybody with no more than the normal ups and downs."

During the year following this record Patty assumed more and more home responsibility, as mother was still not feeling well. Patty preferred to remain in the house after school hours, and when mother would encourage her to go out, she complained that there was nothing to do but "sit on a garbage can." Apparently she felt quite protective toward her mother at this time, and had been able to repress any hostility that she formerly felt.

By this time Patty had taken over almost all the household tasks. She was also expected to supervise the activities of her brother, who often subtly teased her. There was much quibbling about his disrupting Patty's possessions and Patty, when she was sufficiently annoyed, would attack him physically. During that summer both children were away at camp and Patty continued to enjoy this experience very much.

Patty was seen again in the fall when she was in the fourth grade. She seemed nervously eager to please the examiner, and thoroughly enjoyed the performance test given at this time. She received a superior rating on it which reflected her strong interest and good ability in dealing with concrete material and situations. It is evident from these results that Patty functions much more adequately in the performance area than with verbal or ideational material.

Her Rorschach responses at the nine year level are as follows:

Patty's Rorschach Protocol at the Nine Year Level

Performance	*Inquiry*
I 10″ 1. I see like—angels sitting there—an angel on either side.	1. Here and here—they have wings.
2. I see a face. Two bumps, mouth, eyes.	2. Like on a Halloween pumpkin.
3. Two little reindeers.	3. Just the face and top part of the reindeer.
58″	
II 16″ 1. Looks like two caterpillars. (Lower red).	1. Got this here (projections).
2. Then dogs with noses up like that, and	2. Here and here.
3. Two lions with tongues out and	3. Here and here (upper red).
4. Butterfly (lower red).	4. Bottom of a butterfly. The white part (center S) looks like part of it—the wings.
44″	
III 4″ ∨1. A frog with a	1. Eyes, mouth, body up here.
2. Little tie on—a red tie.	
3. Little dwarfs with big things sticking up on the head—with tongues out.	3. (Outer red).
Λ4. This is a man and this is a man—the frog part.	4. Feet, legs, hand, coat, face, mouth.
45″	
IV 6″ 1. A dog with big shoes on.	1. Head, tail.
2. Looks like two skunks sticking up here.	2. (Upper d).
41″	
V 2″ 1. Looks like a butterfly —a black butterfly.	1. Flying through the air.
17″	
VI 4″ 1. Looks like a lion—a lion's skin.	1. Fur side hanging on a wall.
17″	
VII 4″ 1. Looks like two little puppy dogs with ears up and looking at each other and sitting down on a	1. They are sitting on the
17″ 2. Butterfly.	2. Butterfly.
VIII 5″ 1. Top looks like the top of a gray mountain.	1. Parts of a mountain

Performance	Inquiry
Blue part in the middle and orange part at bottom.	
34″ 2. Two pink wolves walking up.	2. (P)
IX 4″ 1. Looks like a little dwarf's face with top of lip here—looking at each other.	1. Standing on a
2. This looks like some place they are standing on.	2. Hill—this is the hill.
X 4″ 1. This looks like two crabs,	1. Trying to get up here.
2. With two people—two little dwarfs holding in their mouth	2. (red).
3. A blue tie, and then	3. (inner blue).
4. Green snakes—two green snakes at the bottom.	4. Crawling up.
5. At the top is a pipe with	5. (upper D).
61″ 6. Two little crabs holding it up.	6. (upper gray)

The "blind" interpretation by the same psychologist is as follows:

"At nine years and eight months of age, Patty's record displayed a new richness: the capacity to react overtly, displaying affect in a socially acceptable manner, a sensitivity to the feelings of others, and a real growth toward self-reliance. The basic elements of exaggerated conformity and distinct compulsive tendencies remained.

"Although she seemed to be somewhat thrown by unexpected emotional situations, she generally placed a premium upon self-control and typically achieved it.

"In spite of the fact that she appeared to be quite curious about the phallus, psychosexual identification was clearly feminine.

"There was nothing to suggest that relationships with people had changed in any obvious way during the year."

Patty continued through the years to assume more and more home responsibilities, and to like school very much, despite the fact that she had to work hard to get the average grades that she received. Patty's grades in Citizenship were consistently the highest on her report card, while academic subjects showed barely passing grades. Mother became concerned around this time about Patty's difficulty with spelling and, through an advertisement in the neighborhood newspaper, obtained a tutor, a college student, to help Patty with this subject. This student and Patty got along very well, and what seemed to be of greater importance than the improvement in the spelling, was the positive relationship between them. They continued to keep in touch with one another for many years after this.

During this year Patty began to worry overtly about her mother's health, and she occasionally expressed concern that her mother might die. Her anxiety had some basis in reality, since mother had begun a series of hospitalizations, some of which were quite serious in nature. Grandmother came to stay with the children while mother was ill, and there was much concern that mother might have cancer.

Patty was ten years old and in the fifth grade when she was next seen. This was during one of mother's illnesses, and Patty seemed tense and quite anxious during the initial part of the interview. She was clutching at a notebook and it was evident that she thought the visit had something to do with her schoolwork. She seemed relieved as well as satisfied when I reminded her of our former contacts and described the research project. As the hour went by she became more relaxed and was finally able to talk spontaneously. Among other things, she said that her father had been transferred to a state further from home; and added, more hopefully than convincingly, that the family will move to him as soon as they can find a house. There were indications that her anxiety penalized her in the testing situation where she achieved a barely average rating on the Wechsler Intelligence Scale for Children. Both performance and verbal scores were below what she had achieved in earlier years on other tests.

Her Rorschach responses were as follows:

Patty's Rorschach Protocol at the Ten Year Level

Performance	Inquiry
I 3″ 1. That looks like a "punkin" face.	1. Eyes, mouth, nose.
2. These two things look like little wolves, foxes (upper d).	2. Their face and some of their body—can't see legs or tail.
3. These two things look like little mountains.	3. Here and here.
	1. (Contd.) This could be the

Performance	*Inquiry*
	"punkin" face and people could take the "punkin" and
25″	make it look like that.

II 2″ 1. Two little bears with noses stuck together.
     2. Two lions up there (upper red).
     3. Down here a caterpillar —rather a butterfly.

1. Little cubs of a big bear.
2. Looks like they are angry— tongues sticking out.
3. A regular butterfly. (lower red)

III 3″ 1. Looks like a skeleton— no, two men standing up on
     2. A bone.

1. Here and here.
2. Could be a bone or a face of a . . . I don't know what to call them—something like a turtle—oh, a frog—just his face.

     3. And a necktie in the middle.
     4. And two little ghosts in the back of them (outer red).

3. Necktie that's a bow.
4. Up in the air, flying.
  a. This could be a whole turtle with a necktie on— legs, face, body—a frog, I mean.

20″

IV 3″ 1. A dog with two shoes on —two big shoes, and
     2. An animal on top of him.

1. Dog's face—here's his eyes— right here is his nose. He has his master's shoes on.
2. I think that's his tail instead of an animal on him.

V 4″ 1. Looks like a butterfly.

13″

1. It all has wings like this and a face with two things sticking out. Q. Flying up.

VI 3″ 1. Somebody killed a lion and this looks like a lion's carpet that they put on the floor.

14″

1. Fur side—got these whiskers out here. I saw in the movies where they kill bears, take the blood out and use them for carpets and put them on walls and everything.

VII 3″ 1. Looks like a butterfly at the bottom and on top of the butterfly on one wing
     2. A little puppy and on the other wing is a little

1. Looks like he's in the air.
2. Two little puppies are on him, being taken for a ride.

Performance   *Inquiry*

22″   puppy and they are look-
      ing at each other.

VIII 3″ 1. Looks like a big candy   1. All colors.
         mountain,
       2. And two big candy bears   2. Bears are brown and black
         are walking up it.   but these are pink.
       3. And through the middle   3. Coming up but it don't come
         is some kind of lemon   out yet.
         juice that runs through
         the middle and out the
         top. It isn't coming out
35″   yet.

IX 4″ 1. Looks like another   1. All colored like—candy
         mountain where juice   mountains—regular moun-
         comes out.   tains are black.
       2. And it's coming out—   2. Could be juice like in five
         lemon juice (center D).   cent package you can get all
                            colors.
       3. Two little men with—it   3. On the top of the mountain,
         looks like a skeleton   drinking the juice with their
27″   nose.   nose sticking out.

X 9″ 1. Looks like two little   1. Just regular worms.
         worms at the bottom.
       2. Then right up above   2. Nose, tail, foot—holding onto
         them is two little puppies   the ghosts.
         (inner yellow).
       3. Two ghosts with   3. You can tell they are ghosts.
                          They don't have no hands or
                          nothing.
                          a. Out here looks like clouds.
       4. A necktie in their mouth 4. A necktie you don't pull
         and a   down—you have it a bow on
                          your neck.
       5. Wishbone.   5. Here.
       6. Two—what do you call   6. Got all their things.
         them—ah—you can eat   They are walking up these
         them but I don't know   ghosts.
         what you call them.   a. These two (upper D) look
45″   (outer blue)   like crabs holding the bot-
                          tom of a pipe.

The "blind" interpretation of this record follows:

"The maturing pattern was interrupted with a display in the ten and a half year record of an anxious tension clearly focused around menstruation. Either the menses had just begun or she had recently learned of them. She exhibited considerable curiosity about sexual activities and seemed to be indulging in new, strong fantasies centering about them. There were hints again of some penis envy, but this was restrained.

"With the new adjustment problem, she seemed to have regressed from the controlled display of affect to a more dependent manner of dealing with other people. Her carefully systematized approach to existence remained unimpaired, however."

It is likely that Patty was reflecting her concern about mother's illnesses more than about menstruation, as was noted in the "blind" interpretation. Mother's physical symptoms, including vaginal bleeding, could have been confused in Patty's mind with menstruation. Patty's partial regression to a more dependent level is, no doubt, directly connected with her fear of losing mother. She was also anxious about father's transfer and longed to get the family together. At this time, grandmother was Patty's main source of strength, but Patty found her worried and anxious about her ailing daughter. As a result, Patty was forced to draw more and more upon her own resources and was paying a toll for this in the form of lower functioning both academically and socially.

The many environmental difficulties in Patty's life continued. Mother was hospitalized every six weeks for brief periods of treatment; and father, who was still working in a distant state, continued to try to persuade mother to join him without success. Mother did go so far as to look over the homes he promised to buy for her, but was still skeptical of the permanence of any arrangement father might make. Patty hoped she would change her mind and that the family might be reunited, but there were implications in Patty's reference to this that mother did not want to leave grandmother upon whom she was so dependent.

At the time of the sixth Rorschach, Patty was eleven years old and in the sixth grade. Although she did not appear as anxious as the year before, she was still initially ill at ease in the testing situation and again had to be reminded that the testing was in no way connected to her academic difficulties.

Patty responded to the request to draw a person by drawing a female figure which had the interesting combination of little girl characteristics in a more sophisticated body. She designated the age of the figure as "nine or ten years." There can be no doubt of Patty's feminine identification, but she likes to think of herself as younger than she is. The male figure, drawn next, was no taller than the girl, had an angular body, and a box-like crotch with short legs attached. The head was large with detailed facial features and no ears. The figure was dressed in sports clothes, had one arm in the air and the other on his hip, and was described as a man "waving to someone." The following are Patty's Rorschach responses at the eleven year level:

Patty's Rorschach Protocol at the Eleven Year Level

Performance	*Inquiry*
I 4″ 1. Looks like a mask, and on top of mask	1. Like two horns on top and mask is made up of
2. Looks like it's two fairies, and put together and makes a mask.	2. Two fairies—standing up and wings are up.
1. (Contd). And on top of mask is two horns.	1. (Contd). Mouth and eyes and the angels make the cheeks and ears of it. Mask itself looks like a cat—a mask of a cat.
32″	
II 4″ 1. Looks like two bears with their noses together and	1. Here and here.
2. At the bottom of the bear is a butterfly.	2. Here's wings and right here is mouth—orange.
3. And on top of them is two lions.	3. Faces and they are mad at each other and looks like they are sticking their tongues out.
20″	
III 2″ V1. A frog. W	1. Here's his feet and here's his body and here's his face.
V2. In the middle of the frog is a bow.	2. A regular bow—girls wear them right here (points to head) and men wear them on shirts and girls wear them in their hair.
V3. And on both sides of the frog there are two little dwarfs. (outer red).	3. Looks like they have real long horns on them—real long mouth and here's their hands. Q. In back of the frog on the ground or in the air—could be on something like a string hanging from the ceiling.
20″	

	Performance	*Inquiry*
IV 4″	1. A little dog with two big boots on.	1. Mouth, eyes, nose. These look like boots—has feet up and doing a head stand.
14″		
V 3″	1. Looks like a butterfly.	1. Wings, face—looks like it's flying and its feathers look like a . . .
	2. On both ends of the butterfly looks like two alligators' mouths.	2. Alligator on each side—looks like feathers are shaped in an alligator way.
24″		
VI 4″	1. Looks like a dead lion, and this is the skin of it.	1. Looks like it's hanging up on a wall and they cut off its legs. Q. That would be the fur side.
25″		
VII 2″	1. Here's a little butterfly.	1. On the ground.
	2. On both sides of the butterfly is two little puppies looking at each other.	2. The puppies are on each side of him with paws up.
19″		
VIII 4″	1. Looks like a mountain with all these colors and	1. Looks like a mountain and looks like
	2. Two bears are walking up on each side.	2. This looks like bears climbing up.
	3. And the mountain is made out of butterflies on top of each other.	3. All different kinds of butterflies shaped to make the mountain.
29″		
IX 8″	1. The bottom is a little hill (red).	1. The way it's shaped round like a piece of ground, rock or a little hill.
	2. On top of it is little dogs on each side.	2. Face, eyes, and ears—body and their paws—body curled up—could be sleeping.
	3. And on top of dogs are dwarfs with real long noses.	3. Hair, nose, mouth and real long noses, real funny shaped.
32″		
X 8″	1. Well, looks like two ghosts holding a	1. Their whole body ain't there —ghosts don't always have a whole body.
	2. Ribbon, a bow in their mouths.	2. A regular ribbon—only it looks like it's torn.
	3. And two crabs beside them (outer blue).	3. Looks like they are on the ghost and holding a stick going up to get those fishes.
	4. And on top of their heads looks like two kinds of fish holding	

Performance	*Inquiry*
5. A pipe, and	
6. Down at the bottom	6. Just little worms that when it
are two little worms.	rains they come out.
47″	a. This looks like a little
	wishing bone.

The "blind" interpretation of Patty's sixth yearly Rorschach record was made by the same psychologist who interpreted the others:

"Patty, at eleven and a half years, continued to display a careful restraint in every phase of existence. She obviously tried to fit everything into the patterns of the known and accepted.

"She appeared to be very much the young lady, rejecting her phallic tendencies and concentrating upon what is considered proper. Some sexual curiosity was evident, but it was well under control, and the tensions of the preceding year had been dissipated.

"In spite of her emphasis upon conformity, she did not appear to have a rigid personality structure and certainly was capable of charming spontaneity. She gave the impression of being very well able to get along with others, both her family and her peers."

As Patty gradually became more relaxed in the testing situation, she was able to participate in a brief interview. When asked what she worried about most, she was quick to say that her main concern at the time was that her mother might die. When she was asked about what makes her angry, she replied, "When something happens at home and mother blames me when I didn't do it. I get real mad and excited and talk real loud." Mother reported that Patty generally ended up in tears on such occasions. There was evidently much pent-up hostility toward mother, with accompanying guilt about her hostile wishes, which Patty had not been able to handle adequately. She could talk quite freely about her anger toward her brother, however, saying that when he teases her, she hits him and tries to hurt him.

Patty referred to her long cherished desire to be an actress or a dancer, but said that she now fears that this is only a dream. She had received a scholarship to a local children's theatre, but nothing much was accomplished there. Patty was embarrassed when she was asked about menstruation. Her mother had told her a little but she had also heard the girls at school talking. She had not started at this time.

In summarizing Patty's personality development from six to twelve years of age, it can be said that the developing pattern of adjustment to life situations through this six-year span of Patty's life is that of conformity and restraint. This is shown in her behavior and reflected in her yearly Rorschach protocols. Her adjustment in the final record is that of a well-adapted girl clearly able to handle the usual life stresses of sibling and parents as well as body changes and onset of menses. She seems to be developing into a normally healthy personality with considerable resilience and potentiality for further growth.

Through Patty's yearly Rorschachs, she shows more clearly than in any other way the changes in her psychosexual development. At six years of age she was still in a pre-oedipal stage of development, as shown by her erotic attachment to both parents and her rivalrous feelings toward her brother with whom she competed for mother's attention.

Father's absence from the home for two years when Patty was between three and five and his separation from the family afterwards may account for the relatively late appearance of the oedipal conflict at the age of seven. At that time Patty gave evidence of tension and anxiety, of hostilities against mother, negativism toward the teacher, and admiration for father. In speculating about her narcissistic needs at this time and later one may relate them to the things that were happening to her at this age.

In the following year, at eight years of age, Patty appeared to use the praise she got for conforming as the main source for energy, which she needed in order to repress her hostility. Since this pattern continued through the years to follow, this may suggest that her solution of her oedipal conflict was not an entirely happy one. Mother's frequent hospitalizations, in addition to father's absence from the home, may have contributed to an exaggerated need to repress hostile impulses.

Despite the excess of energy which Patty invested in conformity and restraint, she had ego strength enough to achieve a good social adjustment and to show growth in self-reliance—new facets in her development at the age of nine. These two facets of her personality continue to grow through the years.

When Patty was seen at thirteen years of age, she was still petite and attractive, but more mature in appearance. Menstruation had begun a few months before. The psychiatrist who interviewed her at this time summed up his impressions as follows:

"This is a very poised, normal, well-functioning girl, a little on the compliant side, with problems—if any—around her inhibition of a reaction against aggressive impulses. She has good interpersonal relations, a strong ego, and a good prognosis for growth. She may be a little demanding or bossy to husband and children, but few problems can be anticipated."

Patty was completing eighth grade and was fourteen years old when she was interviewed again. She was thinking about high school, mainly in terms of social activities, but was not sure she would finish. She wanted to go to visit an uncle in California and see the movie stars since she was still most desirous of becoming a movie star or a dancer.

By the time she was seen at seventeen, these exhibitionistic tendencies had been satisfied in more realistic activities in and out of school. Her interests were numerous and varied—ranging from extracurricular school activities to participating in projects of community organizations. She never missed a school sporting event and enjoyed traveling around the area as a baton twirler in her high school band. Patty was also a hard-working and devout member of the Cadet Corps of a religious group and had attended many of their training camps, national as well as local. Her greatest thrill in this connection was her recent trip as one of the representatives of the United States to an international meeting of the youth affiliated with her church. She had met young people from other countries and visited both Paris and London. Patty still corresponded with many of the boys and girls, and was especially delighted to get letters from a Swedish boy she dated in London.

Despite her enthusiasm and activity in all phases of her life, including school, academic work continues to be difficult for Patty. She has had to work hard for her average grades, but makes no complaint about this since she is realistic in her appraisal of her average intelligence. Until this year she had not even considered college and had been enrolled in the commercial course in high school, anticipating a secretarial job after graduation. However, on her trip abroad, she had heard many of her new-made friends talking about their prospective college plans, and so Patty had decided that she also would like to try it. She has already investigated financial aid and has learned of a number of scholarships for which she is eligible to apply. Her sights are set realistically on smaller, coeducational schools in which the competition will be less acute.

Patty recognizes that her college ambitions are more social than academic. She hopes to get married by the time she is twenty-three. She wants to work for a year or two and achieve some degree of financial independence before she marries, then find a husband with similar church affiliation, a good job, and a determination to get ahead in his work. She would like to have about four children, for whom she and her husband would provide a happy home life. Patty can sew, cook, and clean, and believes she will enjoy doing these in her own home. She is currently dating a boy of a different religious faith and feels that this may pose a problem, since they are becoming increasingly fond of one another. However, one gets the impression in talking to Patty that she has sufficient common sense, as well as inner resources, to deal with this or any other problem that may present itself to her.

Unless one speculates about the unclear role which the maternal grandmother may have played in Patty's development, one cannot help wondering about the fact that this girl has been able to overcome quite successfully the obstacles of an unstable family situation in her development and has been able to grow into an essentially healthy, well-functioning personality. There are indications that Patty early relegated mother to a sibling role and ceased to expect her to be the source of her dependency needs. In the very early days Patty arrived at this solution. There were frequent opportunities for her to turn for help to grandmother, who assumed responsibility for Patty and her brother during the numerous emotional and physical indispositions and illnesses to which mother was prone. As she grew older Patty was also able to turn to other adults, such as teachers, counselors and her minister for acceptance and guidance, thus supplementing her supply of love, acceptance and a feeling of belonging, to the point that she was able to solve her rivalrous feelings toward her younger brother by developing a maternal protective role toward him. One can sense the same attitude developing toward her infantile dependent mother and there is every indication that Patty is becoming the recognized strength in this family unit.

VI : PHILLIP

PHILLIP WAS BORN in New England when mother was thirty-two and father forty-five years of age. The family moved to Pittsburgh, where a sister was born shortly before Phillip's fifth birthday. They live in their own home in a middle class neighborhood of professional and white collar workers. Both parents were high schools graduates, and father had two years of college.

Mother was well during her pregnancy with Phillip, with the exception that she had had undulant fever in the first month of her pregnancy. The baby was full-term and mother was in labor for two days. He weighed nearly eight pounds at birth, but was dehydrated and had the cord around his neck. Because he was cyanotic, Phillip was immediately given a transfusion of mother's blood and kept in an oxygent tent for the first week. Both mother and child remained in the hospital for a month after delivery, due to mother's developing puerperal fever at this time.

Phillip was bottlefed, but he was a poor eater throughout his infancy and gained very slowly. He weighed less than twelve pounds when solid foods were introduced at the time he was eight months old. Clubbing of hands and feet was noted during Phillip's first year of life, and further physical defects were detected in the years that followed.

Phillip did not sit alone until he was fourteen months old, nor did he begin walking until he was two and a half. His physical movements were always awkward and he did extensive falling as he tried to get around during his pre-school years. He talked, however, before his second birthday.

Mother made only mild efforts to toilet train Phillip because of his poor physical condition, and these efforts were not initiated until after two years of age. He developed bowel and bladder control for daytime functions but any attempts at night control were abandoned

77

when it was discovered that Phillip had a severe kidney condition. However, the child himself tried hard to control his bedwetting. On one occasion in later childhood, when visiting in another home, he stayed awake all night to avoid wetting the bed. Mother's comment about this was, "He had lots of mental drive."

Neighbors and friends objected to any attempts mother made to punish Phillip during his early years on the grounds that the boy was "not well." As a result of these comments, as well as her own ambivalence about having such a disabled child, mother's discipline and punishment were inconsistent. When Phillip was criticized or corrected, he often became angry and "wanted to pound things"; but this violence was rarely directed into destructive acts.

Phillip began to attend nursery school before he was three years old. He seemed to enjoy playing with the other children, but this school experience had to be interrupted when the family moved to Pittsburgh. Just before his fifth birthday, at about the time that his sister was born, Phillip started to kindergarten and attended there for one year.

Until this time, parents had not sought medical advice about Phillip's obvious physical disabilities. Now, with his entrance to first grade approaching, they became active in seeking diagnosis and treatment of his condition. After a series of medical consultations, a heart condition was diagnosed and parents were warned that eventual surgery might be necessary.

Phillip's physical handicaps and underdevelopment were accentuated by comparison with the other children in his first grade class. He was unable to play games with his classmates, and there were many other motor inadequacies evident. For example, he became fatigued after walking even short distances. He was often subjected to teasing by his schoolmates because of his physical limitations, and was excluded from their play during this first year of school. This was a source of great concern for Phillip, but he was only able to express this at home.

This, then, was the physically handicapped little boy whose condition had not yet been completely diagnosed when I first saw him at the age of six years and eight months. At this time, he was a small, dark-eyed child with an asymmetrically-shaped head, tiny chalk-white baby teeth, and bluish lips. His enlarged fingertips seemed to be the cause of the fumbling action of his hands, and his speech was slightly infantile. There was a definite enuretic smell about him. His facial expression, however, was alert, and his general body movements, quick. His first grade teacher saw him as an average student "despite a serious heart condition."

Phillip was initially suspicious in the testing situation, but soon became interested in the test material and began to relax. He was consistently cooperative, but it was obvious that he grew physically tired before the session was concluded, and he expressed a desire to terminate. While Phillip achieved an average intelligence rating on the Binet, there were indications that this was a minimal performance and that under less tension he might have achieved a higher rating.

He gave the following responses to the Rorschach cards:

Phillip's Rorschach Protocol at the Six Year Level

Performance	*Inquiry*
I 14″ 1. A flying mouse. 20″	1. Head, hands, wings, legs. Q. Flying.
II 15″　I don't even know what this could be. 16″ 1. A witch?	1. They're playing pat-a-cake.
III 3″ 1. A skeleton. 7″	1. Prancing in the water when they don't have any flesh or anything.
IV 12″ 1. A wolf—legs and head. 30″	1. Head, legs. I don't know what this is (Points to lower D).
V 2″ 1. A fly. 5″	1. Q. Out in the air.
VI 29″　I wonder what time it is. 1. A leaf. (W). 33″ 2. A fly. (D).	1. Here. 2. Looks like a fly up in the air.
VII 8″ 1. Two dogs standing on 2. Some grass. (At this point his lips 15″　grew very pale).	
VIII 10″ 1. Two frogs on each side climbing on 2. Orange and red leaf. 30″ 3. A little house.	1. (P) 2. (lower D) 3. (upper D)
IX 30″ 1. A baby holding 2. A tree. 35″	1. Baby here (red). 2. Q. It's leaves and has a stem. Q. It's green.

Performance	*Inquiry*
X 5″ 1. Reindeers (brown).	1. Up in the sky, prancing.
2. Rabbit.	2. Just the head. (P)
3. Sun.	3. It's round and has things out
I can see some stuff but	on it. (outer blue)
I don't know what it is.	
30″ 4. Two great big animals	4. Head, tails, feet. (red)

Following is the "blind" interpretation given to this record:

"At six years, eight months, Phillip's record seemed to be that of an intelligent child, certainly of better native endowment than the Binet results would indicate. He appeared to have a rich fantasy life, reacting strongly to the environment about him but restraining overt expression of his feeling. The most descriptive word to apply to his behavior is "cautious." He clearly would attempt to conform to convention in any expression of feeling and may often be so concerned about being correct that the observer would appraise his behavior as being vague.

"There was evidence of pretty disturbing sex fantasies. There was a suggestion of masturbation, and the record suggests that he might be enuretic.

"The fact that he regards people generally as being somewhat remote might be a real comfort to him since he also sees them as distinctly threatening. He appeared to be so involved with his personal problems that he probably did not pay much attention to other children except to observe what happens about him. Although there was a rather close relationship with his mother at this time his father seemed to be a threatening figure."

There is no indication in this "blind" interpretation of Phillip's concern about his physical condition. Knowing the history, one might attach more significance in this regard to the "skeleton" response on Card III. That he is able to repress any anxiety in this area is no doubt a reflection of the denying attitude which parents have maintained up to this point regarding Phillip's physical condition.

During the year following this first Rorschach, Phillip's parents made inquiries into the facilities of a well-known diagnostic clinic in another city. It seemed as though societal pressure rather than any change in Phillip's physical condition was influencing the parents to seek more medical assistance for him. Regardless of cause, much more accentuation was being placed on his disabilities than had been the case previously.

When I next saw him, Phillip had changed little in physical appearance and gave the general impression of being a very anxious little boy. He was seven years and eight months of age, but looked and was dressed more like a preschooler than like the second grader that he was. In contrast to his initial suspicious tenseness at our first contact, Phillip came into the testing room this time seemingly quite relaxed and gave evidence of enjoying the experience. He again became physically tired and was obviously relieved when the testing period was over.

Phillip's teacher saw him as an average student in academic subjects, but slower and more awkward in motor activity than the other children in his age group. His drawing of a man on this occasion, was no doubt his own self-concept. The figure was quite small, armless, with a head many times the size of the body, irregular facial features, large bizarre ears, and stick legs. In this drawing, he showed his concern about his inadequate, mutilated physique as well as his feeling that he must somehow try to make up for this inadequacy with emphasis on mental achievement. This was also a reflection of father's attitude at this time; father was pressuring Phillip toward better school achievement. My general impression was that Phillip was beginning to use repression as well as denial as a defense against his anxieties, and was thus able to relate to his environment in a conforming, pseudo relaxed way. His release from tension came in the safety of his own home, where he was able to express his irritation and sometimes indulge in temper tantrums.

He gave the following responses to the Rorschach at this time:

Phillip's Rorschach Protocol at the Seven Year Level

Performance	Inquiry
I 19″ 1. Looks like a ghost to me.	1. Bones, one of things to eat with (upper D). This could be his mouth and wings. When he flies in the air. Q. Flying.
25″	a. (Then sees it as a face with eyes and nose).
II This is one I always had trouble with.	
17″ 1. Fireworks. (W)	1. These things bust up here and look real pretty here. Q. Red and black. That's where they start off.
18″	

Performance	Inquiry
III 4" 1. Couple of monkeys	1. Q. In the cage. Nose, eyes, body, one foot and crushing a
	a. Peanut.
2. With a ribbon between it.	
1. (Contd). Walking, stepping in	
13" a. Puddles.	
IV 4" 1. Fox.	1. Wolf—feet, this is eyes and nose, little tail—things he holds. Q. Getting after somebody—feet are running.
6"	
V 2" 1. That looks like a bat.	1. On top of the ground—just coming out of his hole.
5"	
VI 19" 1. Looks like a fiddle.	1. This is the thing you hold it with and these are the strings and this is where you pound it. (W)
20"	
VII 2" 1. Couple of little doggies standing	1. Ears, eyes, little nose, mouth. Q. Down here and here's his body.
2. On a hill.	
VIII 15" 1. Couple of mouses going to eat	1. Eating grass.
2. Some cheese or something.	2. Grass. Q. It's green.
IX 22" 1. Couple of lobsters standing on	1. These things here—they pick you up and eat you.
25" 2. Some grass.	2. Here's the grass. It's green.
X 4" 1. Lots of little bugs.	1. (Points to each D area).
7"	

The psychologist who interpreted his first Rorschach gave the following "blind" interpretation to the above responses:

"In the seven year, eight month record, Phillip seems to have made rather erratic progress, moving toward a more mature solution of some of his problems but slipping backward in other respects. Again, masturbation is strongly suggested. The intense erotic relationship with the mother which seemed involved earlier was not so evident and the father seemed to be slightly more acceptable to him, displaying some admirable qualities even though still being seen as a rather frightening figure.

"There was evidence of some regressive behavior, probably with oral implications. Pretty infantile behavior certainly would seem to occur sporadically. He would seem to be very dependent and to be retreating from satisfying contacts with people. The quality of change in his record is such that one might wonder whether a psychosomatic disorder might be developing."

The "psychosomatic disorder" to which the interpreter referred was, of course, more than this. In fact, one might refer to it as "soma-psychic." The parents' concern about Phillip's physical condition reached the point where they initiated, during the year following this Rorschach, the first of four diagnostic studies at the nationally known clinic which they had previously contacted. The final diagnosis was that of a very serious heart condition for which the only treatment, surgery, was not recommended because of the great risk involved. Steps toward an operation would be taken only if Phillip started to go "down-hill fast." No restriction of exercise was suggested.

The boy continued on to the third grade, but, during the school year, he made many complaints at home about his "yelly" teacher. The resulting tension in the classroom irritated him. While he was never the subject of the teacher's yelling, he was irritated because the teacher tended to make exceptions for him on the basis of his limitations. Parents wondered whether Phillip really liked school at this time, even though he never complained about school as such. Father helped him with his lessons, and he seemed to enjoy these sessions with father. He was interested in learning, but his parents thought that his struggles with physical handicaps were becoming more apparent at school.

Phillip was again taken for a physical checkup at the diagnostic clinic shortly before I saw him for the third time. He was found to be not in as good condition as he had been the previous year. He continued to play with other children as best he could, but became increasingly short of breath and more cyanotic than he had been previously.

At the time of the testing, when he was eight years and eight months old, he seemed pathetic in appearance and behavior. He was physically restless and seemingly uncomfortable, but always alert and pleasant in the test situation. His reaction time was quick and he often showed a good sense of humor. Phillip spoke spontaneously of his interest in sports, despite his inability to participate.

He seemed to enjoy the Monroe Diagnostic Reading Examination given at this time, and achieved grades consistent with his third grade placement. Again, he gave the impression of a child trying desperately to deny and repress his anxiety and to appear conforming.

Following is Phillip's Rorschach protocol on this occasion:

Phillip's Rorschach Protocol at the Eight Year Level

Performance	Inquiry
I 1″ 1. Bat.	1. Eyes, wings. Q. On the tree.
40″ 2. Two monkeys. (side D).	2. On the tree. Q. Here.
II 4″ 1. Two elephants.	1. In the park. Elephants are stepping on bat.
2. A bat.	2. (Lower red)
3. Two hats.	3. Bobby hats. (upper red)
III 10″ 1. Two monkeys.	1. Drinking water from the pond.
2. Two rocks and . . . a	2. Rocks in the pond.
3. Two cats (outer D).	3. Here and here.
23″	a. Hair bow.
IV 4″ 1. Fox. (Dr.)	1. Face and tail.
20″ 2. Bat.	2. (Indefinite).
V 4″ 1. A rabbit.	1. Just the head.
9″ 2. Bat.	2. The rest.
VI 3″ 1. Wolf.	1. In the woods screaming. (W)
20″ 2. Candle.	2. Fire from it here. (upper D)
VII 3″ 1. Two little kitty cats.	1. Playing together and jumping on the bat.
2. Frog (d).	2. Swimming in pond between two rocks.
17″	
VIII 4″ 1. Two bears.	1. Climbing on a stick of the tree.
2. Fire.	2. Smoke and blaze.
3. Bat.	3. & 4. Lying against the tree.
36″ 4. Tree.	
IX 5″ 1. Two men.	1. On the tree.
2. Trees.	2. Leaves, green and pink leaves, in the fall.
15″	
X 3″ 1. Two spiders.	1. Making a cobweb. (P)
2. Two bugs.	2. (Red)
3. Two alligators.	3. (Upper gray) In a fountain drinking.
40″	

The following is the "blind" interpretation of the above record:
"At the age of eight years, eight months, the Rorschach record displayed considerably more tension. It is by far the most restricted record which this boy produced and suggests a pretty limited intellectual efficiency at this time. There was even a tendency to force his associations toward bizarre concepts, suggesting a reaction to some traumatic experience; the precipitating situation probably occurred sometime earlier (probably more than a year previous to this record) and his overt behavior may have deviated only insofar as his appearing pretty immature at times."

It was learned later that Phillip related his contact with me at this time to his previous medical examinations, which were anxiety provoking to him. It is possible that the short, snappy responses on this occasion could thus have been a function of his dislike and fear of the testing situation. Then, too, the precipitating situation to which the interpreter refers could well be the time, a little more than a year before, that Phillip sensed his parents' real concern about his physical condition. It was at that time that he showed regressive behavior, evidently in connection with the realization of the seriousness of his affliction.

A month or so after the time of the testing at the eight year level, Phillip complained of pains in his legs. He had no control over urination, wetting day and night. A diagnosis of progressive kidney disfunctioning was made during the summer and it was recommended that Phillip have a "home-bound" teacher for his fourth grade work. In October of that year he was hospitalized for three days for further urological study. Phillip was cystogrammed and cystoscoped as a part of this evaluation. Serious heart and kidney conditions were found.

Phillip worked with a "home-bound" teacher through fourth grade, and it was at home, during this period, that I administered the fourth Rorschach and the Grace Arthur Performance Scale. His physical appearance had changed very little, even to the fact that there had been little physical growth since the last contact. Along with the defects noted at the other contacts, there was an added labored breathing on this occasion.

The testing situation was evidently a welcome break in his daily routine and Phillip made superficial attempts to appear happy and content. However, it was quite evident that the boy was uncomfortable, anxious and unhappy. The performance test materials held little interest for him and there was only one item on which he reached his chronological age level of nine years. All other scores were two or three years lower. The rating of low average functioning which he achieved at this time was undoubtedly influenced by his high anxiety level and consequent lack of ability to concentrate on the material.

In general, however, he gave the impression of being better defended and less restless than on previous occasions. There was even some spontaneity and a definite attempt to play the gracious host.

Phillip's responses to the Rorschach cards, which he gave quickly and in a matter-of-fact manner, are as follows:

Phillip's Rorschach Protocol at the Nine Year Level

Performance	Inquiry
I 1″ 1. A bat. 6″	1. Has wings and these feelers. Q. Flying in a house.
II 1. Two elephants holding something.	a. Butterfly.
III 2″ 1. Two men mixing some cement. 8″	
IV 4″ 1. What's this? I don't know what side you should turn it. Looks like a bat and something else. And a chicken or V2. A spider.	2. And a spider this way.
V 1″ 1. A bat—this I am quite sure of. 6″	1. Flying around
VI 1. A bug.	a. A heart (inner d). Q. In your body.
VII 2″ 1. Two puppies sitting on the 2. Ground with 8″ 3. An ant crawling up.	3. (d)
VIII 1″ 1. A fire. 2. Two bugs crawling on something—can't make that out—shaking hands.	1. Fire is usually orange and red. Q. With this other animal.
IX 4″ 1. Two animals sitting on 8″ 2. A green walk.	2. Green stones. a. That's fire.

Performance	Inquiry
X 3" 1. Bugs and bugs and bugs.	1. Down in the water.
	a. Lobsters (blue).
9" 2. Mountain (red area).	2. (Red area)

Following is the "blind" interpretation of the above record:

"The record given at nine years, eight months displayed better control in affective situations, except when they became very pressing. Some of his internalized tension might still reflect direct sexual conflicts. The extent of tension displayed and the internalization, as well as the content of some of his responses, again would raise the question of some psychosomatic disorder.

"In spite of the negative features, this seems a much healthier record than the one of the year before, and the intellectual aspects approached the competence suggested in the first record."

Of course, the interpreter had no way of knowing about Phillip's serious illness. She later explained that she had struggled with the records in an attempt to figure out what was causing Phillip's tension and also what he was trying to "internalize."

Phillip's protests about the lack of a gang to play with and the "loss of companionship" with his classmates resulted in his return to regular school enrollment in fifth grade. His parents had been given a most unfavorable prognosis, and felt that in "marking time" until his death, Phillip should do whatever he wanted and was able to do, so far as school was concerned.

I saw him again in the school setting when he was ten years and eight months old; and, at that time, Phillip immediately expressed his pleasure at being back with the other children. During the testing period, he frequently exhibited a good sense of humor in his spontaneous comments, despite the fact that he was restless as usual.

Phillip seemed to enjoy the test items of the WISC, showing more interest and ability on the verbal scale than he did in the performance area. The results confirmed those found earlier on the Binet and Grace Arthur. He gave the appearance of being less anxious than a year before, and seemed to feel more a part of his environment—he told of being manager of the neighborhood ball team with obvious pleasure. His defense system seemed to be working effectively at this time, with no overt signs of the anxiety which his physical ailment must have been causing.

Mother and father believed, in retrospect, that Phillip even suppressed and denied actual physical pain and discomfort that must have been on the increase at this time. There were frequent outbursts of temper at home, and these seemed to be the release for his increasing tension.

Following are the Rorschach responses which he gave:

Phillip's Rorschach Protocol at the Ten Year Level

Performance	*Inquiry*
I 6″ 1. A bat.	1. This would be his body and there are his wings.
29″	Q. Flying.
II 4″ 1. Elephants and	1. There's two of them standing up and putting their . . .
2. A bug. 10″	2. (Gray part of upper d)—a mosquito.
III 2″ 1. Two men and	1. They're funny—here's one leg and here's another one. Q. Cooking something. a. This could be a pot here.
2. Hair ribbon.	2. Pink.
3. And some kind of a bug. (outer red). 20″	3. Look, spiders hanging down from the chandelier or something.
IV 24″ 1. A pair of feet.	1. Men's feet (all but lower D).
2. And a bug. 35″	2. Looks like he's hanging down. (D).
V 4″ 1. That looks like a bat.	1. He's flying towards a tree I'd say. These are his feet sorta and his wings and antlers—feelers I guess.
18″ That's all.	
VI 21″ 1. A cat and	1. (Upper D). Just his head. Q. His ears.
41″ 2. A bear skin.	2. Fur side.
VII 2″ 1. Two puppies and	1. These are his ears, tail and his head and feet. Q. Standing up on something looking at each other.
2. A bug.	2. He's flying underneath them. Q. Butterfly.
12″ That's all.	
VIII 10″ 1. Well, two mice.	1. These are the mice and they are climbing up something like two bugs.

Performance	Inquiry
2. Two butterflies.	2. The way it looks like he has a head and wings. Other one doesn't look much like one (gray and blue).
30″	
IX 5″ 1. Two dragons.	1. They are real mad at each other. Q. The eyes are not friendly.
2. Stones.	2. (Green and red) Funny odd stone.
35″ That's about all—that's all.	
X 9″ 1. A cliff.	1. Down here is the valley and this is the cliff (center white and red).
2. Lots of bugs.	2. Some are hanging, some are flying.
3. Spider and that's all.	3. (Blue) He's along the cliff—walking on top of it.

The "blind" interpretation of this record follows:

"The record at the age of ten years, eight months displays a tremendous amount of maturing when compared to the preceding one. A very important technique which he has adopted is that of a pretty passive acceptance, both of himself and of his environment. Although the father remains rather disturbing to him, the boy has made a clearly masculine identification. His general perception of people would seem to have a quality of delicate tolerance, which is a most mature step for him to have made.

"For the first time, he displays enough self-confidence to permit himself to consider the display of anger as being relatively safe.

"It is difficult to guess the new source of ego strength. Whether it has been an environmental change, therapy or something else, a truly revitalizing experience has taken place for this boy."

The therapeutic possibility to which the interpreter referred could well be Phillip's release from his homebound instruction and the opportunity to mix with other children at school and in the neighborhood. He continued as manager of different athletic teams as the seasons changed and took great pride in working out schedules and keeping scores. Father, who had become an increasingly important factor in Phillip's life, took great pride in the boy's vast store of factual information. Phillip responded to this by studying the almanac for hours at a time.

At this time, Phillip began to express his anger more directly and openly. "Anything unfair" annoyed him. For example, he would complain that his sister was not sharing properly in a joint responsibility such as dishwashing. However, despite his arguments with her, his sister was probably his closest friend at this time, since his physical limitations directed him toward activities at her age level rather than his own. They often "played story" together by acting out the various roles. They listened to records, pored over comic books, and went to movies together. Although he had only one close boy friend who frequently accompanied them to the movies, he was in good rapport with the neighborhood children, as evidenced by his inclusion in any activity within the limits of his physical strength.

Phillip was in the sixth grade when the last Rorschach was obtained. There seemed to be little evidence of physical growth, and he was still a wizened, physically defective boy with an enuretic odor about him. Although conforming and cooperative as usual, he tended to give curt, snappy answers on this occasion. It was evident that he had little enthusiasm for the test situation.

When I asked him to draw a person, he retorted flippantly, "I'm no artist," but at the same time began to draw. His first drawing was a girl without arms, and he said she was "seven years old—about my sister's age." The face was round, with all features regular and present. There was no neck, the body area was triangular, and there were three buttons down the front and a wavy line at the bottom, evidently indicating the dress trimming. Her legs and feet were stick-like. The boy, "ten or eleven, in sixth grade," was apparently a self-concept. Smaller than the girl, the male figure had a large head with all facial features present, a thin body with three buttons down the front, and legs and arms reenforced with shaded lines. Feet and hands were "scratchy" indications of such.

When he was questioned about his worries, Phillip expressed his concern about his school work, especially arithmetic, and was also worried about what he should get his sister and parents for Christmas. He said that he rarely got angry, and, when he did, he tried not to show it. He added, however, "When my father orders me to do my homework, I could just rip myself apart." His cherished desire was to get a baseball suit for Christmas.

In spite of his many physical handicaps, which portended a most uncertain future, and despite his envy of physically adequate people —his sister, in particular—Phillip seemed to have been able to make a fair adjustment to himself and the world about him. He was fortu-

nate in having a sympathetic and helpful home and school environment.

Phillip's Rorschach responses at this level were as follows:

Phillip's Rorschach Protocol at the Eleven Year Level

Performance	Inquiry

I 5″ 1. Looks like a bat with funny ears and antlers.
   23″   I guess that's about all.

1. Flying.

II 1″ 1. Two elephants clapping their heels, real funny hats and have trunks
    20″   together.

1. Dancing in a circus. Q. Clown hats—little big—I mean little small for them.

III 2″ 1. Two men fighting over a couple of
         2. Pots of gold.
         3. A hair ribbon and I don't know what those
    20″   are.

1. Looks like funny men.

2. Down here.

3. A red hair ribbon for a girl—light red.

IV 4″ 1. That looks like an up-side-down bat with a lot of ears and two eyes—feet (points).
         I guess that's all.

1. Looks like a funny hat.
Q. Standing up.
a. In a tree.

V 5″ 1. Just looks like a bat—so many bats.
   10″

1. Looks like an ordinary bat—tail, ears, face, wings.
Q. Flying.

VI 5″ 1. Looks like a bear rug with wings. (smiles).
         Has a funny nose
    22″   (sighs).

1. Fur—funny nose. Q. In the house.

VII 3″ 1. This looks like two dogs sitting on a rock—looks like they are mad at each other.
    19″ 2. There's an ant hole between them.

1. Here's two puppy dogs and they are mad at each other—standing on rocks. Q. Shape.

2. (S)

VIII 5″ 1. Two chipmunks climbing up a
          2. Big dead bat and

          3. Beautiful fall leaves and stuff down there.

1. Here and here.

2. I don't see his face. Maybe someone shot it off when they killed him.

3. Autumn leaves.

Performance	Inquiry
IX 3″ 1. Two prehistoric animals fighting over something.	1. (upper D)
2. Water gushing out between them.	2. Gushing from down here. Q. The ground.
20″	
X 2″ 1. This looks like all different sorts of bugs.	1. Looks like they were all on the ground.
2. Ants.	2. (Brown) Looks like they are hunting for food.
3. Crabs.	3. Ready to hit someone.
4. Caterpillars.	4. Green. Q. Walking together like they are in love.

Following is the "blind" interpretation of the above record:

"The changes taking place in the previous record continue in that obtained when he was eleven years, nine months of age, but it would not be surprising if people near him might have occasional doubts. His willingness to express anger fairly openly may at times cause his behavior to appear rather brash, in contrast with some of his earlier tense withdrawal. His emotional display may occasionally produce some anxiety in himself, but he really has achieved a pretty good integration of his newfound freedom. When he is not confronted with any external social pressure, he would appear to be a pretty composed individual.

"He seems to have some rudiments of self-criticism evident in his dubbing so many of his concepts as "funny." His selection of descriptive words in other concepts points to this interpretation rather than suggesting a paucity of capacity for self-expression.

"Overtly, he would seem to display the gang interests and scorn for females which is typical for his age group.

"The record would seem to contain many ego strengths and the capacity for future growth. Without knowing more specifically what his problems and his means of recovery have been, however, I should be unwilling to hazard a guess as to the kind or extent of stress he might be expected to withstand."

In reviewing Phillip's development through the six year span covered in the preceding story, one sees a physically ill child whose illness caused anxiety that increased through the years. Reflected in his Rorschach protocols is a desperate attempt to deny and repress this anxiety, with almost unbelievable success. Parents supported him in his defense, enabling him to live as normal an existence as seemed possible for this boy. Although he is described as "wanting to be with people," one gets the impression that Phillip's motivation was more an unfulfilled desire to be accepted than an actual enjoyment of interpersonal relationships.

Phillip's Rorschachs point up clearly that he, himself, could not deny his inadequacies completely, and that he was, at least unconsciously, cognizant of the fact that he differed appreciably from other boys of his age. Because his defects kept him from doing what the others could do physically, and because his many sieges of illness required him to be at home much of the time, his closest relationships through the years were confined to his immediate family. As his physical health became more impaired, he clung to them even more desperately, despite his constant conscious attempts at independence. He tried to lean on mother; but she seemed to deny the demands of a handicapped child. Father, with his sometimes unrealistic academic demands on the boy, was a constant source of mixed fear and challenge for the child. Phillip's most positive relationship seemed to be with his sister. He seemed to experience his most satisfactory and non-threatening contacts with her during this preadolescent period.

Phillip was interviewed by a psychiatrist at the age of thirteen. At that time, he was described as "undersized, frail, but vigorous, with a moderate asymmetry in face, posture, and gait. His face, neck, teeth and fingers were all distorted and his shoulder girdle indicates some wasting."

The psychiatrist went on to say that Phillip was "euphoric in mood and appeared to deny all difficulties. It was not possible to elicit a history of any serious illness. He volunteered, in general questioning, that he was smaller and less strong than the average—but not much! In fact, he felt he was as healthy and happy as the next boy. His wishes for the future were vague. He would like to travel and/or be a TV camera man. He likes TV and movies, enjoys space ships and Bob Hope.

"His concept of the 'worst possible thing' was to be 'never able to move around or go outside—like having polio or maybe 'cause you just couldn't move.'

"The one remembered dream at this time was being assigned an 'impossible task—having a thousand comic books to read in an hour for a reward of $1,000.' "

The psychiatrist thought that Phillip had made a good outward adjustment to his handicap. However, "he needs to face up to his realistic limitations better than he appears to, or he will be riding for a fall—probably a depression in three to ten years."

A little more than a year later, Phillip died. He was in bed only two days in the final stages of his illness. The cause of death as recorded in the death certificate: "Kidney failure—lower urinary obstruction due to 'median bar' deformity. Contributory—congenital heart disease—tetralogy of Fallot."

His Rorschach records give us a better understanding of what was going on inside Phillip than he himself had ever been able to recognize, much less verbalize. A second child psychiatrist, who had access to the preceding case material as well as the Rorschach protocols, made the following formulation of Phillip's personality development:

"Phillip was an anxious, physically ill, somewhat immature boy who was necessarily dependent to a great extent on his family and was very close to mother, whose anxiety and guilt about him led her to react to him in an inconsistent, yet controlling manner. Mother herself used denial of the boy's limitations to herself and projected this expectation onto Phillip. His close erotic relationship to mother, coupled with fear of father and his wanting to conform to father's intellectual expectations of him, as well as conflict and guilt over masturbation and castration fear, led to a persistent enuresis on the boy's part. He used denial over his conflict of dependency and oedipal strivings, and looked upon himself as an entirely adequate normal boy. This view was probably reenforced by fantasies of a sexual and power-operation nature where all the obvious defects and conflicts were negated. His use of tight control over aggressive, hostile and affective responses at earlier ages later became better integrated as he was able to make contacts outside the home with teachers and classmates. Affectivity was often handled by outbursts at home with generally good control outside. His need to be liked by others led him to be agreeable and conforming and gave him a sense of pseudo-adequacy. Sibling rivalry was repressed initially with much castration anxiety present. Later he was more open in expression of hostility.

"Conflicts over dependency, oedipal strivings, castration fears, death fears were handled by denial, fantasy of a wish-fulfilling nature, internalization of aggressive, hostile feelings, and constriction with use of some compulsive defenses. He also used intellectual defenses—striving to know many things and facts which, however, were unrelated to school, where competition with peers was involved."

VII : ADELE

ADELE IS THE ONLY CHILD of an upper middle class family. Mother, a junior college graduate, was twenty-four years old and father, who graduated from a large eastern college, was twenty-nine at the time of the child's birth. She weighed six and a half pounds and was given both the breast and bottle during her early months of life. She was then weaned to the bottle and baby foods without difficulty.

By the time Adele could walk alone and talk, which was around her first birthday, mother had already started toilet training. Mother now thinks that this was too early, since the child continued to be enuretic for several years. As she was unable to cope with this problem and was much concerned by it, mother took Adele for a physical checkup; but the doctor could find no physical basis for her enuresis.

In addition, Adele liked to suck her thumb at night. Mother dealt with this concern by confining her to a "snuggle ducky" so that the girl could not continue this activity. Another "nervous" habit which mother also considered nasty was that of blowing bubbles. This one, however, persisted until Adele was nearly a year old.

Adele was a very active toddler and mother felt the need to watch her continually. Despite this constant vigilance, Adele fell out of the second-story window when she was about two years old. No injuries were sustained, but mother was so upset by this fall that she reported having nightmares about the incident for several weeks afterwards.

It was evident that mother, who is a meticulous and compulsive person, was under considerable strain during Adele's first two years and tended to project her own anxiety onto the baby. The family lived with the paternal grandparents during this period, and they were not only critical of mother's "strictness" but also tended to indulge the child. There was considerable tension generated by the grandparents' behavior and attitude, and many arguments between mother and father about this.

Father is a somewhat passive, dependent person—the only child

95

of possessive, well-to-do parents. He was called into military service when Adele was slightly over two years old, and mother and Adele followed him to a camp in a Southern city. It was then that Adele developed feeding problems. Her previous good appetite and interest in foods diminished to a desire for milk alone. Mother tended to relate this to the hot climate, but also acknowledged that there was some connection between this regression on Adele's part and the tension within the family unit. Besides the very crowded living conditions near camp, parents were much concerned about father's uncertain military future. There is the added possibility that Adele missed the stability of the grandparents' home and the attention which she received from them there.

Father was sent overseas shortly before Adele's fourth birthday and was out of the country for more than two years. During his absence, mother and child returned to Pittsburgh to live with a sister-in-law whose husband, mother's brother, was also overseas. There was a daughter about Adele's age in this home, and the two mothers were much upset by the constant squabbling between the two girls.

The news of uncle's death in action was, of course, very disturbing to the household. In order to lessen the increased tension and turmoil, both children were sent to a private nursery school which they attended for a year, beginning when they were four and a half years old. The following year, Adele attended kindergarten in a progressive school where she reportedly got along well with the other children.

Little is known about the handling of Adele's sex curiosity. Mother reported that she had never asked any questions, but it was evident that Adele was quite interested and had picked up a good deal of such information during her preschool years. There was a problem of masturbation at one point, but mother tended to minimize it in the telling —she considered it another one of those "nasty" habits that mother had to squelch.

Adele was given her first Rorschach when she was in the first grade of the same progressive school where she had attended kindergarten. At this time, when she was six years and eight months old, she was a large, well-built girl with blue eyes, light-brown hair and a serious, almost unhappy expression on her face. The teacher praised both her school work and her ability to use spare time constructively.

Adele cooperated only fairly well in the testing situation. She scored in the superior range on the Binet intelligence test, with indications that she might have scored even higher had she been more interested and better motivated. She grew impatient during the Rorschach when faced with the inquiry, and wondered pointedly if it were not time for her to join the other children.

Her Rorschach responses were as follows:

Adele's Rorschach Protocol at the Six Year Level

Performance	Inquiry
I 9″ 1. This looks like a girl with	1. Legs put together. Dress and you see her legs through the dress. Q. Hands up and her head is stuck back of her like this.
2. Mud sticking all over 29″ here.	2. (Why mud?) It's splashed in here and all over.
II 4″ 1. Dark sky with red mill 12″ stuff (fire).	1. The darkness of the sky. Q. It's red where the mill stuff is.
III 11″ 1. Same thing (dark sky and red mill stuff).	a. This is a design.
2. I see a bow on it right 12″ here.	2. Loops here and here's a loop and this is a knot on.
IV 2″ 1. Dark sky.	
2. Man sitting down. 10″	2. I don't know what he is sitting on—has a crazy head.
V 1″ 1. A butterfly—or kind of 20″ a bird.	1. Butterfly, here's wings and head. Q. On the paper.
VI 6″ 1. It has a butterfly on it.	1. Butterfly is on the stick.
2. Here's a long stick that's pulled out of the ground, with	2. It's dark and it's splashed—
20″ 3. Mud on it.	3. It's wet and splashed—and it's up in the air.
VII 3″ 1. Clouds.	1. Big and round.
10″ 2. Wool—piece of wool.	2. Not made up—it's fluffy.
VIII 15″ Got to do all these cards? Umph—I don't know. Oooh.	
1. Two animals climbing on	
2. Colored rocks.	
30″ 1. (Contd). See the two bears?	
IX 13″ 1. A picture, that's all— 15″ that's just scribble, scrabble.	1. That's a design—all colors.

Performance	Inquiry
X 15″ 1. A beautiful design.	1. (W)
2. Branches and green leaves.	2. Leaves and sticks.
3. Two blue spiders on it.	3. Here and here.
	a. Trousers. Q. Working trousers with cuffs turned up
30″	(lower green).

Following is the "blind" interpretation of this record:

"At the early age of six years, eight months, Adele's identifications are markedly feminine. Although the mother is somewhat confusing to her because she appears to have adopted masculine attitudes that are emphasized by the father's passivity, or it may be prolonged absence from the home. The family situation seems to be fairly stable at this time. Adele, herself, has mixed feelings. She feels sad and inadequate but reacts against this by being quite outgoing. Sex appears to be a somewhat dirty thing to her and she may use certain compulsive mechanisms to overcome this feeling. There is also some use of reaction-formation which seems to be her chief defense at this age. Because of the defenses she is utilizing, she may be having trouble with her peer group, being somewhat different from them."

At this time, there were suggestions of deep tension in Adele which the examiner felt were related to events at home. Father had just returned from overseas, and the family was having considerable difficulty getting settled and adjusted to one another. They were again in the paternal grandparents' home. Mother reported that Adele had continued to wet the bed and the family doctor could still find no physical cause for this. Mother could not recall that Adele had asked any sexual questions, but one wonders what fantasies the child may have had in regard to the relationship between her parents at the time of their reunion. There were, no doubt, delayed oedipal feelings, since father had been absent from the home since shortly before the child's fourth birthday.

Not long after this, Adele obtained a place in the enriched academic program sponsored by her school. It was in this setting, where she worked with other children of correspondingly high intelligence, that she gave her second Rorschach at the age of seven years and eight months. Her teacher described Adele as "a very pleasant, active child at all times, a good worker and gets along nicely with her classmates."

Her drawing of a man at this age was like that of a much younger child and gave little indication of her high intellectual ability. Anxiety factors were noted in several features of the drawing, such as the oversized head, which suggested pressure, either from herself or environment, for high intellectual functioning. The absence of hands and feet suggested fear of her own aggressive feelings, as well as fear of aggression from the environment. Feelings of inadequacy and castration were further indicated in the drawing. There was evidence that the child's anxiety was, in part, related to her curiosity about the sexual relationship between her parents.

Adele's Rorschach responses at this time were as follows:

Adele's Rorschach Protocol at the Seven Year Level

		Performance	Inquiry
I	2″	1. An angel. Something like a girl. Legs, arms	1. Q. Right in here. Two legs and come in, shaped and goes
	28″	—a boy maybe.	in (runs finger over).
II		This doesn't look like anything, do you think?	
	19″	1. Looks like a bird with his middle shot through.	1. W
		2. Something like flames.	2. (upper red).
	48″	3. Point like the top of a rifle.	3. middle d.
III	2″	1. Skeleton of two men and	1. One leg, awful skinny and funny looking head.
		2. A bow tie and	2. Just a bow.
	15″	3. Flames, see?	3. Here (outer red).
IV	2″	1. Giant with no head.	1. Look at his big feet and no head.
	5″		
V	1″	1. A butterfly.	1. Always have these and these.
	2″		
VI	4″	1. Little butterfly.	1. (upper D).
		2. Long bone or something.	2. (center D).
	19″	3. Wind blowing clouds all around.	3. Rain clouds. Q. Black.
VII	7″	1. Clouds and	1. Sort of smoky all around going different ways.
		V2. Little girl and little boy hopping on one leg. One going one way	2. Here and here.

Performance	*Inquiry*
and one going another	
20″ way.	

VIII		This doesn't look like anything to me—oh, yes—	
		1. Two bears walking on	a. Inside of animal. Q. Skeleton bones, whee!
	25″	2. A mountain.	
IX	8″	1. Waterfall, but not the color of one.	1. White and it looks like water —Q. Water looks like it's coming down dripping all over the
		2. Ice cream cone.	2. Strawberry ice cream cone.
	33″	Bah (baby talk).	
X	7″	Pretty.	
		1. Spider—two spiders.	1. Cause they have all legs.
		2. Beetles—two beetles.	2. (Brown).
		3. Two butterflies.	3. Yellow butterflies.
		4. One huge bug—I don't	4. (Green).
	28″	know what it is.	

Following is the "blind" interpretation of this record:

"At seven years and eight months of age, Adele's identification begins to lean toward the masculine role. She is trying to deny her feelings and perhaps exert some control over them. The father now has assumed the role of authority and she, in her sexual confusion, seems to be moving away from mother. Her control of her feelings may be channeling her tensions into the physical symptoms and she may be showing symptoms of enuresis at this time. She is still a dependent girl and reacts strongly to this with denial. Her peer relationships at this time may be better than they were at the age of six years and eight months but at this time they are also somewhat tenuous."

Adele continued to participate in the enriched academic program of the school during third grade. Her academic achievement, measured when she was in the third grade, while slightly better than average, was however, below what could be expected from her superior intelligence. Despite this failure to work up to capacity, she was able to get A's in all her subjects, liked school and, according to her teachers, was well liked by the other children. She continued to be a healthy, husky child.

In the testing situation, at the age of eight years and eight months,

Adele's manner was abrupt and somewhat tomboyish, but she was always superficially cooperative. There were indications that she was trying at this time to identify with the male role. Adele seemed preoccupied at times during the testing period, showed a tendency to give up easily on difficult items or to hesitate before attempting new tasks.

Her Rorschach responses were as follows:

Adele's Rorschach Protocol at the Eight Year Level

Performance	Inquiry
I 2″ 1. That looks like an angel with wings. Let me try it another way. (Mumbles) Leg—hands—angel with no head looks like wings 35″ are torn. W	1. Right here—two legs, shape, wings are ripped.
II 7″ 1. Looks like two giants with 2. Blood around them. (Mumbles). I couldn't 34″ really say what that is.	1. Their knees are like this together. Q. Hands are together.
III 3″ 1. Looks like two men. 2. A bow tie. 1. (Contd.) Half to one and half to other and 26″ they pull.	1. Both had the same tie on and they pulled back and ripped their suits. 2. Red bow tie.
IV 3″ 1. Looks like a giant sitting on 2. A big log— 18″ 1. (Contd.) or a bear.	1. Giant—look at the big feet, legs, stump. Head is funny and reminds me of a giant.
V 2″ 1. Looks like a butterfly, 10″ period.	1. Wings, head with ears.
VI 5″ 1. Looks like a little butterfly sitting on a V2. Bear upside down with 23″ two legs together.	1. Here is butterfly.
VII 6″ V1. Looks like two girls with no head and no legs.	1. Must be angels. Q. Waist, skirt and one of their legs.

Performance	Inquiry
2. Big butterfly.	
3. Hey, that looks like clouds to me that are going together and ready to break out for rain.	3. (W)
34″	
VIII Nobody can tell me that.	
16″ 1. Two pink bears going up the side of	1. (P)
2. A wall—a very funny wall if you ask me.	2. Look at different colored bricks—this must be different colored stone and white stone on them.
	a. I'd say it was mountain with different colored stones.
20″	
IX 20″ 1. Looks like green and pink and orange clouds.	
V2. Fountain.	2. Here the water comes up out of it and that (green) is background, bushes, pink water.
V3. Tree, fairy tree. Could be a maple tree.	3. Bush, roots.
X I had an answer to this one last year, I remember.	
20″ 1. I guess these are two spiders—two blue spiders.	1. Long legs.
2. Looks like way down under the ground. W	2. Might be bottom of ocean —different colors of fish.
35″	

The "blind" interpretation of this record follows:

"At eight years and eight months of age, Adele's conformity appears to be faltering and she is easily stimulated to show her feelings. She is ambivalent about her masculine identity and reacts against it with a show of aggression. The father figure, still an authority, has taken on some sexual significance. Sex is a stronger stimulating force at this age, and she is reacting against it by denial and by attempting to present a facade of extreme goodness to hide her anxiety and emotional confusion. Symptoms of enuresis also appear at this age. Parental relationships at this time appear strained; the mother is still a phallic, masculine-type person; and the father has become a sexual symbol that is anxiety-producing for Adele. Her peer relationships would be marked with ambivalence and hostility to males."

The home situation had been fraught with considerable friction during the year preceding this record. Father was having difficulty establishing business connections and mother, unhappy about not having her own home, was complaining about this constantly. Adele tended to withdraw from these battles and to express anger at both parents on occasion. She seemed to adopt a kind of sibling relationship to them, looking to grandparents for the source of her dependency needs.

Adele remained in the progressive school through a semester of fourth grade. It was then that the parents decided to build their own home. While deciding on a location for the new house, they moved into an apartment in a section of the city far removed from the paternal grandparents. Adele complained bitterly that the apartment was not a home and that she had no friends to play with nearby. Most of her summer was spent in her room, immersed in comic books. Her parents became concerned about her increasingly withdrawn behavior and sent her to camp for a short session, hoping to compensate for her lack of friends in the new neighborhood. Adele did not enjoy the camp experience; but in the fall, after she had enrolled in the neighborhood school, she seemed to "come out of her shell." She became active and energetic, both in and out of school. One of her activities was selling newspaper subscriptions for which she won a trip to Niagara Falls. Her parents were delighted with this improvement in her behavior.

It was early in her new school career that Adele gave her fourth Rorschach, at the age of nine years and ten months. The current school situation was a decided contrast to the former progressive school setting; even testing conditions were unfavorable, due to a resistant principal and a disinterested teacher. The Grace Arthur Performance Scale, given at this time, was administered under adverse conditions, and the resulting score was far below Adele's former intelligence rating on the Binet examination. The discrepancy between this average performance with the concrete items of the Grace Arthur and the superior ability previously demonstrated with ideational items of the more verbal Binet, may have been in part the result of this inadequate testing environment; but there were many indications of emotional factors which seemed to be crippling Adele's over-all functioning at this time. It is possible that she was reflecting the emotional strain incurred by the unsettled condition of the family home life, as well as by the separation from her grandparents, the real source of supply for her dependent needs.

Following is Adele's Rorschach protocol at age nine years and ten months:

Adele's Rorschach Protocol at the Nine Year Level

Performance		*Inquiry*
I 10″	1. That looks like a headless angel with torn up wings. She has a skirt on and doesn't have any feet.	1. Dead.
34″		a. This looks like eagles. They are carrying her.
II 13″	1. Two bears dancing together and I don't know what the red is. They don't have any heads, either.	a. They look like chickens. Q. Roosters if they are red like that.
33″		
III 17″	1. Two men that had	1. (P)
	2. The same bow tie on	2. (P)
	1. (Contd.) And they pulled away from each other and it ripped. Their legs are pulled away far back.	
	3. There are two spiders on each side. They have feet out and stinger out. (red).	3. (outer red)
44″		
IV 20″	1. Looks like a great big fat man sitting on	
	2. A stump or stone. That's all I can say.	
40″	1. (Contd.) With great big feet.	
V	Is that the right way? Let's see—(slants, looks on back).	
30″	1. This looks like a—butterfly, yes, a butterfly.	1. Looks like he is flying. Doesn't have a head either.

	Performance	*Inquiry*
VI	Huh, humph.	
15″	1. Oh, it looks like a dead bear and he's hung up by feet and there's	1. Bear skin or deer skin. Q. Skin side.
28″	2. A butterfly behind his legs.	2. (upper D)
VII	This is the one I remember.	
20″ V1.	Two girls without heads—each of them has one arm and one leg—holding something and running.	1. (W)
49″	2. Could make it simple and say clouds.	2. (W)
VIII	I must be answering these too quickly.	
20″	1. Looks like two animals walking up	
	2. A colored mountain.	
IX 20″ V1.	Oh, it looks like a fountain that gives pink water (laughs).	
49″	2. And the green and orange are the walls.	2. Of the fountain
X	There is a lot in this.	
19″	1. Two blue spiders.	1. (P)
	2. Looks like cowboy's legs without the rest of him.	2. (Lower green).
	3. Couple of orange clouds.	3. (Outer orange).
	4. And yellow poodles—don't they look like poodles? Except they only have one leg in front.	4. With noses up and back legs stretched. Have tails up in air.
	5. Green animals running off—I don't know what kind.	5. (Upper green).
77″	6. Clouds around.	6. (Red).

The interpretation which follows was made by the same psychologist who interpreted Adele's other protocols:

"At nine years and ten months of age, Adele appears to feel threatened by her feelings and is unable to present the facade of conformity that was her mainstay previously. She seems to deny the responsibility of growing up by wanting to participate with people on a younger, more immature level. She is still struggling with her masculine identification and feels marked threat from the mother figure because of her interest in males. Sexual aspects of the father figure have been supplemented by those of authority. Sex is again repressed but she feels impotent and anxious. Symptoms of enuresis are again evident in her record. Denial and repression are again operating here. She at this time seems to be still quite hostile toward males and indifferent to females and female activities."

During the following summer the family moved into their new home in the suburbs of still another section of the city. Adele repeated the camping experience of the preceding summer, but was only mildly interested by it. In her transfer to the school in her new neighborhood, she repeated a semester of fifth grade, since there was no mid-term promotion in the new district. Her parents objected to this, but Adele gave no indications of either boredom or resentment; she liked the school and the teachers, and continued to make good grades. Adele also entered into many extra-curricular activities, where she showed signs of competitiveness.

At about this time mother got a job to supplement the family income. She had many complaints about Adele's lack of interest in doing anything around the house and her failure even to keep her own room tidy. Mother's high standards of cleanliness and order were discouraging to Adele and the child seemed to take out her resentment at forced, increased responsibility by making only the feeblest attempts in that direction.

When she was tested again at the age of ten years and nine months, Adele was quite critical of her failures and aware of her successes in the test situation. Her performance on the WISC followed her former pattern of superior ability with verbal material, and slightly better than average ability with more concrete material. New learning was the highest ability demonstrated. There were still many indications, however, that anxiety interfered with her optimal functioning in most areas.

Her Rorschach responses at this time were as follows:

Adele's Rorschach Protocol at the Ten Year Level

Performance	Inquiry

I   Oh dear, I just don't . . .

7″   1. Looks like a girl with two wings—she doesn't have a head—wait a minute.

1. Looks like she's flying around up in the clouds.

2. Those wings look like bears sorta—the head sorta, but

2. Ear and the nose—looks like he's climbing up a mountain.

3. The wings look like wings, just the pair.

53″

3. Just wings. Q. Bigger than butterfly wings.

II 16″   1. Looks like two bears dancing sorta. That might be a

1. No head.

2. Lobster or crab up there—shaped like it.

2. Red things here and here.

3. That could be a spider —only it's red and a queer looking spider.

3. Legs—red as a spider doesn't appeal to me.

III 6″   1. This looks like two men sorta bowing and have a

2. Big barrel in their hand and their leg is separate from their body.

2. Sort of apart maybe.

3. Bow tie in middle and it looks like it's just

44″   ripped off the coats.

3. Q. Because of jagged around here. Something screwy. They could have been attached.

IV 4″   1. That looks like a pair of big feet with legs sitting on a stump. I guess you could call it a giant—it looks furry. Maybe an ape, you could call it sitting on

1. No face but I guess it's the front—the feet are sorta turned there—a giant.

2. The stump.

40″   Maybe I'm not growing up.

2. (Lower D)

V 3″   1. This looks like a butterfly when I turn it this way.
This doesn't have too much in it.

1. Flying, I guess—wings are out.

Performance	*Inquiry*
2. Looks like rabbit's ears up there.	2. Rabbit's head too.

10″

VI 2″ 1. This looks like a bear skin hanging on a wall —two legs together.

1. Furry. These would be legs.

29″ 2. A butterfly behind the feet.

2. Trapped behind the bear's feet.

VII 4″ V1. Looks like two girls dancing and hanging

1. Hands, waist, only one leg.

V2. Onto a cloud. One leg is missing.

V3. Whole thing could be an ordinary cloud.

3. Fluffy and odd shaped.

V4. This up here could be a caterpillar or butter-

4. The body would be that. (lower d-D)

35″ fly up there.

VIII 3″ 1. Two pink—well I guess —they could be mice or guinea pigs—last time I thought they were mice—crawling up a

1. (P)

2. Mountain.

2. Rugged and jagged.

V3. This way it could be a colorful waterfall when they turn the lights on.

3. I just can't think what that is.

IX 7″ V1. Well, they look like two heads—this here (red). Gee, could be a

1. Men, I guess.

V2. Cave or cavern in there between the orange.

2. Go in.
   a. I have a new idea. This could be a pipe and this is the fountain (red).

48″

X 2″ 1. Looks like two blue spiders.

1. Crawling on the grass.

2. Looks like a pair of cowboy pants right here (lower green).

2. Bowlegged legs.

3. Could be a bow tie in

3. Just a blue tie.

4. Between pink clouds.

5. Pink clouds could be a vest.

5. (DS)

6. That could be a crab— those two brown.

6. They're brown and have things coming out.

50″ 7. And a wishbone.

7. Here.

Following is the "blind" interpretation of this record:

"At the age of ten years and nine months, Adele appears more helpless and less sure of herself and appears to be using fantasy for stabilization more than she did previously. Again she appears to be afraid of growing up and feels inadequate because of an all-encompassing mother figure. Her identification is still masculine and she is still striving against it by showing much hostility toward males. She shows more sensitive awareness of the sexual aspects of the father figure even though he still appears as an authority. Although she is aware of sex, she appears to be repressing her feelings. Her feminine identification with mother causes her physical tension and anxiety. Her interest in males is marked on this record. On this record also enuresis and sexual desire are somehow combined and if this girl is enuretic it appears that it might be as a substitute for sexual feelings. Faltering repression appears to be her only defense here. She may attempt to relate to feminine-like males but will be unable to get along with masculine males of her peer group and is possibly still indifferent to females of her peer group."

During her first year in the third school Adele became more and more active in and out of the classroom. The teachers all commented on her energy and interest in many areas. She had grown into a large, sandy-haired, blue-eyed girl—not pretty but attractive in a "horsy" sort of way. She appeared eager to do the right thing, but anxious that she might not be doing so. At the same time, she seemed to be a basically hostile little girl who projected her hostility onto her environment.

When she was seen again at the age of eleven years and nine months, Adele had just entered the sixth grade. She was quite hesitant about answering any of the examiner's questions, especially when they had to do with anything she considered personal. She did not like to talk about menstruation and simply said that her mother had told her about it—but not everything. She was not looking forward to this. Her identification struggle was still quite evident at this time: she was not sure she wanted to grow up, nor was she sure that she wanted to be a woman.

Adele's drawings at this time reflected this ambivalence. She decided to draw a girl first because it was "easier to draw a boy." There was much erasing on both figures. She put mittens on the boy's hands because, she remarked, she could not draw hands. This was said despite the fact that she had already drawn the hand and fingers of the girl. Evidently her frustrating attempts at male identification made boys seem threatening to her.

During the testing period Adele asked spontaneous questions about the research project; most of them seemed to be self-oriented.

The following Rorschach responses were given at this time:

Adele's Rorschach Protocol at the Eleven Year Level

Performance	Inquiry
I I always see the same thing it seems to me. (Shrugs). I don't know but I always see it. Are you supposed to look at it one way?	
29″ 1. I still see a girl with no head.	1. See here's the waist and the legs are sort of profile. Q. Looks sorta like an angel. These could be wings.
2. Seems to me that looks like a bear with wings.	2. Nose—here looks like a wing, but that doesn't look like a bear. Q. See, about to his . . .
1. (Contd.) These look like sorta hands sticking up. Sorta silhouette of her. I suppose, I don't know.	
3. Could be a butterfly —a big one.	3. Wing and the middle. Q. With his wings spread. Q. Flying, I suppose.
101″ Well, I suppose that's all.	
II 5″ 1. These there sorta look like seals—I don't know, chickens.	1. This looks more like a seal— his head's up like he is balancing something. (upper red)
2. This looks like a spider or a butterfly or something like that.	2. Spider of some sort. Q. Just these things down there. (lower red).
3. Looks sorta like two hands up in the air together—a bear or something.	3. Looks big and bulky like a bear. Q. His foot is raised and he doesn't have a head. Q. Hands are raised and together, like they are dancing or something. a. This looks like a duck— see the mouth. (d)

Performance	*Inquiry*

<4. Oh, I just had a new idea. A rabbit with two ears—of course he's all out of shape.

75″

4. See the ear and this is a little tail. Q. He looks like he's running—this is the front leg and this is the hind leg.

III 4″ 1. Looks like he's pulling and

1. Looks like they have tuxedoes on. Q. Pulling and bow tie snapped off. See, it's jaggy here—looks like it was hitched on both of them and it snapped out.

2. Bow tie broke off.

1. (Contd.) Looks like a skeleton and his legs are out of joint.

2. Red one.

3. Of course this could be a . . . butterfly. More butterflies around here. (lower D).

45″ I don't see anything else.

3. That looks sorta like a body only the body of the butterfly is long. Q. He must be flying because they don't sit in midair.

IV 7″ 1. These look like two big feet. This looks like a bear. Looks sorta like a bear skin on the floor or something. (Looks at card edgewise).
I suppose that's all. I suppose I should see
42″ more on these.

1. Just a big bear sitting on a stump. Q. Looks so big and furry. He could be a skin on the floor but it looks more like he's sitting on a stump— back view because he doesn't have a face.

V 13″ 1. Oh, this looks like a butterfly. No matter how I look at it, it still looks like a but-
35″ terfly.

1. Looks like its body has two things sticking up. Q. Flying.

VI 5″ 1. This looks like a bear skin hanging on the wall or a deer skin.

1. Bear.

2. This looks like some kind of decoration— could be a butterfly —I have butterflies
33″ on my mind.

2. Looks like he's pinned be- hind the bear—he's by the bear's paws.

Performance	Inquiry

VII   12″   Heh.

V1. These look like girls with only one arm and one leg.

1. Looks like each going in the opposite direction, have ahold of whatever this is (D).

A2. This looks sorta like a girl with hair out on her forehead. I don't know what this thing is sticking up for. (upper D).

2. Hair is upswept on her. Q. Just looks like a head.

V3. This looks sorta like a cloud.

3. Over their head—sorta like an overcast low cloud. (lower D).

51″

VIII   This is the one that always stumps me.

9″   1. This looks like a rat —that's what I always said. I don't know. This confuses me.

1. Here's his back leg, other legs. Q. Looks like he's climbing up on something.

2. There's a skeleton of some sort in there. I can't figure that one out—that puzzles me.

2. Looks sorta like a stomach of a person.

43″

IX   V8″   V1. This looks like a fountain sorta— sprays up (uses her hand). Trying to.

1. See it spray up—never saw one spray red water.

<2. This looks like sorta hair, eyes go in and big nose.

2. Do you see it? Man's face. (red)

50″

X   5″   1. This looks like a bowlegged cowboy outfit.

1. Just up to the waist—a cowboy. (lower green).

2. This looks like spiders—big blue things.

2. Middle of spider with legs going out. Q. Crawling around.

3. This looks like a French poodle—see his nose and tail— bet nobody else figured that out—it's stupid.

3. This little nose, head, tail and the leg. Q. He's sitting.

4. This looks like a sort of vest. Sides of a vest—I don't know.

4. Pink one—see only a little bit of it.

Performance	Inquiry
5. That is—bow tie, but it's too low.	5. It's too low.
54″	a. Oh, I see something representing a wishbone.

The comments of the "blind" interpreter of the above Rorschach protocol were as follows:

"At eleven years and nine months of age there is marked confusion of Adele's feelings and mixed emotions. She feels passive and inadequate and is seeking some balance for her sexual urges. There is a need to be hostile and to castrate males to deny her feelings for them. The father is still an authority, but there is some affect hunger for him. Sexual threat also seems to be associated with the father but this is as much a desire on her part as it is a threat from him. Her relationship to the mother is somewhat incomplete and is confusing to her. Her feelings are being more directed toward self. Enuretic symptoms reappear here on this record. Males again are a source of sexual interest and she may appear both shy and hostile to males, alternating her feelings toward them. She still feels inadequate as a female and indifferent to females of her own peer group.

"It appears that this girl is identifying with her father because of his passivity and because he is less confusing to her than her mother, who has evidently usurped the masculine role and masculine attitudes. She feels so mixed in her feelings toward males that in order for her to get along well she would have to undertake some sublimation of her feelings toward males. She might find some stabilization in socially acceptable male activities which were to allow her to compensate for being a female and would allow her partial identification with males and a way of working out her hostility in an acceptable manner. The thing I think of in connection with this is sports activities which would give her a sense of competition and reward. Also, she might seek out a career which had about it certain masculine attributes and would allow her to foster independence and prove herself as adequate as males. It appears that she would not readily welcome marriage and might have a rather stormy marital life unless she could work out some of the confusions and feelings about male-female relationship."

Five years later, when Adele was seventeen years of age, she accepted an invitation to come in for an interview at the Center. She was about to begin her senior year in high school, and during this session many of the predictions made by the interpreter on the basis of her early Rorschachs were given confirmation.

Adele, at seventeen, is a tall, handsome, well-built girl who appears most mature and intelligent. On this occasion she looked suntanned and athletic, but at the same time quite feminine and well-groomed. Despite the fact that in a group situation she acts quite self-possessed, there were times during this face-to-face interview when she seemed to lack the poise and self-assurance of many less gifted children. For example, when she was asked to draw a person, she reacted with more resistance and a greater number of negative comments than did many other young people in the study. She said that she felt drawing was her least adequate area of achievement and seemed considerably threatened. In fact, art is the only school subject in which she has ever fallen below an A—"and I got out of that subject as quickly as I could."

Adele has many current interests and is engaged in many activities. At the time of the interview she had a summer job as a waitress and salesgirl in a neighborhood dairy store. She was offered job opportunities in the city but had chosen to work in her neighborhood for several reasons: the hours of eleven to five were convenient; there was no carfare involved; and she could further save money because she was provided with lunch and a uniform.

She is now the chief cheerleader at her high school and practices with five other girls every Saturday morning during the summer months. She models teenage clothes at one of the large department stores and is the representative there for a teenage magazine. She sings in the church choir and is in a school choral group that goes out of town on tours during the winter. She has engaged in church activities since moving to the neighborhood despite the fact that her parents are non-church goers. For two years she was a local swimming champion but her numerous current activities prevent her from keeping up her practice. Since she is now too old to compete in the junior swimming group, she is hesitant to enter in competition in an older group without practice. She is a straight A student and is competing with another girl for first honors. She was tapped for the National Honor Society during her junior year which had just ended.

Adele feels that she gets along well with both boys and girls—"in fact, I can get along with anybody." She goes to shows with her girl friends, they have slumber parties, "so-called"—and do other things together. She dates both doubly and singly. She has a boy friend in whom she is quite interested—in fact, they talk of marriage as soon as they have finished college. He is two years older than she and already in college. He was a straight A student in high school and first in his class. Adele thinks he has influenced her thinking and behavior more than anyone else in her life. It was he who kept her interested in doing her best in her school work. Next year Adele plans to go to a girls' college near the one he is presently attending.

Adele said that she gets along well enough with her parents since they let her do pretty much as she pleases. Although she rarely talks over her problems with them this is not a new situation since she never did depend on their advice very much. When she talked about them Adele gave the impression that she was talking about peers.

Adele speaks confidently about her status ten years hence—she sees herself as a college graduate, married with three children. So far, this competitive girl has been able to achieve top honors in most areas of her life. However, a feeling of inadequacy in any area makes her quite uncomfortable and she handles such feelings by either avoiding or ignoring them. Fortunately, this maneuver has worked simply because there are so many other areas to which she can turn and there feel adequate. The final solution of her identification struggle may pose a problem in marriage that she will be unable to avoid.

Adele's Rorschach protocols throw much light on her personality development. Her early feelings of unworthiness and guilt were brought out in her very first response at six years of age. The source of these feelings was also suggested later in the record. Since we have access to the historical material, in which mother was vague and evasive about Adele's sexual interests and the way in which these were handled, it is not surprising to see that Adele, at this very early age, considered sex "dirty" and tried to rid herself of thoughts and actions connected with the subject. She received little help from her immature parents, whose needs seemed to be as great as Adele's. She tried repression, then reaction formation as defenses against her anxiety, but these were not successful. All of this is shown in her records through the years.

In the serial Rorschachs we see what is not as clear in the history—a vacillation in her relationship to parents, when she attempts from time to time to identify with one parent or the other: a phallic but overtly feminine mother, and a passive but overtly masculine father. In the early years, she succeeded in identifying mainly with their immaturity, and showed in her Rorschach responses her feelings against growing up. The enuresis about which mother was concerned appears on the Rorschach to be related to her fear of her sexual aggressive urges. That these urges are related to her fantasies about the parental sexual relationship is also suggested. There was an indication of such feelings in her drawing at seven years of age, and again at eleven.

There was further evidence in Adele's sixth Rorschach that her struggle through the years had not been in vain. Before twelve years of age, she thought of herself, and accurately so, as a peer of her parents, and had assumed a fairly comfortable identification in a competitive, somewhat masculine role. It was during these latency years that she began to attend church and Sunday School, even though her parents were non-church people. According to the Rorschach, in this attempt at piety and good conduct, she got help in handling her sexual-aggressive feelings.

That the prognosis given at the time of the sixth Rorschach is not applicable so far as Adele's later ideas about marriage are concerned, is not due to lack of skill on the interpreter's part—unless it be that he failed to see the great effort that she was putting into her adjustment problems and that there seemed to be no indication of this struggle subsiding. Although she is still a competitive, penis-envying type of girl at seventeen, she seems to have achieved her greatest satisfaction in her relationship with a boy friend whom she respects and feels has been the greatest influence in her life. She seems to have become more aware of her feminine characteristics, and is able to integrate these comfortably with her masculine qualities.

Just as Adele has grown between twelve and seventeen years of age, we can expect changes in the next five years before she plans to be married. Such changes may well be in the direction of still better adjustment to her feminine role, and result in a satisfactory marital relationship.

VIII : EDGAR

EDGAR IS THE SECOND of four children in a family that lives in one of the city's wealthiest sections. His mother's education included one year of college, and his father is a very successful physician. The whole family is highly religious.

In giving information about Edgar's early development, mother referred to a well-documented scrapbook about her children's activities. The entire interview was sprinkled with references to her first child, a girl, who died suddenly of an acute infection ten months before Edgar was born. As she leafed through the book, mother mentioned that she had never noticed before that many of her comments about Edgar in his early months were relative to his sister and to what she had done at the same age. Her comment on this was, "Perhaps I was too sentimental," but mother added that she feels that her upset over the first child's death might have influenced Edgar's development.

Despite mother's intense grief, she was in good health during her pregnancy with Edgar. He weighed over eight pounds and developed nicely. He walked at ten months and was putting words together at eighteen months of age. As an infant, Edgar was entirely breastfed and, although for a short time, he was given a bottle at night, he was completely weaned at around sixteen months. He never sucked his thumb, as did all of his siblings. Mother recalled that toilet training had been fairly easy, but she did not remember just when it was accomplished. There was occasional bed-wetting.

Father entered the army when Edgar was fourteen months old and he remained in military service for the next four and a half years. Mother dwelled on the impact this experience probably had on Edgar, relating it to the fact that Edgar almost worships his father. Father's leaves from duty were brief, and throughout this four and a half year period he was only with the family a total of about a month. Just before father left for service, mother learned that she was again preg-

117

nant. She was quite distressed during this interval and realistically had many pressures upon her: Father was terribly busy curtailing his medical practice just before leaving and spent little time at home. When Edgar was twenty-three months old, father had his first visit with the family. He came home for the new baby's christening. In father's absence, mother had tried through letters and pictures to keep father posted on the boy's development, and during this visit Edgar and father spent much time together. Edgar accompanied mother and grandparents to the airport to see father off. Mother spoke of this as an experience she will never forget, but she wishes she could. The moment the plane door closed, Edgar cried pitifully. "It was a heartbroken cry—you couldn't control him—he sobbed and sobbed—no one who heard or saw him had a dry eye." A similar response recurred when father left from a visit when Edgar was around four years of age. He was inseparable from father until the evening he knew father was leaving. He then refused to go with father to visit friends, and complained that he was too tired to go. While father was briefly out of the house, Edgar coaxed mother to give him a bath so he could go to bed. Later, his parents found him quietly crying. These incidents were upsetting to parents also. Mother said that Edgar was not a "lovable" baby (she was trying to say "cuddly"), but he had a pattern of wanting physical contact, particularly with father. Mother claimed that he could not go by father without giving him a pat under the guise of a playful fight. She added that even as a preschooler Edgar had always "loved men—women bore him," and mother related this to father's extended absence. At this age, Edgar also "loved to pretend" and "had a vivid imagination." He and mother used to play a game of picking out things in cloud formations.

Edgar was twenty-one months old when his brother was born. Since father was away, the maternal grandmother helped mother during her confinement. In this confusion, mother could not recall Edgar's specific response to his brother's arrival but she said that since infancy Edgar has been "rough on him."

Edgar had no playmates in the neighborhood and because of this he started to kindergarten at four years of age. Toward the end of his second year there a baby sister was born into the family. Edgar was much more accepting of her than of his brother.

Around the time of his sixth birthday, Edgar started to first grade. He seemed to like school and his teacher observed that he "had a keen sense of abiding by the rules." While in first grade, at the age of six years, eight months, he gave his first Rorschach. At that time he was a tall, thin, alert-looking child who seemed to be quite tense and anxious. Edgar achieved a slightly superior rating on the Binet intelligence test but there were indications that this was minimal. His restlessness and inability to concentrate seemed to penalize him quite definitely.

Edgar gave the following Rorschach responses at this time:

Edgar's Rorschach Protocol at the Six Year Level

Performance	Inquiry
I 7″ Looks like ink.	
1. Looks like a deer's head. Ink spots all around—these dark spots around.	1. Because of the holes for the eyes—and the horns.
V2. Could be a bat. Have I got it upside down? Now it looks like a bat upside down —looks like the wings 75″ of it.	2. Hanging upside down on a tree sleeping in the daytime.
II 27″ 1. A caterpillar (upper red).	1. Just the head. Q. Has fur going out.
2. This could be . . . what do you call those things with things sticking out . . . a porcupine.	2. Leave these on there and it could be. Q. Just the head. (lower red).
3. Eagle.	3. Here (indicates whole blot).
4. This way, two hats— see these two hats?	4. Looks like clown hats. Q. Round like that (upper red).
5. A leaf—somebody cut 85″ a hole. W	5. Going in and out like somebody cut a hole.
III 2″ 1. Got two men—one got	1. Lifting a basket of clothes.
2. Basket.	
3. Got stuff falling down —leaves.	3. Here (outer red).
4. Bow in the middle.	4. Red bow.
V5. They have both got 43″ their hands sticking up.	5. Two men sitting at a desk. Q. Natives or black men.
IV 10″ 1. A gorilla—fur—	1. Parts of a gorilla—everything but his hands. Q. Could be sitting on that stump.
45″ 2. Part of a tree trunk.	

Performance	Inquiry
V 2″ 1. That looks like bird— some kind of bird—got wings, got feet, got big things sticking up.	1. The whole thing. Q. Here.
2. These horns could be hair from a girl's head	2. Whole thing—black could be hair—long. (dW).
35″ —hair could be on it.	
VI 15″ 1. Looks like feathers. (D)	1. Different colors of black.
V2. Looks like two men with arms.	2. Head, arms. a. Stem of a bow. Q. Like Dave Rubinoff's.
35″	
VII 6″ 1. That could be a deer head.	1. Horns, nose, paws, black nose. (upper ⅔).
2. This could be fur 27″ here.	2. Has all different colors of black. (lower ⅓).
VIII 2″ 1. Could be skull with	1. (Inner D).
2. Two bears going up.	2. (P).
3. Parts colored pink, parts colored orange and parts colored green, two lines sticking down and parts are white. Not very much 30″ on that to see.	a. Or could be tonsils. Q. They're pink.
IX 4″ V1. Like an umbrella.	1. A pink one and got a stem on it.
V2. This is like green, pink leaves—got lines and white around.	2. A tree.
V3. Holes in some of it is like a man's head—a 32″ pumpkin.	3. (Inner d).
X 5″ 1. Pink and blue and green—well this is like brown, white, yellow.	1. The whole thing.
2. Looks like bones sticking out like horns—a green thing like that 30″ there.	2. It's a rabbit. a. Roots.

The "blind" interpretation of this record is as follows:
"At the age of six years and eight months, one question immedi-

ately leaps up; why is he so careful? The child's good intelligence is pretty evident and yet the heavy form emphasis and inhibitory tendencies about expressing himself imaginatively are more impressive. One gets the feeling of quite a conforming youngster because of the passivity of movement that is expressed and that he is not in particularly great psychological pain. At the same time he is being very careful and losing out in spontaneity and creativity. He is particularly careful in the realm of reactivity to environmental stimulation where he initially freezes, then shows a tendency to overreact impulsively to what's going on around him. His controls here are not what they could be and affect does leak out. It is possible that he inhibits so much that he has trouble getting into social situations and surveying and learning from them. This child is operating a little on an "all-or-nothing" principle in responding to his environment.

"Identifications are more feminine than masculine. One wonders about a boy seeing a "pink umbrella" but there is some depression about this which may become more manifest and facilitate a more masculine switch later. The main defense seems to be generalized inhibition and repression and this is hindering his development. His affectional needs are expressed for both parental figures and though fairly extensive, are well controlled. One hopes for greater satisfaction of these and helpful support in being less constricted."

Around the end of his first grade year, Edgar began to get children's diseases. When he was ill he did not complain; he just wanted to sleep and to be left alone. Mother reported that she was puzzled by Edgar's hysterical reaction to getting enemas when he was ill. She thought that this was probably related to the fact that she did not know how to give one—perhaps, she "hurt" him. In view of the historical material and first Rorschach, one cannot help but note at this point that mother seems to be a person of much self-recrimination and hypercautious in the way she extends herself to others. The influence of her personality on Edgar's, including her guilt for any less-than-perfect interaction that they might have, seems both extensive and obvious.

Edgar did not make as good progress in school as his intelligence seemed to warrant. His first grade teacher thought of him as shy and easily embarrassed, with unintelligible speech at times.

By the time of his second Rorschach, he was in the second grade and was retarded in his school achievement. This teacher also considered him slow in relation to other children, but pointed out that

Edgar was willing to undertake any tasks assigned him, and assumed responsibility readily.

In the test situation he was ill at ease but cooperative. His Goodenough Draw-a-Man was quite immature for his age as well as for his intelligence level manifested in his Binet score the previous year. The drawing was crude, without hands and feet, and suggested castration fears. It also indicated that Edgar had poor contact with his environment and a fear of his aggressive impulses.

His Rorschach record follows:

Edgar's Rorschach Protocol at the Seven Year Level

Performance	Inquiry
I 8″ 1. Looks like a bat.	1. Inside and the wings on it. Q. He's out flying some place.
10″	
II 10″ 1. Looks like two noses and this doesn't look like nothing.	1. Shaped like, not the color. Q. Of a person (upper red). a. This could be a design. The colors in here and the black.
13″	
III 6″ 1. This looks like two people lifting	a. Two drops of rain. Q. Coming down. (outer red) b. A necktie. Q. Shaped. (P)
2. A basket.	
IV 5″ 1. Looks like a nut or apple core or something like that. (lower D). 10″	1. An apple core. Have lots of stems sticking out.
V 2″ 1. Looks like a fly of some kind.	1. Out in the wind.
VI 9″ 1. This looks like something you blow a fire with. DW	1. (Seemed to change from a D concept to a W as he talked.)
2. And this looks like a piece of ground or clay you make things with. 14″	2. (W)
VII 6″ 1. This looks like a design. 8″	1. It's just drawn. Just made a picture in kindergarten.
VIII 3″ 1. Looks like two bears going up	1. (P)
15″ 2. A piece of a hill looks like.	2. No special kind.

Performance	Inquiry
IX 7″ 1. Another design made out of clay.	1. All different colors of clay.
X 1″ 1. Looks like two spiders.	1. (P)
2. Some leaves.	2. (green).
3. Looks like some ants and	3. This is an ant (lower brown) a. and that's a fly (wishbone).
4. Some flowers.	4. (Yellow) Growing out of the trees.

Had a tendency to lose his first concepts—and get confused in the inquiry.

The following is the "blind" interpretation of this record:

"At the age of seven years and eight months, it would seem that the support that Edgar needed was not forthcoming and the result seems to be one of further constriction and one in which the expression of feelings or admission of thoughts is not allowed. He is trying very hard to control himself in all spheres and is doing this so rigidly that he is missing aspects of relationships, feelings and thoughts that could help him and sustain him. Previous defenses are intensified and effective controls are probably lowered because he is ill-prepared for new or unusual stimuli in his life.

"With such tightly drawn controls, the boy cannot go on as he is. His environment will impose new and further stresses on him and he is not allowing himself the experiences that will help him cope with his future. It would seem that he sees himself as a bad boy trying to keep all his feelings, particularly in regard to his parents, who may be fomenting this attitude, carefully in check."

In our notes on Edgar's life at home, we have no evidence of a warm and outgoing relationship between him and his family. Possibly mother, who had given information on only difficult circumstances in both her life and Edgar's, was not capable of extending warmth and affection. And father, who was a busy doctor, may have still had little time with him even after his return to the home after military service. These speculations seem merited mostly on the basis of our lack of historical data on the subject and on the basis of Edgar's first two Rorschach records.

Edgar continued to have difficulty with his school subjects—reading in particular. He went to remedial reading classes in third grade;

and, when he complained of a blurriness in his eyes, a medical examination revealed a fusion difficulty which might well have been related to his reading problems. Edgar took eye exercises for a year and the difficulty was cleared up. Mother reported at this time that Edgar never used his eye difficulty as an excuse when he was criticized for his lack of reading skill.

When he was seen for testing during this year in third grade, Edgar was outwardly conforming, but he put forth minimal effort and gave up very easily. He would return to the task, however, when the examiner gave him encouragement.

The results of the achievement tests given at this time showed him to be a half year below his grade placement and much farther below his potential ability. This inadequate functioning was, no doubt, related to the anxiety that was more evident on this occasion than in earlier clinical contacts.

Following is the record of Edgar's Rorschach responses:

Edgar's Rorschach Protocol at the Eight Year Level

Performance	Inquiry
I 9″ 1. A bat.	1. Wings and there's the body. Q. up in the sky flying.
2. Two leafs. Can you take things off it?	2. Two leaves.
50″ 3. Core of an apple.	3. (upper center d)
II 12″ 1. Part of the throat. W	1. Like in my daddy's book.
2. Looks like a butterfly down there.	2. Red.
22″ 3. Looks like two caps up here.	3. (upper red).
III 4″ 1. Looks like two men lifting a	1. (P)
2. Basket.	2. (lower center D)
22″ 3. Bow in the middle of it.	3. Here.
IV 3″ 1. Shoes on the bottom.	1. (side D).
2. Inside of a nut up here.	2. (top d)
3. After you've eaten all off	3. (lower D)
29″ the apple.	
V 8″ 1. A bird flying.	1. (P)
2. Up here looks like rabbit ears.	2. Just the ears.
24″ 3. Feet down here.	3. Of a butterfly.

	Performance	Inquiry
VI 20″	1. Looks like a blanket down here. (W)	1. Flat. Q. Colored.
	2. Feathers.	2. Eagle (upper part of D).
24″	3. Stick.	3. (center D).
VII 6″	1. Animal with heads turned. Paws of an animal. Head of an animal.	1. Same animal. (upper ⅔)
20″	Ears of an animal.	
VIII 8″	1. Looks like two animals there.	1. Climbing up this
30″	2. That looks like a point of something up here.	2. Mountain. Q. Point of mountain.
IX 26″	(Slants).	
	1. Two holes there (middle d).	1. Holes in wood.
40″	2. Trees up there—in the winter time. (orange).	2. No leaves.
X 2″	1. Spiders.	1. On the wall. (P)
	2. Ears.	2. Here. (lower green)
	3. Bone of an animal. Green things are	3. (upper gray). Here and here.
62″	2. (Contd.) Eyes in a rabbit face (P).	

The "blind" interpretation of this record is as follows:

"By eight years and eight months of age, one wonders how the defense pattern has been able to stabilize itself because the pattern of the previous years is there without as much of the anxiety and tension. Even more than before, Edgar is not being too fussy with exactitudes of control, tending toward ambiguous forms. He is not looking at his world as perceptively as before though he is careful about just what he will respond to. He stays away from human percepts except where he is in safe, obvious and familiar grounds.

"He is still largely not responding to environmental stimulation but is tending to heed his inner life which is, as would be reasonable from all his inhibition, rather immature. He is responding more slowly and selectively to his world. With the decay, food, and anatomy responses, one wonders about the anxiety outlet. It is possible it may be in morbid fantasy preoccupations now aborning, in eating and food preoccupation and/or in a somatic disorder. It is possible that all three serve to drain off tension as his constricted front seems to become stabilized and compensated with acceptance of this mode of life in the form of decreased ambition. This boy is tending toward a character disorder."

When mother was asked at this time about Edgar's interest in sex, she remembered only that he had asked simple questions at an earlier age. She felt that she had answered them adequately at the time, but he had not made any inquiries further into the subject for more than a year. One is again dubious as to mother's ability to handle this subject satisfactorily, both from the point of view of information she must give to another individual and from the point of view of her affective reactions to this subject. Edgar's lack of further inquiries on this subject might give a more realistic indication of how well this was handled than does mother's own statement.

At nine years, nine months of age, Edgar had grown to be quite tall and handsome in appearance. He seemed more self-confident than the year before, but he was still quite tense at times. The timing that was necessary in administering the Grace Arthur Performance Scale seemed to make him anxious and impulsive. His rating, however, was in keeping with his former Binet score of slightly superior. Evidently he has equally good potentialities in both the concrete and verbal areas.

His Rorschach responses on this occasion were as follows:

Edgar's Rorschach Protocol at the Nine Year Level

Performance	Inquiry
I 4" 1. Core of an apple.	1. (upper center dr).
2. Dress right in there.	2. (lower D).
3. Branches of a tree.	3. (upper center d).
4. Elves' caps.	4. (upper side d).
5. Wings here.	5. Just the wings (don't see the
42"	birds). (D).
II 10" 1. These look like legs.	1. Of a bug (dd in lower red).
2. Thumb caps.	2. Dentist made them for kids that suck their thumbs.
3. Shell or fish or cactus plant—because of the needles right there.	3. (lower red).
50" V4. Right here a deer.	4. Horns and nose. (lower red).
III 6" 1. Some people holding	1. (P)
2. A basket.	
3. Pin or butterfly there.	3. Butterfly. Q. Any kind. I don't know the kinds.

	Performance	Inquiry

Performance | *Inquiry*

4. Legs of horse on bottom. — 4. (lower side D).

5. That looks like a head of some sort. — 5. Dog (outer red).

42″   6. A whip or something like that. — 6. (dd on outer red)

IV   5″   1. Shoes. — 1. (lower side D).

2. Horns. — 2. (upper side d).

3. Core of an apple— somebody has eaten the apple. — 3. (lower D).

4. Arms r i g h t there, they're sticking them out. — 4. (Same as horns).

42″   5. These look like little pipes going over there. — 5. (dd on lower D).

V   6″   1. Whole thing looks like a bat turned around— horns. — 1. Back's to you (standing up). Q. Horns of bat.

2. Feet of the person or animal. — 2. Animal. (lower d).

3. Wings of some sort. (side D). — 3. Eagle, just the wings.

48″   4. Roots. — 4. (outer d).

VI   2″   1. That looks like a tomahawk. — 1. Eagle, feathers, there. Could be coming out of tomahawk.

2. That looks like bugs coming out of them. — 2. (d)

1. (Contd.) They look like feathers of some kind. — 1. (Contd.) On tomahawk.

3. Tips. Like the janitor uses to pull things out with. — 3. (lower dd).

VII   5″   1. Looks like bunnies' ears. Shape of head. — 1. (upper ⅔).

2. These look like things that stick up in a cave. — 2. (d on "head")

1. (Contd.) Paw of bunny and face of bunnies. — 1. (Contd.) Same bunny.

3. Head of some funny animal peeking out there. (Dd) — 3. Lamb—feet and grayish (part of lower D).

42″

Performance	Inquiry
VIII 4″ 1. These things here look like some kind of animal. Feet of animal there.	1. They look like they are trained, go up the thing themselves.
2. That looks like some part inside your body.	2. Color (lower D).
3. That looks like a hill these animals are climbing up.	3. In here.
4. These look like feet of something right there.	4. Butterfly's feet. (dd at top).
5. These look like the shape of a skeleton.	5. Dead person. (inner D) (skull).
52″	

IX 16″ 1. Looks like bones after you have eaten something—fish.	1. Upper d.
2. This looks like a head of some kind of man that has a mustache on.	2. (red area).
54″ 3. Holes you drill in a board.	3. Here is the board (inner d).

X 2″ 1. That looks like a spider.	1. Legs. (P)
2. That looks like a bug right there.	2. (Green). Green worms.
3. Them blue things look like the axle of a car.	3. (Center blue).
4. Lion standing there.	4. Color makes it a lion.
5. Fish.	5. (Outer yellow).
6. Cherries.	6. (Wishbone).
52″ 7. A green animal up there.	7. (upper green).

The interpreter had this to say about Edgar's record:

"By the age of nine years and nine months, it would seem that Edgar has worked out resolutions of the "much ado about nothing" sort. He drives himself to function and to produce but warmths and nuances are simply not there. All that is there is a sort of shell of the beginning of an ego structure that was never completed because the engineer was afraid to spread out, look around, and utilize all the possible resources about him."

According to mother, Edgar seemed to "wake up mentally" and showed a genuine interest in learning shortly after the time when the above Rorschach was administered. He enjoyed parental encouragement and actually enlisted their assistance on occasion, but he always insisted that he do the actual work for himself.

At the time of his fifth Rorschach, Edgar was a tall, attractive, blond boy who was fairly spontaneous in the test situation. Although he twisted about in his chair and looked bored at times, he continued to try to appear interested and was always cooperative. He thought he was getting along all right in school where, although he did not like arithmetic, geography and history were his favorite subjects. His rating on the WISC, administered at this time, was slightly higher than on previous intelligence tests and therefore confirmed the fact that this boy had a high intellectual potential.

His Rorschach responses were as follows:

Edgar's Rorschach Protocol at the Ten Year Level

Performance	Inquiry
I 3″ 1. Bat.	1. Whole thing. Q. Face right there.
2. And that looks like the core of an apple.	2. Right in the center. (D).
3. And that there looks like these antlers.	3. Just the antlers.
4. Two caps.	4. Up here. (upper side d).
38″ 5. Wings (side projection).	5. Different wings from bats.
II 2″ 1. Two thumbs. (upper red).	1. Just looks like a thumb like my sister's when she gets through sucking it—all red.
2. That there looks like a mouth or something—you know them tweezers.	2. Mouth of the tweezers when they open up. (center d).
3. Looks like a sea shell. (lower red).	3. All shaggy and wore out—just came in from the sea.
4. Two elephants' trunks with elephants' head 42″ and elephants' ears.	4. Standing up probably—can't see the leg.
III 2″ 1. Two people holding	1. Might as well make them men.
2. A basket.	2. (lower center D).
1. (Contd.) Ladies' shoes.	
3. Two things on sides look like bugs.	3. I don't know. Q. Peculiar shape, and long.

Performance	Inquiry
4. And that looks like a bow tie.	4. Bow tie with something wrapped around it.
1. (Contd.) Two heads and a neck.	
V5. These might look like butterfly wings too.	5. (Red) Turn it upside down —just the wings.
36"	

IV 6"
1. Looks like core inside of a nut.	1. (upper d). Just looks like the inside of a nut.
2. Two big shoes.	2. Here and here. (lower side D)
3. Little limb of trees hanging over.	3. (upper side d)
4. Duck face.	4. On the end of the limb (dd)
5. Core of an apple.	5. (lower D) You know when you eat it off.
6. Bug with feelers— them things sticking out.	6. (Bottom of D) Eyes and feelers down there. (dr)

41"

V 2"
1. Bat—bat wings with two little feet—feelers on bat.	1. Whole bat wings and inside of him. W
2. Head of rabbit.	2. Here. (upper d)
3. Looks like legs—them things there—without feet. That's about all. Doesn't have much on it.	3. Human being legs. Q. Make it a man (lower d).

26"

VI 3"
1. That looks like an Indian thing he clubs over the head with.	1. Feather sticking on there. (upper D).
2. Looks like Indian skin.	2. Stretched it up. (W)
3. Bugs down there.	3. (d)
4. Like beaks on an eagle.	4. (lower dd)
5. Whiskers up at the top.	5. (upper dd).

47"

VII 2"
1. Looks like two rabbits —two ears, two feet and a body and a head.	1. Could be like all pounded into rock (a statue).
2. That there looks like the core of an apple.	2. (lower d).
1. (Contd.) Looks like they are holding	
3. On two rocks or something.	3. (lower D).

40"

VIII 3"
1. Like beavers or some kind of an animal on the side.	1. Climbing a rock. a. That mountain there.

Performance	Inquiry
2. Looks like two heads there.	2. Make it a skeleton (skull).
3. Them there look like two legs or something.	3. Peoples' legs. (upper dd)
4. That looks like a spider's web.	4. See them things in there hanging over. (upper gray)
5. Two wings, maybe they are. I don't know. (55″)	5. I can't remember.

IX 7″
1. Looks like two heads there. An animal or something.	1. (lower D).
2. Like twigs on a tree.	2. (upper d).
3. Like carrots (orange)	3. Round and fat at the bottom.
4. Like bombs or torpedoes.	4. Shaped like (inner D).
5. Something inside of something. Right there.	5. Brace holding up a room or something (middle line).
1. (Contd.) That looks like a statue—you know them statues. (41″)	

X 5″
1. Head of a rabbit,	1. Here. (P)
2. With two little bugs on it.	2. Just look like bugs. Make it a moth.
3. Crabs with feelers,	3. Here and here (gray).
4. Fighting over a hunk of something.	4. Make it a fish head. (top D).
5. Spiders.	5. (Blue).
6. Spider web.	6. (Brown).
7. Two little dogs there.	7. (Yellow) Sitting and showing off.
8. That would be the limb of a tree.	8. (Red).
9. Shoe there maybe. (Outer yellow)	9. Thin, yellow things. Q. Shape of pointed toes.
10. Bugs right there.	10. Can't find the bugs.
11. Little animal right there. (50″)	11. Here. (outer orange).

The comments of the interpreter are given below:

"At the age of ten years and eight months, one envisions a basically constricted young person rigidly trying to be outgoing and contact his social environment but having very little to give and no ability to receive from it adequately. There is cognizance of this and tension arising from it. Some of this is bound in the somatic and gustatory areas and in his compulsive picking and searching behavior as he tries to get roots. Unfortunately, his tendrils are not well developed or strong enough to find aspects of his environment to hold to.

"His extreme control and affect repression are working sufficiently well so that he is in no danger of serious pathology but it leaves an undoubtedly unhappy, insecure youngster, who is probably unable to do anything much about it. It is doubtful if his peer relationships have ever been happily adequate. He has so little grasp of emotional give and take, of social interactions, of exchanges of feeling and warmth. It is possible that he may have a limited number of equally socially and emotionally inhibited friends with whom he has a formal facade of friendship."

Edgar had become increasingly antagonistic toward his younger brother through the years. They had shared a room for many years but there were constant fights over the arrangement. The younger boy was outgoing—of a completely opposite temperament from Edgar, and possibly, for this reason, much more readily accepted. "He knows just what to say to people," was mother's comment.

Edgar continued to seek help with schoolwork from his parents. Mother gave him his spelling lesson for practice, but looked on this as "spoon-feeding," since she felt he should have outgrown this long ago. The boy was quite tense in school but continued to try hard to make good grades.

At eleven years, eight months, Edgar was in the sixth grade and gave the appearance of a tall, lanky, superficially pleasant boy. Underneath this exterior, however, he seemed very tense and constricted, and had a tendency to stutter. He said that the only thing he liked about school was gym, and he played center on the basketball team, which he enjoyed. His main worries at this time were about his tests at school; about breaking things at home for fear of a whipping (since his parents were very strict); and about missing someone on his paper route because his boss would "bawl him out." He got angry when someone hit him, because he was not allowed to hit back.

His human figure drawings at this time indicated that he had a very poor concept of himself as an immature, inadequate person. Edgar had been given little opportunity in his early years to develop into a self-confident, effective personality. He seemed to defend against the anxiety created by this situation by becoming more and more constricted.

His final Rorschach record follows:

Edgar's Rorschach Protocol at the Eleven Year Level

Performance	Inquiry
I 3″ 1. Bat wings and	1. Just the wings. Q. Oh, I don't know—just looks like them.
2. Like a core of an apple.	2. That thing there sorta—it looks like one. (upper d).
3. Little hats—tall dunce hats like. (Tendency to stutter). That's	3. (Not on any one). Tall and pointed at the top. (side d)
29″ about all.	
II 2″ 1. Like two thumbs sticking out up there at the top.	1. A person. That's the only things that have them. Q. I don't know.
2. Like an elephant's trunk there. (P)	2. A lot of the elephant head with no ears or eyes. Q. One comes up and down like that.
3. Like icicles sticking out—them red things.	3. These hanging down like that. Q. Straight. (dd on lower
24″ That's about all.	red)
III 2″ 1. Two people carrying	1. Holding on a basket. Q. I don't know. Q. Women, I guess. Q. Shoes on them.
2. A basket.	
3. Bow tie in the middle.	3. Like that, see. Q. A red one.
1. (Contd.) Shoes on the people.	
4. Like some animal with a long tail. (outer	4. He's just a picture of one. Q. Just drawn on there.
23″ red).	
IV 2″ 1. Core of an apple. (lower D)	1. Just looks like one.
2. Little big feet.	2. Elephant's, I guess.
3. Two arms hanging down.	3. A person's with no hands on them.
<4. Nut shell up there— like you see inside a nut.	4. Inside of the shell. Q. Middle part between the meat. (upper d)
V 3″ 1. Some kind of animal with wings on—horns, two legs.	1. Standing still.

Performance	*Inquiry*
2. Legs on this, wing here like—and that's about it. (Straightens cards).	2. Horse or cow. Q. Just the legs. (lower d).

VI 2″ 1. Like one of them Indian blankets.

2. Some fur off some animal. ("feathers")

3. A dog's head up there.

22″ That's about all.

1. Leave the middle thing out. Not all around. Like you get in the store.

2. Some kind of skin and fur. Q. Just piece of fur.

3. Eyes, nose. (upper d)

VII 2″ 1. Rabbit ears.
2. Paws of some animals.
3. Face of something.
4. Core of an apple in
21″ there and that's it.

1. Just the ears. (upper d)
2. Some animals. (side dr)
3. Some animals. (dr)
4. (lower d).

VIII 2″ 1. Two animals and
2. This looks like the head of something.

28″ 3. Legs up there—feet.

1. They are climbing something.
2. I don't know—one of them things they chisel out of rocks. Q. Animals. (outer d).
3. Rabbit, I guess. (dd on top D).

IX 6″ 1. Like antlers of a reindeer.

2. Raindrop right there. (orange)

3. Some animal's head. (lower D) And that's
30″ all.

1. Just the antlers. (upper d).

2. A big one (orange). The way they are formed—you see them in pictures that way. Q. Standing still—they don't stand still but it's painted that way.

3. Like little eyes there, mustache and that's about all.

X 1″ 1. Two crabs.
2. Little animals up here —two of them—fighting over something, a bone.
3. Like axles on cars. (inner blue)

4. Two dogs.
5. Kind of worm.

1. (P). Q. Long legs on them.
2. (Gray).

3. See round things on either side and little pipe like on top.
4. Sitting up. (inner yellow)
5. One of them green kind of worms—I don't know their name. (P)

Performance	Inquiry
6. Rabbit's head.	6. Here. (P)
7. Like a foot or something. (outer yellow)	7. That yellow things—somebody big with a great big foot.
8. Cherry thing—like two cherries hanging from a stem—that's all.	8. In here. (wishbone)

The final comments of the psychologist who interpreted Edgar's Rorschach records are reproduced verbatim:

"Toward parental figures, there seems to be only a feeling of unfulfillment in his Rorschach responses at the age of eleven years and eight months. There are recurrent themes of nurture and succorence which were really not given. Edgar is clearly an emotionally deprived child who has never received and so now cannot either transmit or receive emotional ties with others. The six-year-old who was almost a full, rich person, has turned into a rigid, selectively perceptive, hollow youngster. He has the barest trappings of a male sexual identification but it is far from full or complete and is only indicative of a slight shift from an asexual level. Relationships with both sexes have been disappointing but the male, perhaps a little less so.

"This child is tending toward a fairly unhappy adulthood because of the emptiness of his childhood. At the end of the chain of records is an indication of a counterphobic diminution of fearfulness about the male sexual role and a tendency toward a comparatively unrestrained passively affectional drive in this area. He may be able to find some emotional props in a heterosexual relationship, though he perceives the phallus as something less than safe. It is possible that he may be the passive partner in a homosexual relationship which will probably be quite unfulfilling emotionally. This is a lonely wanderer who is probably discontent and feels unfulfilled and is not sure what is missing and not filled in his life. It is difficult to foresee great success for him, for he is likely to be so bogged down in the minutiae and production that he cannot plan adequately. It is more difficult to see him genuinely happy or having found a satisfactory and adequate niche in life."

Edgar has been seen three times during his adolescence; the last occasion was around his seventeenth birthday. It was obvious from his remarks and his attitude that he had come to see me only because of parental pressure.

During this adolescent period, Edgar had been described by mother as an exceedingly strong boy who did not heed his own strength in his rough play with his siblings, and particularly with his sister, who is six years his junior.

His chief interest is in sports—those with direct body contact. He was thrilled when he first made the football team and anxiously anticipated the first official game. As with any special event, he got "fussed up." Under such conditions, mother said: "He is restless, can't sit still and has trouble sleeping."

Mother added, "I do the same thing myself," as she described the extreme tension in Edgar under these circumstances: he "gets into knots—gets silly—excited, wrings his hands and is 'harder' on his brother—just all keyed up." Prior to the current incident Edgar had last manifested these symptoms in anticipation of the family's summer vacation in Florida.

Edgar's mother spoke of her increasing awareness of his present maladjustment. However, she said that he does much work around the house for her—mowing the lawn, spading, and heavy physical work. "He isn't a lazy youngster," she added. He apparently hates housework, but will help mother "when the chips are down." He enjoys surface neatness about the house, but he usually shoves everything into a closet to achieve this. When his mother requests his assistance, he will help her; but he complains loudly about his sister, whom he thinks is a "spoiled brat"—she should help.

Mother also referred to Edgar as a "big-hearted youngster," where money is concerned. Although he would never think of paying much for an item for himself, he recently paid nineteen dollars for a Meerschaum pipe for father, who had only casually expressed an interest in one. He had also given mother a gift of a course of sewing lessons recently, since she had occasionally mentioned that she would like to take one.

Edgar had a paper route until recently, but he gave it up because he needed the time for football and studying. He saved most of his money that he earned from the paper route and had recently added another hundred dollars from mowing lawns. He is only mildly pleased with his bank account of more than six hundred dollars. Edgar's interest in working is diluted by his hating to meet people; he preferred to deliver the newspapers and have his brother do the collecting.

Edgar detests dances and music, and he never sings. In addition to his nervous mannerisms when experiencing great anxiety, he bites his nails. The nail-biting has increased since twelve years of age. He does this biting in preoccupied fashion, although it is worse at times, without any apparent cause. Mother feels that Edgar really needs punishment at times. He is particularly sensitive to being hit or slapped, so deprivation of TV or going some place is the main type of punishment. Apologizing for some action of his is one of the worst things that Edgar can be forced to do. He isn't remorseful and doesn't think that he should act like he is. This moralistic trait is seen in other experiences of Edgar. He intensely dislikes swearing.

He is extremely fond of men and elderly people, and in amusement, mother told of an incident revealing his devotion to an elderly great aunt. On a hot day, she casually mentioned how good a beer would taste. Edgar volunteered to go buy her one. He was turned down by the bartender in his attempted purchase, so he asked a nearby shoemaker to purchase it for him. Mother could think of no other circumstances that would motivate Edgar to exert himself in relation to people as much as he then did.

Edgar attends church and Sunday School regularly, but he doesn't participate in the young people's activities. He resents mother's volunteering his services at Sunday School and verbally threatened to shirk on her promises. He gives money regularly to the church but refuses to enclose it in the customary identifiable envelope, since he does not want credit for his offering and says it's no one's business how much he donates.

Edgar speaks of his vocational ambition as medicine. His admiration of his father leads him to this choice. When younger, he always spoke of a specific job for himself. His choice varied from a scissors grinder to a streetcar conductor to farmer. Around twelve years of age, he decided to be a doctor, and wants to go to a local university. He hostilely jokes with father, saying that then he too can claim he has to go to a meeting when he wants to avoid any other commitment. Edgar "has been schooled in expecting that Daddy can't go," or do something with the family because of his practice. Father now spends more time at home, however, than when Edgar was younger.

The father-son relationship is described as quite unusual. There is much bantering between them with Edgar often being flip. He protests father's ideas and tells him that he has "rocks in his head," although he supposedly has an intense respect and admiration for father. He cannot pass father without giving him a punch, encouraging him to "go ten rounds with me." Mother fears what would happen to Edgar if father would have some severe misfortune—injury, illness or death.

Edgar has no friends. This distresses his parents, particularly mother, who is hopeful that Edgar's interest in sports will bring the development of some friendships. Recently, when a co-player on the football team had three teeth knocked out, Edgar telephoned him to learn of his progress in recuperating. However, he gave no indication of developing this interest further when father suggested having this fellow come over to the house. When acquaintances stop to talk with him as he works in the yard, Edgar greets them coldly. Mother tries conscientiously not to interfere, but she mentioned that she is tempted to invite groups to the house or to encourage Edgar to go visiting.

He does like it when his parents entertain and enjoys adult company in the house. He seems, on these occasions, to enjoy simply sitting in the same room quietly, but when someone directs himself specifically to Edgar, he then becomes animated and joins in an active conversation with the adult involved.

In our interview, when he was seventeen, Edgar seemed embarrassed and poorly poised. He is a healthy-looking boy who wears an inexpressive smile much of the time. However, as he smiles he clenches his fist, rubs his hand and even blushes at times.

Edgar was an extremely difficult boy to interview, since his answers all seemed to be directed by a need to be conforming. His main interest, in his own words, was "horsing around." He has few friends —one or two fellows he "horses around" with, though. He does not like girls and wouldn't even care if there were no girls. He plans to go to college because "you can't get anywhere without going," and will be a doctor, like his father. Edgar goes to a military academy summer school every summer and he enjoys "horsing around" with the boys there.

This boy's overemphasis on "horsing around" may serve several purposes. It prevents him from becoming aware of feelings of hostility towards women, father, and his younger brother, by allowing him to live in a childish world where life is rosy and serious things do not really matter. It prevents him from becoming aware of his unconscious fear of being overpowered. This fear is expressed in his dreams. At the same time, it may be a veiled expression of homosexual feelings: these feelings are suggested by his close relationship to boys—or at least a desire to "horse around" with them—and by his apparent indifference to the sexual side of girls. It allows him to remain a little boy and thus avoid the realization that his adult or adolescent achievements, in school as well as out of school, are poor. Finally, it might be an expression of hostility, a teasing of the interviewer, who represents authority and whom he has been asked to help in the interviewing situation; i.e., he is not going to say anything.

Although a considerable amount of information was conscious to Edgar, his behavior seems to be at the twelve to fourteen year old level, rather than at the seventeen year level. He is unable to enter into any constructive activity, or to form any mature relationships with boys—much less girls—or to succeed in school as a first step in achieving his future goals. In all probability, the only positive thing that can be said for him at this time is that his defenses, while preventing him from growing up, also prevent him from being overwhelmed by what may be a considerable amount of unconscious hostility.

By way of summary, the reader will note that in this particular case, while the Rorschach records of Edgar are not incongruous with the other pieces of information that we have, they obviously do not allow us the depth of perception that can usually be expected. It is possible that the situation is inherent in the somewhat sterile characteristics of the boy himself, and in his moralistic and compulsive upbringing. It has always been more important to parents that Edgar not "get into trouble" than that he have a chance to develop any personality traits that might lead to a richer, less inhibited life. That his dependency needs have never been satisfied and that he has many hostile fantasies in this regard are important reflections in the Rorschach records. As a result of this hostility, Edgar seems to overreact to both parents in a propitiatory manner feeling that he must buy their love. It is evident that he has only a very brittle intellectual control against these unconscious feelings. This type of control is staunchly supported and held together by both parents, who are in constant fear that his impulse life will break through. This fear has evidently been transferred to Edgar, since he docilely accepts such restrictions as summers in a military school, and fears any interpersonal relationships which may counteract the family's rigidity. As I write this, I have just heard that Edgar has received an appointment in one of the national military colleges and he is now headed toward a military career—a continuance of environmental rigid controls.

IX : MOLLY

MOLLY IS THE THIRD in a family of five children born to Southern Negro parents, who had migrated to Pittsburgh before their marriage. The family resides in a low-rent housing project to which they moved more than ten years ago from the slum home in which all the children were born. Father is an unskilled laborer whose income necessitates a limited standard of living for his large family.

When she was interviewed, mother, who seemed to be of low intelligence, had difficulty relaxing in the presence of a white interviewer and expressed her resistance to this in a passive way. She frequently acted embarrassed or self-conscious, and seemed to discharge her anxiety through inappropriate giggles and laughter. However, underneath this strained exterior she gave the impression of having considerable warmth for her family and repeatedly expressed a desire to have them be conforming.

Mother confined herself to replying to direct questions about Molly and rarely made spontaneous elaborations of any statements. She had been well during the time she carried Molly, and the child was born in a local hospital after several hours of labor. Molly weighed nine pounds at birth and was breast-fed for the first year. Mother described her as a good eater, although she was a "fussy baby—she's fussy now."

As to toilet training, this was initiated before one year of age. Molly "learned good," according to mother; she was completely trained for bed-wetting prior to age one and informed mother of her daytime needs by the time she was sixteen or seventeen months. Reportedly, Molly walked alone by thirteen months and talked in single words by fourteen or fifteen months. Mother denied that there had been any nail-biting or thumb-sucking, although Molly, who was present throughout the interview, did considerable chewing on her fingers at this time.

Mother seemed to be unable to comment upon the kind of things

Molly liked to do before she started to school. She could give no general description of Molly's preschool days, mentioning only that she liked to do "stunts" at about four or five years of age. Molly entered kindergarten around the age of four and a half, and she attended there for two years before she entered first grade in the same school.

Shortly after she had entered first grade, when Molly was six years and nine months of age, she was given her first Rorschach. At that time, she was a small-statured, immature little girl who wore her hair in tiny braids all over her head and was not very clean in either body or clothes. She was pleasant and cooperative in the test situation, but her cooperation was that of a hyperactive, talkative preschooler whose attention had to be brought back to the test material constantly. Her teacher reported that in the classroom Molly was neither defiant nor negativistic but that she was a problem in that it was difficult to get her to conform to any routine work—she seemed unable to concentrate.

Molly's performance on the Stanford-Binet, given at this time, resulted in a mental age of five years and three months: she based at the 4-6 level, with three successes at year 5 (Picture Completion, Paper Folding and Definitions); two, at year 6 (Vocabulary, Mutilated Pictures); and one, at year 7 (Similarities). She had no successes beyond this level, and the resulting I.Q. of 78 suggested definite retardation. There was some indication in the test results that at one time Molly might have had a higher potential.

Her Rorschach responses were as follows:

Molly's Rorschach Protocol at the Six Year Level

Performance	Inquiry
I 10″ 1. Tree. W	1. Here.
60″ 2. Man. D	2. Head, hands.
II 7″ 1. Fire.	1. We got fire like that—looks green—no, yellow.
2. House—sidewalks, strips, chimney.	2. (upper d).
3. Boy coming out of house.	3. (Denies).
95″ 4. Water coming down out.	4. (S).
III 5″ 1. Dumplings — head — foots coming off.	1. (black area).
2. Fire burning—getting on	2. (red area).
70″ dumplings' head.	

Performance	*Inquiry*
IV 3″ 1. A billygoat—arms, foots, holes.	1. Head, neck.
44″ 2. Something coming to get him.	2. (lower D).
V 4″ 1. A bear—gotta left foot —gotta ears sticking up, don't got no hands, hands fell off—something coming up after him. 42″	1. Bowlegged foots.
VI 4″ 1. A billygoat—looks like his arms is on fire. Something coming from his neck. Looks like he ain't got no foots. Looks like he ain't got no clothes on. 51″	a. Eyes—it's a cat. (d)
VII 2″ 1. Looks like dogs.	1. (upper ⅔).
2. Looks like a house they are going in.	2. (d)
3. Smoke's coming out of chimney. Dogs have a tail. House got a lot of grass. 50″	3. (whole).
VIII 2″ 1. A tree and	
2. Two mouses climbing up a big tree. Here is an animal coming back down—one of his eyes is broke. 50″	2. Could be dogs coming up to eat something off the tree.
IX 6″ 1. Burning all of him up— all the house up.	
2. Boys fell down—two boys fell down. They were looking at the fire. Fire began to burn the boy. 44″	2. Pink.
X 6″ 1. The fire burn the house all to pieces.	1. (W).
2. The goats be running.	2. (brown).
3. Ears be sticking up— got no hands. 30″	3. (green).

Following is the "blind" interpretation of this record:
"The first record of this child is quite immature, emotionally and

intellectually for a youngster of six years, nine months—more what one would expect of a three or four year old. There is nothing within the protocol to suggest better ability than the Binet I.Q., though the pervading sense of anxiety and violence might mask better basic resources. Right now, either the family stability or her own role within the family is so threatened that Molly is preoccupied with her personal problems. Fears and feelings prevent an objective non-personalized view of her world and few defenses are emerging yet. Molly's interest and motivation is towards a protective relation with parent figures rather than her own peer group. Her needs and anxieties are too great to permit real participation in groups of her age, though her hostility might well find expression here. With her mother she appears to have a more secure and satisfying relationship than with her father. One wonders whether the family unit is intact.

"A youngster with so much insecurity and so few defenses might well present an overt behavior problem. She is not yet ready in any way for school."

The first grade teacher considered Molly too immature for first grade, but since she had been in kindergarten for two years, she was promoted on age, as well as size. She was unable to relate to the other children on their level, and this improved little with time. She gradually learned, however, to be less hyperactive and more conforming to the class routine and was promoted to second grade, again on age.

Little is known of Molly's home life during this year. Her next sibling, a sister, was in kindergarten at this time, and showed signs of better intelligence and adjustment than Molly.

When she was seen for a second interview at the age of seven years and nine months, Molly seemed much more subdued in her relationships than the year before. Her behavior was most immature, however, and her teacher saw her as greatly retarded in school achievement—in fact, the teacher felt that she had not even made a beginning.

Her drawing of a person confirmed the low intellectual rating found on the Binet the year before. The figure consisted of: a large head with the only features being large circles for eyes and two straight lines above them for eyebrows; a long truncated body with no arms; legs which were drawn in sections, perhaps to represent trousers; and feet of different sizes.

Her responses to the Rorschach cards were as follows:

Molly's Rorschach Protocol at the Seven Year Level

Performance	Inquiry
I 7″ 1. Butterfly. (Dr) 10″	1. (Confused about outline).
II 5″ 1. Santa Claus (D) 7″	1. Hat, body, legs.
III 3″ 1. Donkey (D) 7″	1. On a tree. (lower D).
IV 4″ 1. Wolf. 7″	1. (W).
V 5″ 1. A deer. 7″	a. Tagger, teeth, tail.
VI 5″ 1. Rabbit. 8″	1. He have this. Q. Feathers. (Rubs hand over card). Goes over him to make him warm.
VII 4″ 1. Two doggies. 5″	1. On a rocking chair.
VIII 3″ 1. Two pigs. (P) 5″	1. Climbing up on the tree.
IX 5″ 1. Two leaves. (D) 7″	1. Fall—fall off the tree. Q. Looks like when they fall off and get red.
X 5″ 1. A fire. 7″	1. (red).

Following is the "blind" interpretation of the above record:

"There has been a marked change in this child from the age of six years, nine months to seven years, eight months. She has either protected herself from her fears and hostilities through a massive repressive defense or there has been a drastic change in her living situation. In either event, the personality structure is more constricted: there is effort towards control and conformity, though it is an inflexible, brittle control, and overt behavior problems are still to be anticipated. Considered with the first protocol, this record fairly well establishes her intellectual capacity, as well below average, her thinking is arbitrary and stereotyped, and she is at a disadvantage in perceiving and interpreting her world. Relationship with mother that seemed rather close at six is more remote now. One wonders now whether she is living with her parents or in an institutional setting. Her dependency needs remain strong and apparently are poorly met. She continues infantile perceptions and speech patterns. Perhaps she is a little more ready to become a member of a group but her immaturity and apparent deprivation make such an adjustment difficult."

The inference in the above interpretation that Molly is an institutionalized child probably stems from the fact that Molly appeared to feel deprived and rejected at this time. This might well have been true, since she was reacting to mother's obvious disappointment at her failure to achieve in school as well as to the threat of a younger sister's greater academic ability. Not only the Rorschach record, but also Molly's drawing at this time pictured a child with feelings of unworthiness and consequent rejection, and with a fear of the anger that accompanies these feelings.

Considerable pressure was being put on Molly to achieve, not only by her teacher, but also by mother, who compared her lack of progress with the younger sister's better school adjustment. Although she was quite unhappy, Molly never refused to go to school, and seemed to enjoy the companionship of the younger children as they all went to and from class. However, she was not promoted to third grade since she had not even made a beginning in academic progress. Her sister had started into first grade and was already "breathing down Molly's neck."

When she was seen at eight years and eight months of age, Molly presented a dull, unhappy appearance. She showed real pleasure, however, upon recognizing the examiner. When she was completely unable to perform on the Monroe Diagnostic Reading Examination, she was obviously most uncomfortable. The teacher saw her as making no progress academically, and felt that she was even too immature for her second grade placement. At this time the possibility of recommending Molly to the special class for retarded children was considered by the school authorities.

Molly's responses to the Rorschach cards at this time follow.

Molly's Rorschach Protocol at the Eight Year Level

Performance	Inquiry
I 2″ 1. A butterfly. W	1. Flying—black.
14″	
II 3″ 1. Fire.	1. Color like fire.

Performance	*Inquiry*
2. Looks like a man.	2. Head, body, foots—looks like he's sitting down but he's standing up.

39"

III 4" 1. Ribbon.
2. Fire right here.
42" 3. Two little goats.

1. (red).
2. And here.
3. Sitting down.

IV 5" 1. Looks like a man—some hands—got his eyes shut
29" —got some legs.

a. Tails
(side d).

V 2" I memory this one.
1. Looks like a bunny, it's
9" a bunny. W.

1. Wing. I saw a bunny that flies.

VI 21" I don't memory this one.
1. Looks like somebody standing up. Oh, that's a
45" cat—got whiskers.

VII 2" 1. Two little doggies.

1. Have tails, some ears, mouth, eyes. Where is the foots?

22" 2. A butterfly down there.

VIII 5" 1. Two pigs climbing up.
2. A tree.
3. Some bricks
18"

3. Made like bricks—we have those at our house.

IX   1. Looks like trees—stems.

1. Tree is green and turns brown.

2. What do you call them? Looks like big brick stones.
48" 3. Got some eyes—they're big eyes.

3. (S)

X 4" 1. These look like spiders.
2. Something flying.
25" 3. Looks like a man.

1. Crawling.
2. The brown.
3. (W)

Following is the "blind" interpretation of this Rorschach protocol:
"At eight years, eight months, we see evidence that Molly is becoming aware of her limited capacity and is feeling the pressure of environmental demands. Despite her intellectual handicap, she tries to satisfy these pressures, makes a real effort to comply, even if she can only identify the blot as "something." Confabulatory, confused

and arbitrary thinking is present: good judgment is apparent only infrequently. There are efforts at control and conformity, occasionally successful.

"Since the first protocol there has been a shift from releasing her feelings in an outgoing direction—impulsive and uncontrolled as that may be—to withdrawing from the environment and working out her problems in wishful childish fantasy. Now Molly is less prone to impulsive or explosive outbursts; unacceptable overt behavior is less likely, though a generally immature response is to be expected. Some progress has been made in identification, though self-concept is still confused and poorly differentiated. Aggressive content is being replaced by more passive concepts, suggesting that this is the role she is gradually adopting.

"Men seem more meaningful though certainly no more manly than women, another shift from the initial record that cannot be accounted for without further information."

There were many squabbles at home between Molly and her younger sister, with the sister usually the victor. Molly got along better with the other siblings in the family, but her relationship with them was neither so close nor so positive as with this next younger sister. Mother consistently tried to impress all her children with the need for them to conform and to repress all aggressive feelings, since she saw this as the only way to get along in a "white" world.

Molly was a short, poorly-dressed little girl with a sad, dull face when she next came for her interview, at the age of nine years and nine months. At first she did not recognize the examiner; but later she said, "I remember you now but I don't know your name." There seemed to be some evidence of a visual difficulty since she bent her head very close to the test material. She also indicated a short attention span, and showed neither persistence nor any attempt to grasp the meaning of the test items.

Her scores on the Grace Arthur Performance Scale ranged from below five on Knox Cube to nine years on Healy I and the resulting P.Q. was 69. The poorest ability demonstrated was attention span, while a sensitivity to her environment was her best. This combination of qualities, no doubt, contributed to her unhappiness since she could sense the poor quality of her performance but was seemingly unable to improve it.

Her Rorschach responses were as follows:

Molly's Rorschach Protocol at the Nine Year Level

Performance	Inquiry
I 4″ 1. Butterfly. W 21″	1. Flying.

II   7″ 1. Fire.
         2. Head
      70″ 3. Bears.
	1. 'Cause it looks like it.
	2. (centered).
	3. Sitting down. (D)

III 11″ 1. Black is a man.
         2. Bow in the middle.
         3. Fire up here.
      55″ 4. Piece of wood.
	1. Sitting down—a leg.
	2. (red).
	3. (upper red)
	4. (lower side D).

IV   9″ 1. Looks like a tree.
            Something holding him
      60″   up.
	1. Tree—middle holds up the tree.

V 8″ 1. This looks like a rabbit 42″ —got a wing on him.	1. In the air. (W)
VI 14″ 1. Looks like a hole in the ground and 40″ 2. Something in the middle.	2. A fox. (upper D).
VII 24″ 1. Looks like two little dumplings and they are down on this thing that 54″ 2. Looks like a butterfly.	1. Animals.
VIII 6″ 1. Something climbing up a tree. 30″ 2. Got red down here and orange.	1. Animal. 2. Fire.

IX 20″ 1. Apples down here.
         2. Something green right here.
      47″ 3. Orange.
	1. (red).
	2. Leaf, trees.
	
	3. Looks like some people talking.

X   3″ 1. Looks like little worms down here.
         2. Fire here.
         3. Something in the middle of it.
         4. Looks something like mosquitoes.
	1. (green).
	
	2. (red).
	3. Like a bow. (inner blue)
	
	4. Got long legs (blue).

Following is the "blind" interpretation of the above record:

"At nine years, nine months, Molly gives the most erratic record of the series. She appears to have made real progress in integrating affective control and in identification aspects of personality development. Self-concept still seems to be that of a "little" person; there is growing evidence that she is establishing a passive role but feelings of inadequacy are less diffuse. There again is an increase in successful socially adaptive efforts and greater conformity of thinking—a real gain in a handicapped person. These trends, however, are not firm and more immature reactions are common when her situation is complex or threatening.

"The inconsistent aspects of personality development are reflected in the uneven use of intellectual resources, raising the possibility that the Binet I.Q. may be a somewhat low estimate of capacity had this youngster enjoyed a more favorable environment."

Molly had been promoted to third grade, but there had been little academic progress during the year. The sister had passed her and was now adopting a protective role, defending her against verbal attacks by other children and trying to help her with her school work. Mother still had difficulty accepting Molly's retardation and continued, without success, to encourage her to do better. When, at the end of this year, Molly was recommended for special class assignment, she was most unhappy about it because of her mother's disappointment in her.

By the time that Molly was visited the following year, she reportedly liked her new assignment to the special class in her same school. She was then ten years and eight months of age; and, although she was still generally dull and sad in appearance, she showed some enthusiasm when she talked about the work she was doing. She told of making a skirt for herself, describing it as "striped and comes up this way."

Molly achieved a Full Scale I.Q. of 68 on the Wechsler Intelligence Scale for Children which she was given at this time. Her verbal I.Q. was 68 while her performance I.Q. was 74. She showed an increased attention span in the test situation—due, no doubt, to the fact that she was finally placed in a school situation where the work was within her grasp.

Her Rorschach responses were as follows:

Molly's Rorschach Protocol at the Ten Year Level

Performance	Inquiry
I 30″ 1. A candle.	1. (Denies).
50″ 2. Looks like a butterfly too.	2. Q. In the air.

Performance	*Inquiry*
II 14" 1. Two little donkeys. 27"	1. Sitting down.
III 7" 1. Fire. 9"	1. Burns like that—(pointing to black.)
IV 9" 1. Tree. 17"	1. Leg part, arm part, head part. Q. Of a tree.
V 5" 1. Rabbit. 8"	1. Bunny rabbit—wings—flying in the air.
VI 8" 1. Kitten. 15"	1. Black part, neck part. Q. Standing up.
VII 4" 1. Two little doggies sitting 14" 2. On a rock.	1. Here and here.
VIII 79" 1. This is a tree. 110" 2. And this is mountain.	1. (upper D). 2. (lower D).
IX 21" 1. Fire.	1. 'Cause it looks like it—fire stands up like that.
X 16" 1. Two little green worms down here. 2. Looks like spiders. 3. Little donkeys (inner blue).	1. (P) 2. (P) 3. Up on this wall.

The "blind" interpretation of this record is as follows:

"After some reduction, at years eight and nine months in the tension and constriction that suddenly appeared at year seven, Molly, at ten years, again gives a restricted record. Moreover, the quality of her responses is poorer than before and there is a regression from the gains in identification noted in the pevious year. Babyish speech patterns have decreased but perception is still infantile. However, Molly seems more self-conscious regarding her inadequate functioning and is turning to evasion as a defense. Identification aspects of personality development and emotional resources now seem to lag even below the projected mental age. One pictures her in an environment that is not meeting her affective needs nor supplying adequate identification opportunities, while perhaps unrealistic pressures increase her sense of inadequacy. She reacts with some socially adaptive responses and perhaps childish fantasying but has relatively few such resources and impresses me as an unhappy child, withdrawing as she fails to find satisfactions in her social contacts."

The interpretation above gives an apt picture of Molly's functioning at that time, and a suggestion of the pressure she felt. Her special class placement was ignored by mother, either through ignorance or in an attempt to deny Molly's retardation; but the child continued to be the butt of much teasing among the children on her way to and from school and in the neighborhood. Mother gave her somewhat inconsistent support in standing up for herself, since she allowed Molly to fight back if she was attacked in her own yard, but not elsewhere. At times, Molly would grumble at her mother, but she was much more compliant when her father spoke—"She knows better than to argue with her father."

Although she was fairly well-developed physically, Molly presented a pathetic appearance at eleven years and eight months of age. She was poorly dressed in a short, soiled jacket and blue jeans, and her hair was most untidy. She was forced to breathe through her mouth because of a bad cold, and this, coupled with her running nose, gave her face an even duller look than usual. Molly made every effort to be cooperative in answering the interview questions, but she had difficulty formulating her answers and looked very unhappy. Her feelings of general inadequacy were evident in her behavior.

When she was asked about her worries, she expressed concern over getting along with the children with whom she plays, saying, "I don't want to fight and I'm always afraid they will start a fight." In response to the inquiry about what makes her angry, she replied that she gets "mad" at her younger sisters when they "mess up" the house and then leave it for her to straighten up. She admitted that she got angry at mother but, "I can't do nothing to her—she'll beat me up."

Molly needed a great deal of encouragement on the Human Figure Drawings. She erased continually on both figures and was not satisfied with the finished products. Her first drawing was of a twelve-year-old girl. The body was short, plumply rounded, and top-heavy in appearance, and the arms were close to the body and too short. The legs were drawn in close proximity to each other. Four buttons down the front of the trunk were the only indications of clothing. This drawing manifested, quite obviously, Molly's feelings of insecurity, inadequacy, and fear of aggression.

The figure of the boy, thirteen years of age, was somewhat similar to that of the girl. Attached to a rounded trunk with three buttons down the center were: a head smaller than that of the girl, with no nose or ears; curved lines for arms which were attached to the lower edge of the trunk and gave the effect of "hands in pockets"; and legs with a wide space between them. She had considerable difficulty with the boy's legs and was concerned about their being so far apart. Although Molly denied any knowledge of menstruation, she seemed aware of sex activities and concerned about what may happen to her as a girl.

Molly's Rorschach Protocol at the Eleven Year Level

Performance	Inquiry
I (Looks on back—smiles —sneezes).	
47″ 1. Looks like a butterfly to 58″ me.	1. Looks like his wing and his body. (W)
II 27″ 1. Fire. 32″	1. 'Cause it looks like it.
III 15″ 1. Two little donkeys on it. 21″	1. One of his legs—face—looks like other legs.
IV (I don't know. I ain't wearing my glasses and that's why.)	
45″ 1. Maybe it could be a tree. 47″	1. Trunk and this looks like one of its branches and this looks like its head.
V 10″ 1. Could be a butterfly. 12″	1. Wings. A butterfly don't have no ears. Q. In the air. Q. Flying (W).
VI (I don't know what that looks like. Encouraged).	
52″ 1. Looks like a cat—got 55″ whiskers.	1. Head—whiskers. Just this part up here (D).
VII 13″ 1. Two little dogs on 18″ 2. A hill.	1. Sitting on a hill.
VIII 60″ 1. Looks like one of those— I forgot what you call it. Looks like one of those . . .	1. Looks like they are climbing on something. Q. Bricks.
61″ something like a cow.	
IX 37″ 1. This looks like some green grass. I don't know what this looks like.	1. Green grass.
71″ I don't know what this looks like.	

Performance	*Inquiry*
X 5″ 1. This looks like spiders— right here.	1. They are stuck on this.
2. These look like little worms.	2. Green. Q. On the ground.
I don't know these.	

The "blind" interpretation of this record is as follows:

"There appears to be little change from age ten years eight months to eleven years eight months. Neither protocol indicates any strengthening of the progress noted at year nine years nine months. Instead, feelings of anxiety and inadequacy have become more diffuse and destructive to ego development and intellectual functioning. She seems resigned, anticipating little success or acceptance from an environment that has not, from these records, offered her many positive experiences.

"Anticipating the future adjustment of any subject is difficult and particularly hazardous in the case of a dull child, less capable of meeting the stress of everyday living and more dependent upon environmental support. Molly lacks self-confidence and ego strengths, her identifications are passive and immature, and there has been little progress in any area of personality development over the past two years. Under the stress of adolescence, of greater expectations, of increasing independence, one questions whether Molly can make an acceptable or satisfying adjustment except under most favorable circumstances."

During the next year, Molly continued to be the "low man on the totem pole" in a family that itself felt inadequate and unable to stand up against environmental pressures. She moved on to a special class in a junior high school setting, and was, fortunately, getting some pleasure from what she was learning of a practical nature in this setup. When I invited her to come to the Center for a visit, mother was unwilling for her to come the four blocks alone. I suggested that I come for her in a car and that she might want to bring one of her sisters along. This was evidently a big occasion for the family, and when I arrived everyone was excitedly getting the two girls ready. Once we were in the car, Molly volunteered spontaneously that I had come for her on her (thirteenth) birthday. She also said that she liked school and her teacher better this year than she had the year before. This teacher was "learning her more—had learned her to do arithmetic and even to read."

Molly was interviewed by a child psychiatrist at this time, and his report was as follows:

"It was tough to interview this pathetic, yet naively happy, lonely, little thirteen-year-old Negro girl. What she denies of her inadequacy is quite harmless—her career aims—to 'be a good housecleaner' are appropriate enough to her limitations to keep her out of trouble. If she has the good fortune to have strict parents who are God-fearing and religious, she can get enough satisfaction out of 'goodness' and 'compliance' for awhile to keep from having to resort to more punitive asocial methods.

"She will perhaps have some difficulty with boys—at present she deals with her concrete, very limited fantasy life by denial, 'I just won't get married—ever—I'll be alone and take care of myself just like my aunt.' The paradox that she also has a mild illusory boy friend now doesn't bother her because logic is not one of her vices.

"She thinks of her troubles mainly in fears of somatic pain or punitive oral gratification difficulties. Her worst trouble is that she can't eat as much now as she used to be able to.

"Guilt is at a very low level so her prognosis for good adjustment without asocial behavior is excellent. Unfortunately, she is likely to be victimized by, or because of, her low intelligence. I believe she is primarily retarded, not emotionally disturbed."

Another child psychiatrist, with access to all of the case material, made the following formulation of Molly's personality development:

"The central factor in the consideration of this child's personality development is the well-established subnormal intellectual capacity. It gave one strike against her—if not two—from very early in life. Born a large (nine pound) infant, the third of an eventual five siblings, we have no definite information regarding emotional deprivation or difficult management except that she was 'fussy.' The impression remains from the data that the mother supplied the affective needs in this period of life with reasonable adequacy. The quite early toilet training can be assumed to be syntonic with this Negro family's cultural pattern and, therefore, not of itself 'traumatic.' Yet, considering the eventual evidences of retardation, this child may well have had a delayed neuromuscular development. If so, such demands for motor compliance were accomplished at the price of an early recognition by the ego of its own helplessness in the face of inner (physiologic) urges. There is, of course, considerable later evidence of the ego's brittleness and this child's relative feeling of inadequacy. Especially did she become afraid of hostile impulses, both by her own admission and collaborated by the mother's statements. At any rate, by age six-and-a-half, at the time of the first Rorschach, she showed extreme concern about her body and its integrity, e.g., the several responses concerning the body, things missing from the body, things going into or coming off (the body). This concern appears to transcend strict 'castration anxiety,' to wit, the interesting comment, 'one of his eyes is broke.' Furthermore, the frequent reference to 'fire' as a single response and in connection with other responses is interpreted to reflect an awareness of the danger and inadequate control of these, her own, primitive physiological internal pressures. She would seem then to have felt quite vulnerable and attacked.

"For a while beyond age six-and-a-half, the parents and society apparently did support and aid her development, judging from definite disappearance of this type of response in the protocol at age seven-and-a-half.

"The 'massive repression' hypothecated by the Rorschach interpreter would appear correct. Such probably resulted from the necessary, rather strong social pressures of the first grade. It is also significant in terms of the conforming type of character structure that eventually evolved by early adolescence, i.e., this period was a turning point and forewarned the trend of further development.

"On the basis of the general gradual improvement then noted up to age ten-and-a-half (with some 'good' popular and human responses seen, Card III, at nine-and-a-half), we must assume that the environment accepted and even enjoyed the little girl for a while. The gains made in this period, though not ideal, added sufficient ego strength to carry her into adolescence where she is last reported to be making at least a socially acceptable adjustment.

"Yet this lull in the storm was destined to be short-lived. By ten-and-a-half the protocol shows on the same Card III, where a year before she could see people, at least as people popularly see them, a return to the old "fire" perception. One can guess with strong conviction that by eleven-and-a-half the menarche had been reached (if not actual menstruation, the early hormonal changes of pubescence) and that the ego again felt threatened, as it had at six-and-a-half, by powerful psychophysiologic impulses. Had she been more successful in her ability to handle them the first time, presumably so great a regression would not have been necessary. Likewise, had she had the resource of greater intellectual capacities the outcome would not have been the same.

"The role played by the parents is not entirely clear. The protocol at this point suggests poor identifications. She denied the 'father card' altogether. However, judging from the social history, the mother seemed to be giving as much as she could, and probably both parents were giving quantitatively enough for a child with an average I.Q. On the other hand, the organic factor cannot be completely differentiated from the environmental effects upon this individual. The additional social factor of placement in a special class at about age ten may well have produced loss of self-esteem and self-doubt. Yet clinically, at that time, Molly seemed happier about school. The mother, when giving the social history, completely avoided mentioning the special class and one wonders how well she accepted it. Although denial is a common response for a mother with such a child, it can result in definite unrealistic expectations of the child. Indeed, the mother's (and father's) failure to accept this daughter's mental retardation would have been highly significant in depriving Molly of adequate emotional support. This factor may well account for several interpretations of various protocols to the general effect that Molly is in an essentially rejecting milieu—perhaps an institution. To speculate further, by eleven it was probably less easy for everyone to overlook the mental retardation, even though moderate, hence people became more demanding. Nonetheless, I deem it fortunate and helpful in strengthening Molly's already difficult personality development that she was placed in a special class at that time in her life.

"Finally, it appears that Molly reached a state of equilibrium by eleven-and-a-half. She compromised between people and fire on Card III with animals (donkeys). She had finally relinquished the rather pathetic though concretistic fantasy of a flying rabbit on Card V (though she still wonders: 'A butterfly don't have no ears'). This equilibrium seems to have become the character structure of the conforming person at fifteen who is not really happy but who does not get into serious trouble, who still has occasional bursts of anger when the brittle defense cracks under pressure of misunderstanding. I would agree with the psychiatric evaluation that her limited goals and homely accomplishments are her greatest asset—though life seemed to have offered more to Molly at birth."

Molly accepted my invitation to come for a visit at the age of seventeen, but never put in an appearance. When I called her again, she was pleasant but evasive, saying that she was no longer in school. She was unable to accept my explanation that the visit had nothing to do with school. The school authorities informed me later that Molly had been excused from school at sixteen to take a job. She had achieved her cherished goal of "housecleaner," and was doing menial cleaning jobs in an institution near her home.

X : ALLAN

ALLAN IS THE YOUNGEST of four children in a family where his near-est sibling is fourteen years his senior. At the time of his birth, his parents' marriage was already close to dissolution, and mother refers to her pregnancy with Allan as the "dirty trick my husband pulled" to keep her from leaving him. Both parents, by this time, were already in their forties; and mother had been waiting for her opportunity to leave father for many years.

Father was an unstable, itinerant carpenter with two years of high school education while mother, who had had three years of normal college training, had been a school teacher before marriage. Since the three older children were born within the first four years of mar-riage, mother had been helpless in the face of her husband's lack of responsibility toward providing for his family. She grew bitter with the years and warned father that she planned to leave him as soon as the children were in high school and, therefore, less dependent upon her. Mother believed that father thought a new baby would curtail the divorce plan, but she said Allan's birth could merely delay it.

Allan weighed ten and a half pounds at birth and the delivery was difficult. Mother was disappointed when she was informed she had a son; she had gone so far as to promise her fourteen-year-old daughter a sister when she came back from the hospital. However, this older sister was delighted with Allan and "mothered" him from the start: she took complete care of him except when she was at school.

The boy was breastfed for two months and then changed to a bottle because of mother's diminished milk supply. There was no feeding problem—"everything agreed with him"; and, even as an infant, he was "put on a diet" because of his obesity. Allan walked at nine months but talking was slow. Mother started toilet training at about seven months, with success.

Her major concern about him at this time was his thumb-sucking

158

which continued until Allan was ten years old. She scolded him continually about it and later, as a last resort, pointed out the damage to his upper jaw development. Allan did not stop, however, until after he had been taken to an orthodontist. The attachment placed in his mouth on that occasion was irritating to Allan's thumb and he gave up the habit. The gadget was kept for two or three months; when it was finally removed Allan did not return to thumb-sucking except when he was frustrated or embarrassed.

When Allan was three years old mother left home; she took him and his sister with her at this time. The oldest boy was in military service, and soon after mother's departure, both father and the second brother also joined the armed forces. After several months' absence, mother returned to maintain the home for the two younger children. She later obtained a divorce, but mother was quite vague in her discussion of this.

The sister, who was now in her late teens, took care of Allan while mother worked. There was never any explanation to Allan about his father's disappearance from his life, and he has never asked mother about this. In fact, his mother believes that Allan was never even concerned about father. However, when Allan was about five, father returned from service and tried to effect a reconciliation with mother in a turbulent scene to which the boy was a witness. Even after this occasion where many harsh words were exchanged, Allan and mother did not discuss the situation. A second such episode occurred some time later and resulted in father's departure from this part of the country. Mother and son have never made any further reference to one another about these traumatic incidents.

Shortly after this time, Allan started to first grade. He was first seen in the testing situation a few months after the beginning of school and was six years, eight months at the time. He was a short, round-faced little boy, immature and unhappy looking, but very eager for the examiner's acceptance and approval. He appeared anxious and depressed in spite of the fact that he was cooperative throughout the session. He achieved a slightly superior rating on the Binet examination. Allan's teacher described him as a "good student but unable to concentrate when instructions are given. He daydreams and sucks his thumb occasionally." Such behavior apparently reflected Allan's anxiety about parental relationships, his father's disappearance and his mother's lack of communication and understanding.

Allan's first Rorschach protocol follows:

Allan's Rorschach Protocol at the Six Year Level

Performance	Inquiry
I 24" 1. A stone—or could be when you put glass in the furnace. It burns up 60" and gets like this.	1. Glass.
II 28" 1. Looks like a clock when the place where the hands go round is 65" knocked out.	1. (W).
III 14" 1. This looks like ice—this down here.	1. It's white. (lower D).
2. Cat fish (upper red).	2. Cat fish is red.
45" 3. Bow.	3. Here.
IV 28" 1. Looks like a scalp of 55" something.	1. An animal, all chopped up.
V 6" 1. Wings of a bird.	1. The whole bird.
2. Looks like a rabbit or 35" something.	2. Head and feet.
VI 28" 1. Looks like ice when 35" snow comes.	1. Looks frozen and white.
VII 20" 1. Ice. 32"	1. Frozen snow—white.
VIII 40" 1. Looks like two cats fooling on 50" 2. Ice, trying to pull it down.	1. This is the ice and here are the cats.
IX 65" 1. It looks like a head of 70" something.	1. Two holes like eyes—a deer (points to horns).
X 70" 1. Looks like a kind of animal pulling this ice down.	1. (Upper D). a. Head of a rabbit.

Following is the "blind" interpretation of this record:

"At year six, Allan demonstrates a basic constrictive pattern, in a setting involving much blocking and a markedly dysphoric mood. The constriction here is not at its peak, and he shows some hints of potentials for a freer approach to the expression of feelings, as well as hints of substantial striving to come to grips with some externally imposed psychological trauma. His primary mode of dealing with the anxiety-arousing aspects of his experience is by reducing his awareness of them, rather than through easy motor discharge of the anxiety attending threat or through binding the anxiety, once aroused, through motoric or symbolic processes. In this Rorschach, avoidance and denial are very prominent and of themselves are not sufficient to stem his burden of anxiety, resulting in much blocking and felt discomfort. His early efforts at internalization here appear to be ineffective in dealing with tensions.

"Many of my formulations about Allan are pinned to the hypothesis that he suffered some recent trauma regarding his father shortly before this first Rorschach was taken, most probably the death, desertion, or serious incapacitation of the father. He is hungry for adult affection, and seems to be developing propitiatory, hostility-denying maneuvers in respect to authority figures."

As the interpretation suggests, Allan is struggling to repress and even to deny his inner feelings. This struggle leaves him little psychic energy for responding adequately to the world about him. He is fast developing a constriction that may continue to bind him through the years.

During the year following this first contact with Allan, his older brother returned to the home from military service for a brief interval. Allan was devoted to him and followed him around. Soon after, however, brother married and left the home. This was followed shortly by Allan's sister's marriage and departure. Allan missed these siblings and found his sister's leaving especially difficult since she had been the person closest to him up to this time.

After this, mother took Allan to work with her because she could find no other way of having him cared for. He was always obedient and well-mannered, never gave her any trouble and never interfered with other adults at her place of employment. Mother seemed little aware of what was going on with Allan at this time, since he never discussed anything with her. He seemed to get along all right in school but had few friends and stayed much to himself when he was not at school or with mother at her work.

One has the picture of a sad, constricted little fellow, afraid to express himself for fear of further and complete rejection. First father rejected him, then brother and sister, and he was now afraid of losing the last possible source of his unmet dependency needs, his mother.

When Allan was tested at the age of seven years and eight months, he had changed little in appearance, unless it was that he looked more unhappy, and even more eager to please the examiner. There was a complete lack of spontaneity throughout the session. His drawing at this age revealed his insecurity and feeble ineffectual reaching out for affection. The male figure, with outstretched arms, wears dresslike apparel with large buttons down the front, and a masculine hat with feathers attached. Allan's drawing gave indication of his failure to have reached a solution of his sex identification struggles.

Following are his Rorschach responses at this time:

Allan's Rorschach Protocol at the Seven Year Level

Performance	Inquiry
I 7″ 1. A face.	1. Eyes, these look like ears, neck. (WS)
28″ 2. Big butterfly.	2. Whole thing.
II (Smiles faintly, frowning at the same time—squints his eyes and forms words with his lips.) (Encouraged.)	
180″ (After much encouragement.)	
1. Rabbits (upper red). A little bit like rabbits.	1. These are legs (white) and that's his paws. There's his mouth, these look like ears. Looks like he's jumping.
182″	
III 110″ 1. Looks something like an animal or something.	1. Looks like a duck. Eye, mouth, neck, body. One leg but don't see the other (omits lower D). Q. Standing up.
2. This looks like a butterfly or a bow.	2. Bow. Q. Red.
2′30″	
IV 52″ 1. This looks like an animal.	1. Eyes, mouth—just the head.
62″ (lower D).	
V 65″ 1. Grasshopper.	1. Ears, legs. I don't know what this is (wings)—not part of it.
72″	
VI 55″ 1. Looks like a little bird up here. (upper D).	1. Wings, eyes and nose. Q. In the air. Q. Trying to go high.
57″	
VII (Turns head to one side after two minutes of steady looking. Frowns considerably, always	

Performance	Inquiry
looking at picture—tilts	
3'10" card a little).	
1. Looks like some kind of animal right there.	1. This looks like a lion or something. Leg, eyes, nose and mouth (upper ⅔).
3'25"	

VIII	(After encouragement).	
1'52"	An animal here.	1. Looks like a red bird or fish
1'55"		Q. An animal walking.

IX	(Same behavior of tilting head, squinting, frowning but always with eyes on card).	
3'22"	1. This looks like a snowman right here.	1. (Inner D). Here's his eyes. Looks like he's sitting in
3'39"		snow all right.

X	28"	1. These look like worms.	1. Two green worms.
	36"		

The "blind" interpretation of this record follows:

"At year seven, Allan shows increase in passivity constriction, and a need to maintain security through not extending himself, which appears to yield some slight gain in comfort at the expense of spontaneity. He has not yet abandoned attempts at integration of his internal feelings through being aware of them, nor hesitant feelers to the outside world, but he appears to be on the way toward this. He relies heavily on an avoidant, passive approach to many stimulus situations, with great emphasis on suppressive and repressive devices. There is almost a complete lack of willingness to reveal his associations, and his basic root systems of passivity and reaction formation are already in strong appearance at this age.

"He shows an interest in relating to people and would probably enjoy a number of superficial contacts with peers, but is curtailed greatly by fear of rejection, passivity and a lack of genuine reflection of feeling. He continues to search unsatisfactorily for a satisfying father image, and tends to identify with the mother at this time."

During the year following this Rorschach record, when Allan was around eight years old, he continued to be much alone. There was little contact with other children after school hours, as mother took him with her to the neighborhood movie, where she was employed. Communication between mother and Allan was still limited. He never asked questions and mother had no idea when he became curious about sex-related facts or where he got his information, if any.

He was next seen at age eight years, eight months and at that time he appeared quite small for his age. He talked with infantile speech, such as "wound" for "round," but there was much more spontaneity during this session than there had been the year before. He gave the impression of actually enjoying the Monroe Diagnostic Reading Examination, and was interested, cooperative, and persistent in all phases of it. The results showed that his school achievement was above his third grade placement, with more than a grade's advancement in arithmetic. He showed some compulsive traits in his need to stack all test items neatly as he completed them. Allan's teacher reported that he lacked friends at school; he seemed to fear the boys' rough games and was much more comfortable watching the girls in their play.

His Rorschach protocol follows:

Allan's Rorschach Protocol at the Eight Year Level

Performance	Inquiry
I 50" 1. These look a little bit like cat's ears.	1. (d).
67" 2. Top of deer's horn.	2. (d).
II 11" 1. If these weren't red and you put an eye there it would look like a rabbit standing on its hind legs.	1. (upper red).
2. This here looks like the 42" bottom of clippers.	2. (center d).
III 10" 1. If you put an eye in there it would look like a man with one foot and	1. Here and here. (P)
40" 2. Here's a bow.	2. A red one.
IV 32" 1. If you put two eyes there it would look like an 51" alligator head.	1. (lower D).
V 10" 1. It looks like a rabbit standing on two hind legs. If you put an eye it 34" would be.	1. (D)

Performance	Inquiry
VI 45″ 1. Up here it looks like some object with wings 73″ flying.	1. (Upper D).
VII 20″ 1. If you put an eye in here and a piece here it would look something 40″ like a lion. (upper ⅔).	1. Laying down or something.
VIII 22″ 1. If these two things were brown and you put an eye would look like a a mouse.	1. Looks like he's climbing up something.
IX 47″ 1. These down here (part of orange) look a little 79″ bit like crabs' pinchers.	1. (Upper d).
X 10″ 1. That looks a little bit like two green worms. (Yawns).	1. (P)

The interpreter had this to say about the above record:

"By year eight, Allan has comfortably established himself in a markedly constrictive pattern, experiencing his greatest security from anxiety, and a higher degree of comfort and confidence in his mode of relating than he shows on any previous record. He now seems to believe firmly that the tiny 'neatened up' world which he sees bears a substantial relationship to reality, and this comfort offers him a modicum of confidence in at least the superficial contacts he establishes with others. We find Allan experiencing his greatest freedom from anxiety through adoption of a compulsive pattern in dealing with his associations. It is a rather primitive compulsive pattern having as its essential goal, prevention of awareness of unwelcome urges, and avoidance of coming to grips with many aspects of his experience, rather than the developmentally more advanced compulsive orientation of binding the anxiety in a world freely-experienced through precise ordering or through all-encompassing contact. At this time, Allan appears to achieve considerable security in his confidence that he can control unwelcome fantasy through this device, and apparently also, through finding that the modicum of independent assertion which he begins to show here is not met with the environmental retribution or punishment which he has been anticipating.

"At year eight, Allan seems to feel more comfortable with his role and can tamper with it, since he seems to be relating to persons with less anxiety at this time, although in a limited way. However, he tends to over-identify with the goals of adults for him; and his sense of weakness and vulnerability to external retributive assault if he should express his impulses freely or oppose adults firmly is apparent."

Sometime during the year following the third Rorschach, Allan's sister, her husband, and year-old baby came back to live in the home. Allan was distressed when the baby bothered his possessions and often resorted to yelling at him. There was no reference by the mother to Allan's relationship to his brother-in-law, but one could conjecture a resurgence of oedipal feelings, since there had been no opportunity to work these out before this. At this time mother took a full-time job as a cook in a restaurant and during mother's working hours Allan was looked after by the sister.

When he was tested at the age of nine years and nine months, Allan was unkempt in appearance. He talked and acted effeminately but was most affable and tried hard to please. He did not show the same persistence in the test situation as he had the year before but this could have been a function of the test material. Allan achieved a slightly lower rating on the Grace Arthur Performance Scale than he had achieved on the more verbal Binet examination; but the discrepancy seemed due to lack of real interest and an inability to concentrate on some of the test items, rather than lack of potentiality. Following is his Rorschach record at the nine year level:

Allan's Rorschach Protocol at the Nine Year Level

Performance	Inquiry
I 9″ 1. That looks like a face. This sorta looks like horns of some animal. (Frowns).	1. Eyes, nose. Horns on top of his head—I can't see his mouth. Here's his ears.
II 2″ 1. This on it looks like a rabbit. His ears and face.	1. Jumping off on something. (upper red).
2. This looks like another one if there was a longer 31″ ear up there.	2. He's standing some place (P).
III 10″ 1. This looks like the face of a duck on each side.	1. Here is head, body, and legs down here.
2. And this (outer red) looks like an animal in 39″ the water or something.	2. Up in the air.

Performance	Inquiry
IV 20″ 1. This looks like some kind of an animal with mouth open.	1. Head and some of the body —about to here.
V 6″ 1. That looks like a butter- 20″ fly.	1. Wings, legs, head. Q. On the ground, standing up.
VI 6″ 1. This looks like a large animal with wings on the 35″ side of his body.	1. Standing up in air and there's his wings and his long body. (W)
VII 7″ 1. Here looks like a lion with part of his back cut 29″ out.	1. Standing on the ground and somebody just took a piece and cut out of him.
VIII 3″ 1. This looks like a rat walking over some dirt 30″ on each side.	1. Spaces and holes through the middle of it and he's stepping over it.
IX 17″ 1. This looks like a gorilla —something like his face 43″ on the side (red).	1. Big face, the head, and a little bit past the neck.
X 7″ 1. This looks like the face of a rabbit.	1. a. Green things is coming up to him. Q. Like worms.
2. Two little animals on side.	2. (Upper gray).
3. This looks like an animal I saw in the museum that goes in water—has 65″ legs on side of his body.	3. (Octopus).

The "blind" interpretation of this record follows:

"At year nine, Allan shows an immediate reduction in his sense of security with only slight relaxation of his essentially passive and constrictive orientation. There is, however, a gradually increasing tendency to bind anxieties through less primitive modes and to attempt to gain perspective on himself and his problems through the use of fantasy. This graduation never achieves a high degree of success in allowing him comfort, and he easily retreats to his underlying core of passive-avoidant devices. His partial abandonment of his compulsive approach (out of disillusionment of its utility? out of its inadequacy to deal with the reality problems which he must face?) and slightly greater use of fantasy are attended by an increase in social anxiety. He continues to attempt to maintain autonomous striving, but with the revival of oedipal fears, some phobic organization of stimuli occurs, although not as a thorough-going defensive pattern.

"This revival of oedipal concerns at the ninth year is most unusual, (even though we have long since found out 'everything ain't so latent in the latency stage') and suggests the return of a father-figure, most likely the introduction of a new father-figure. These fears are likely driving him into more substantial relationships with his peers at this time."

Mother continued to work full-time as a cook, and left sister in full charge of the home and of Allan. The boy had few friends at school or in the neighborhood. He went regularly to Sunday School but made no social contacts there. Allan spent much of his time in his room working on solitary projects; there was only one boy friend with whom he occasionally shared his interests. He continued to make good grades in school and, while mother was proud of his achievement there, she complained that he took little responsibility and cited examples of her need to nag him to do simple household tasks. Allan never talked back to her—he just said he forgot. He had taken a paper route during this period and mother reported him as being "tight with money."

When he was tested at ten years, seven months, Allan was still small for his age but very neat and clean in appearance. He was pleasant and eager to please as usual. He whispered to himself as he worked on the WISC, but seemed blocked and preoccupied on several occasions. He evidently grew tired for he yawned unashamedly, like a much younger child. He again fell short of the slightly superior intellectual rating obtained on the Binet at the age of six.

Allan's Rorschach responses came tantalizingly slow, as if he might be resisting unconsciously, although his outward behavior was agreeable and cooperative:

Allan's Rorschach Protocol at the Ten Year Level

Performance	*Inquiry*
I 16″ 1. These could be some animals, the face and den some kind of leg down there. (Frowns and points and then puts finger in his mouth). (Points again).	1. Head there (upper d).
V2. Can that be the head of a little dog or some-	2. Head and neck.

Performance	*Inquiry*

thing? (Lower d).
(Head to one side.)
(Encouraged him to
170″   lay it down.)

II 8″   1. These could be some   1. (Upper red.)
            kind of rabbit or some-
            thing jumping.
         2. And this could be an-   2. He's standing there and has
            other rabbit with ears.   two legs and ears coming up
            (P)   and here's the outline of his
                                             face.

III 5″ 1. These could be ducks   1. Head and neck. Q. Should be
            or something sitting   another leg.
            right there.
       V2. That could be an ani-   2. There should be another leg.
            mal   or   something   (outer red).
            jumping up in the air.
         3. Could you have some-   3. A round red one. (Laughs).
            thing that isn't an ani-
            mal? Well, that looks
            like a bow tie.
101″   (Frowns and searches
            diligently).

IV 8″   1. This could be some-   1. Cut the little prongs off right
            thing like an alligator.   around here and put two
                                            eyes here.
         2. Or could that be a   2. It was curled and started to
            snake or something   move.
            crawling out of that?
            (d).
         3. Couldn't that be a   3. Looks like some kind of ani-
114″   head?   mal—just his head. Q. Might
                                            be a dog. (lower side d).

V 7″   1. This whole thing there   1. Standing on a flower, little
            —it could be a butter-   things come out of his head
            fly.   —he's standing and opened
                                            up his wings.
         2. If you could cut right   2. If you cut that off and put
            over there (one entire   an eye in there and thicken
            side) that could be the   the leg. Q. Maybe a lion—I
            head and that could be   don't know . . . a dog or a
100″   the legs.   lion.

VI 22″   1. That could be an ani-   1. (upper D).
            mal or something there
            and the wings.

Performance	Inquiry
(Frowns and looks intently at the card.)	
2. Could that be an animal's head? (lower d).	2. Looks like it could be the head and it's cut up right at the head—could be a St. Bernard.

120″

VII 8″ 1. That could be an animal with part of it cut out (upper ⅔).

2. (Studies card.) Could that be an animal's head that had horns
99″   on?

1. Head, one of legs and looks like piece of him gone and three of his legs cut off.

2. Looks like they took the skeleton of a bullock and took the eyes out and set him there. (lower white space)

VIII 7″ 1. These could be two animals here walking.

2. Couldn't that be an animal's head right there? (outer d).

1. Could be a rat.

2. Head of a duck—cut off at head with a little ribbon around his neck. Is that all I said?
  a. That could be an animal sitting there with his
112″   mouth and his eye (red).

IX 3″ 1. Couldn't that be an animal's head there (red) and he has prongs coming out of his mouth?

2. Could that be an animal like a deer and antelope with horns coming out (orange)?
138″

1. Looks like he has an eye and out of his mouth a prong. (Demonstrates.)

X 7″ 1. Couldn't that be the head of a rabbit?

2. These could be some kind of animal—looks like it's jumping.

3. Couldn't that be some kind of animal if you cut that side off (half of inner blue)?

4. That could be a green snake—some kind of snake.

5. That looks like a horse's face.

1. (P)

2. (upper green).

3. Head (dd in center) leaning over. Looks like two legs.

4. (P)

5. (upper gray)

Performance	Inquiry
6. That's something if you cut that off (inner part of outer blue). See his mouth and his eyes are open.	6. (dr in outer blue) a. Right here looks like a little rabbit or mouse or something running. (brown).
166″ 7. That looks like a duck or something when it is sitting up.	7. (inner yellow).

Following is the "blind" interpretation of this record:

"At year ten, there is a substantial change in the form of Allan's constriction, although its meaning appears to me to be consistent, i.e., the former massive constriction now changes into a more active 'flight into reality,' but of an essentially stereotypical, overly conventional, superficial variety. He does allow himself contact with more elements in his environment, suggesting some increase in flexibility and surface allocentrism. There is a strong suppressive and compulsoid orientation, however, which allows him superficial contact with a broader diversity of objects but does not allow him greater ease in dealing with the strong feelings which many of these objects stimulate in him. His has now a well established passive, stereotyped approach.

"His maternal dependency and needs to propitiate authority figures, in particular male authority figures, would scarcely earn him leadership status in a latency age group. Because of his propitiatory needs, restraint of strong feelings, and increasing need to make superficial contact with those around him, he might well find a position of leadership in an adult-dominated children's group, e.g., student council, Sunday School leader. However, in the informally organized play groups of which he would be a member, his lack of assertiveness and his dependence on adults, would reduce his popularity as a potential leader, if he is, as I suspect, a member of the lower social class. He shows slightly more 'push' and assertiveness, somewhat greater freedom in establishing contacts with others, with a stirring of sexual interests; but his 'sense of being different' and his hesitancy in actually investing strongly in others of his age allow him little freedom for other than superficial relationships.

"Allan shows phobic associations around the father-figure and warns himself about the exposition of sexual strivings which further support the supposition that a new father-figure has entered his life. There is guilt about and concern that his unexpressed hostility toward adults will become apparent to them. His relationship to mother has strong aspects of hostile-dependency. He experiences her as powerful and threatening (and thus obedience-demanding throughout all his early years), but concomitantly unable to supply him with the income of affection which he needs to feel secure in his relationships with others. There is resentment toward the mother-figure for her inattention and incapacity to satisfy his affectional needs. There is also some awareness of his closeness to the mother (apparently based on the former absence of other figures for each of them to relate to), and hesitant striving to exert autonomy and separate himself from the mother. This is, for him, an ambivalent striving.

"He searches for a father-figure, or more appropriately for the ideal father, but this search appears to be unavailing and he is continually thrown back upon the image of his mother as his major identification object. He identifies diffusely with those who would correct him, and with the aggressor in others who insist upon conformity and 'being nice' in him."

Allan's home life continued through the next year much as it had been since his sister and her family moved back, freeing mother for her full-time job. He communicated very little of his thoughts and feelings to his family. Mother assumed that he enjoyed school, since he brought home good grades, but she knew or seemingly cared little about his peer relationships. Allan continued regular Sunday School attendance, but refused to participate in any social events connected with the church. He and his one close friend, with whom he shared similar introversive interests, enjoyed tinkering with "ham" radios. Mother had never discussed with Allan her need to work and commented that "he didn't say too much about it." He had his paper route at this period, which provided him with limited spending money. In describing Allan's limited verbalizations to her, she commented, "He's not too confiding—you have to draw things out of him and ask him direct questions." At moments of irritation with Allan, mother threatened to send him to live with father and she was surprised that she detected no reaction to this threat. Mother considered Allan different from her older sons—"he's more like an only child."

When he was tested at the age of eleven years and seven months, Allan was a pleasant, smiling, neatly-dressed boy who looked somewhat effeminate and talked with a lisp. He was most cooperative in the test situation, even though his interest seemed to lag and it was evident that he was weary before the end of the hour. It was difficult for him to concentrate on the material, but he denied being tired, and insisted that he enjoyed the test. When asked to draw a person, he first drew a girl eleven years old, his current age, and when asked to draw the opposite sex, drew a smaller nine-year-old boy. Feet, hands and face were in profile, while the bodies of the two immature figures presented a front view. These drawings suggested a feminine identification with which he was not satisfied.

In a brief interview, Allan was able to express concern about his school work, that he gets angry when he has difficulty with his homework and that his sister always comes to his rescue and helps him. He was also able to say that he worried about his father and wondered about him often. Allan denied that his mother and father were divorced; he said that they were simply separated and he hoped his father would eventually return.

His responses on his sixth Rorschach were as follows:

Allan's Rorschach Protocol at the Eleven Year Level

Performance	Inquiry
I 7″ 1. Could look like a butter-fly—this could be its body and the wings.	1. Looks like he could be alive. Q. Well . . . looks like he's flying.
2. And then on the side here could be a bear—its face—facing towards here on each side.	2. Looks like he's jumping out. (D)
3. Whole thing could be a face.	3. Like a leopard—his face and here's the ear. Q. Looks like if you could see the body he would be jumping at you.
4. There's a little animal's face here, the mouth (de).	4. Looks like his mouth could be opened—like a dog howling.
II 6″ 1. This could be two little rabbits with little ears.	1. Looks like the—could be one rabbit on ice with reflection in the water—could be on a pond. Q. Looks like he's walking over the ice to get to the other shore.
3. That could be a face if you take this side off—looking at the top of its 45″ head (center d)	3. Head of a young alligator could be.
III 12″ 1. This looks like it could	1. A sea horse. Q. Looks like

Performance	*Inquiry*
be—what do you call them in the river—a body and one of its legs.	it's in the water. Q. I don't know whether they swim or not. (side red).
2. Here could be a duck with two legs and face up here.	2. Looks like they are standing looking at each other.
3. This might be the face of an animal climbing up a wall. Face and body.	3. (Half of lower center D)
4. Here could be a bow tie —with it tied in the middle.	4. No particular kind. Looks like you draw a person and put on a bow tie and then erased the lines of the person it was on.
58″	

IV	7″ 1. Here could be the top of an alligator. Top side of its head.	1. Because the head is long and not as wide as a dog and eyes are up farther than usual animal. (D)
	2. Here could be a dog with mouth open.	2. Standing up on two back legs and howling. (lower side d)
44″	3. Might be a snake coming down out of its hole.	3. (upper side d)

V	4″ 1. Here could be the butterfly with wings wide open.	1. It's getting ready to fly.
	2. And if you take the wings off here could be a rabbit.	2. Standing up walking.
	3. Face with two legs sticking down here. (½ of blot).	3. Lion's face—standing up. Q. Lion has hair around its face.
	4. This might be the face of a collie dog sticking out the side. (de).	4. Hair going over its head.
65″	5. This could be the outline of a devil. Its horns, nose and mouth come around (de near ears).	5. Could be a little bit of its body and front of its legs. Q. Could be standing up walking towards each other.

VI	6″ 1. This could be something like an animal with wings—face and wings over this side.	1. He might be in the air flying. (W)
	2. This might be the face of a dog with head up	2. (side d)

Performance	*Inquiry*
and howling on each side.	
3. This might be something like a face of a dog with nose coming around and their body sticking out.	3. (upper D)
65″	

VII   6″   1. This might be a lion with its legs and a V-shape cut out of it.

     1. Face and hair around its neck and V-shape cut out.

2. Here may be an animal sticking out and then (upper projections)

     2. Approximately one-half of the animal—might be sticking up in the air and if he was a water animal he could be coming out of the water.

3. Maybe a face with nose coming around there—a porcupine with its pointy back. (de on D).

     3. Face—there in the woods and another animal coming up to him and when another animal comes after a porcupine, he sticks these quills up.

70″

VIII   4″   1. Here may be a river rat climbing some logs.

     1. Don't see logs.

2. Here may be a duck with its head sticking out on each side.

     2. Here and here. (side d)

3. Here may be a frog with its mouth coming in and going around.

     3. This could be the face, mouth, eyes. (lower red D)

4. This could be an animal with short piece off— legs down here and head up here and has wings.

     4. (upper gray)

76″

IX   5″   1. Here could be an animal with a big tooth sticking from the top of it on each side (red).

     1. He could have four legs and be standing but his hands wouldn't be right—maybe he's sitting down.

2. Here could be a rhinoceros with a long nose and tooth sticking out (green).

     2. A silhouette of the head.

3. Here could be an animal with a pointing nose.

     3. Shows his body but not his legs. Pointed nose, mouth with this (projection) not connected on. Q. May be on the ground sleeping.

Performance	Inquiry
4. This looks like it could be a face with that (S). Its mouth and two eyes right there (upper part 80″ of green area).	4. In fairy tales they have stories of the North Wind— could be a picture of that with him howling—mouth open and two eyes.

X 4″ 1. Here could be a water crab (blue) and

                            1. May be on the top of the water. Q. The white part could be the water.

2. here could be a little animal with a sharp point on its head.

                            2. Could be walking up a little hill. (inner yellow)

3. Rabbit with ears sticking up.

                            3. Just the silhouette of his head.

4. And here could be a green snake.

                            4. Looks like they are crawling along the ground.

5. Here's another rabbit with face coming around and its nose.

                            5. (outer yellow)

6. Here could be a rat jumping or smaller animal jumping.

                            6. (outer orange)

7. This could be another animal jumping (brown).

                            7. If it had horns it could be a deer. Q. Long, the body, their long legs and long neck.

8. Animal here with face and here and legs pointed straight.

                            8. (Upper green). Could be a small silhouette of a buffalo.

9. Here could be a face with hair. Face and here's a face here.

                            9. Maybe a human. Q. A boy. Q. Could be laying in bed. (lower part of red)

10. This could be two ducks sticking out with a face.

2′30″

                          10. (Inner blue). Legs could be on a ground and heads over a ravine looking down.

Following are the final comments of the interpreter:

"By year eleven, Allan has again obtained a higher degree of structure and comfort in his conception of the world and himself but he is still unable to allow himself free fantasy or relationships with other persons which are not of a shallow, passive, "on the fringe" sort. Warm affects, despite this opening up of his mode of relating, still do not appear to be allowed free expression or even awareness. His 'flight into reality' is well entrenched and expanded. Passivity, reaction-formation, in the service of impulse control are great. Of positive import here, he shows some increase in attempts to attain some ego-buffering through the freer use of fantasy, but this is entered into hesitantly, and he retreats rapidly from it in the face of the ready appearance of phobic objects.

"Allan has incorporated a passive-feminine mode, rather thoroughly, which should earn him little respect from his male peers. He appears to yearn for more substantial relationships with others here, and to have glimmerings of sad awareness of his maternal dependence. He continues to involve himself with the problem of separation from mother with difficulty. He appears obedient to her, hesitant to oppose her authority, achieves for her, but is resentful of her lack of true affection, shows some despair of ever having his dependency needs well met by her, while at the same time experiencing doubt as to his ability to exist entirely independent of her. He has accepted a 'second best goal' of going along with what mother and other important adults say is best. He experiences himself as insufficient in this, knowing that he is expected to stand on his own two feet with somewhat greater ability than he can now muster, attempting such a relatively autonomous position with little confidence and continuing to yearn for more satisfying dependency supports.

"PROGNOSIS: Although Allan's restraint of strong feeling, conformity, press toward establishing superficial contacts, and unsatisfied dependency probably combine to give him an air of advanced social maturity in the eyes of some adults, these trends would not necessarily seriously incapacitate his relating to peers during the age span covered by the Rorschachs, in view of the superficial nature of contacts characteristic of many children during this period. They are trends, however, which do not prepare him well for the development of richer, more intimate relating in adolescence and adulthood. His ability to find a satisfactory father-figure or father surrogate around which to learn greater assertiveness and more support for his autonomous strivings is a crucial feature. He can be expected to continue pacifying adult figures and to be essentially conforming in the demands which they make on him. His search for affectionate support from a maternal figure will undoubtedly continue in his choice of a wife, a wife who will probably be older than he or at least strongly maternal in her behavior toward him. I would predict that he would tend to marry early rather than late, probably in a 'by the boot straps' sudden declaration of autonomy. Occupationally, a position involving superficial personal contacts and highly structured repetitive characteristics with paternalistic supervision would spell the greatest comfort for him. However, his passive feminine orientation is one

likely not to be valued highly in the social class of which I believe
him to be a member and may pose increasing problems for him in
terms of occupational choice as well as general social adjustment. Although he may never qualify for psychiatric diagnosis, should he,
this would probably be either 'passive-dependent character' or 'anxiety neurosis.' "

Following the sixth Rorschach, Allan continued to get good grades
in school but was a lonely, isolate boy, who spent much time in his
room in solitary pursuits. When he was invited to come in for an
interview at thirteen, his mother accompanied him. She had been interested in the research project and wanted to know more about it,
saying that she had thought at first he had been tested for retardation. At this time, Allan was a slender, soft-spoken, mild-mannered
boy, cooperative and persistent in the test situation. He had not yet
given any thought to an eventual vocation. He did odd jobs around
the house and cut the grass, as well as that of the neighbor, with the
neighbor's power mower. He and the neighbor, who is an older man,
were "real good friends"—he "fooled around with him in the gar-
den."

It was shortly after this that Allan got his rating as a "ham" radio
operator and when he was seen a year later at the age of fourteen,
this was his main topic of conversation. He had become so active
in the radio club at school that he was afraid his school work was
suffering. He described his activities in the club and his main interest
in helping other boys get ready for their license examination. On a
repeated Binet examination at this age, Allan scored in the superior
range of intelligence. This is evidently nearer his potential than earlier ratings and evidently reflected his feeling of achievement and
confidence in the things that he was doing at this time. He spoke of
wanting to do something in the electrical field as a vocation but was
pretty sure he could not go to college. He had been saving some of
his paper route money and had over a hundred dollars at that time
but he knew that was not enough even to get started in college.
Mother later reported how "tight" Allan was with his money at that
particular time. He liked, however, to bring home little surprises for
mother, who always insisted on repaying him. About this time, the
sister left the home again, and Allan was again on his own, dependent on neighbors for companionship and supervision. Mother noted
that Allan's grades began to drop as he became more interested in
the extra-curricular activities at school—especially when he spent

so much time helping out with the public address system. Because of this, mother requested of the principal that Allan be relieved of this responsibility if his grades did not get better.

There were many other indications of mother's displeasure with Allan during this early adolescent period. For example, when Allan attempted to repair things or carry out some suggestion that mother made, she became annoyed that he "can't wait" and that he "goes right ahead" without further instructions from her. Mother cited as an example how he did some patch plastering in the basement and how he rearranged the furniture to make room for the Christmas tree as a surprise for her. He even attempted to mend his pants. Instead of receiving any recognition for initiative, or for these attempts to please mother, Allan was severely criticized. Even if Allan were in bed, which was usually the pattern, since mother did not return home from work until after ten o'clock, she would berate him. In such instances, mother often suspected Allan of pretending to be asleep in order to avoid these scoldings.

Allan, at seventeen years of age, was a young man of slight build, somewhat effeminate in looks and manner. He was meticulously dressed and his thick, brown hair was carefully combed. His movements were gentle and his speech soft. His constant smile gave the appearance of superficiality but, at the same time, seemed to be a distinct part of him. He raised his brows coquettishly as he talked. Allan likes to talk and remarked that he has always enjoyed his part in the research project because it gave him a chance to talk about himself.

When he was asked about his interests, Allan said that he really liked all kinds of things. The trouble is, he often likes something very much and becomes very much interested, but this interest never lasts. For example, there was a time when he was interested in bees. His neighbor had given him some boxes of bees and he started to raise them; but he soon grew tired of this. Then he became interested in radio and television. For a while he was "lighting" man in the Stage Club at high school. This was a responsible job, as the stage lighting cost $7,000 and he was in charge of it. He did not explain why he was no longer at that job. Now he likes mostly hunting and fishing. He goes to a camp with the neighbors, who have a trailer, and there he hunts deer with his new Winchester. He also likes to hunt just around the house where he lives. There is a creek, too, where he can fish.

Allan's grades have been increasingly low, and he has some concern whether he will finish high school next year. College is not in his plans.

He has had jobs off and on for several years. He sold newspapers at one time. Now he works in a bowling alley setting up pins. As for future plans, Allan really does not know what to do in the future. He realized just recently that the time is very near when he must choose. He once considered raising bees but he knows "that is really not enough." He would like at times to be a truck driver, but that is really not a good job either. He has also thought of joining the navy when he gets out of school but he does not like the idea of having to stay in the service for three years. Allan has had little experience with girls—perhaps he will date more when he gets a car. He likes a girl that he met at a trailer camp on one of his trips with his neighbors. They write to each other, but she lives some distance. He may be able to go to see her when he gets a car.

In Allan, at seventeen, we see a person of potentially superior ability lacking in both direction and drive. He thinks poorly of himself and unconsciously doubts his adequacy as a male. He harbors considerable anxiety. This had continued for such a long period of time, however, that whatever anxious thoughts reached consciousness are dissociated from the feelings which give rise to them. He attempts to give an impression of well-being which results in a kind of general blandness underneath which his real dynamics are carefully hidden.

Allan had little chance for a normal development from the moment of conception, with mother's attitude that father was in this way trying to keep her bound to him. Deprived of a father whom he did not dare mention, shunted between the two mother figures of mother and sister, with little consideration of his feelings, he grew up in isolation from his peers. All attempts at initiative were squelched to such a degree that he is left at seventeen "rudderless" and without ability to use his very good potential ability. He is unsatisfied with his pseudo feminine identification, but has not made a satisfactory identification with the male role. Without considerable help, he will continue to drift, and in his unconscious and continued search for emotional sustenance, will eventually marry a woman who, like his mother, will dominate him.

Allan's Rorschachs help us to understand why he has not fared so well through the years. In the first record, when he was six years of age, we can see how he was struggling, and not too unsuccessfully, to repress his feeling of extreme dependence on a rejecting mother and his great desire for an unattainable father figure. The psychic energy which went into this defense struggle left him unable to concentrate on his school work and resulted in the daydreaming, of which his teacher complained. We see through the series of Rorschach records a continuance of this struggle, with no solution in sight. His responses gave a good reflection of his passive feminine identification, his intermittent compulsivity, his insecurity and his overconformity as an expression of his feeling that he must please in order to be accepted. His drawings and other test material convey the same impression about him. His inadequate peer relationships were highlighted in the Rorschach. This situation, together with such poor parent-child relationships, are indicative of the somewhat isolated, ingratiating, drifting type of personality that he was presenting during this period. The prognosis made after the sixth Rorschach seemed to be still valid when he was seen at seventeen.

XI : EILEEN

EILEEN GREW UP in a middle class family of moderate income. Father is a professional man, a college graduate, who is older than the average parent of the children in the study. Mother is ten years younger than father and had one year of college. This couple was married when mother was over thirty, and had three children within the first five years of their marriage. Eileen was the second of these three girls and was born about a year after her older sister. Father had wanted a boy but mother, who had preferred a girl in her first pregnancy, was indifferent about the sex of this second child.

Mother, a somewhat crude, brusk and innately hostile woman, laughed loudly as she told how she "got tired of waiting" for Eileen's birth; so two days after the predicted delivery, she took a big dose of castor oil to precipitate labor. Although she heard there was no validity to the "oil treatment," she "got results and Eileen was born that afternoon." Eileen was a healthy baby weighing five pounds, six ounces. Mother added that she likes babies but when they "start monkey-shines—nope!"

Eileen was bottlefed from birth, since mother was never able to breastfeed. In general, she was a good eater. Toilet training was easy, as she imitated her older sister. When mother was giving information about Eileen's development, she compared her constantly with this sister. Eileen's motor development seemed more advanced than her sister's, which mother attributed to the stimulation of an older child on a younger. Once Eileen had started to crawl, at about six months, she would not stay in the playpen. She walked around nine months of age; according to mother, "I let her loose, she went." Eileen continued through her early development to surpass her sister in motor skills—learning to ride a bike first, falling less, and usually seeking "tomboyish play."

In regard to speech development, mother conveyed her annoyance with having to listen to a child. She said that Eileen always talked

182

clearly, but mother's timing of this was vague—"average age, whatever that is. Too early as far as I'm concerned. As young as I ever want to hear."

Interwoven through mother's comments about Eileen's early development were more negative than positive remarks. There was a consistent description of the problem she had always been to mother and the unpleasant personality she had always had. Mother's basic rejection of this child was evident. Even as a small baby, "she had a nasty temperament." The evidence of this, as mother saw it, was in Eileen's demanding manner, which mother considered selfishness. As an infant Eileen no doubt sensed this rejection. To illustrate this "unbearable selfishness" of Eileen's at an early age, mother told the following story: Eileen was in the playpen when father arrived home from work. Her sister, who was toddling about, went to the door to greet him. As he picked her up, kissed her, and threw her into the air, Eileen started a progressive tantrum of screaming so father would do the same to her.

Mother related the beginning of self-assertion to Eileen's developing traits of being "antagonistic and a battler." She added parenthetically, "I'm a good one myself." Since the age of two, she has taken toys from her older sister, who readily gave in since Eileen put up such a fuss of screaming and crying. Her jealousy at her younger sister's birth when she was three was marked by exaggerated bids for attention. At about four years of age, mother remembered Eileen as "wanting everything"—other children's toys, articles in the stores, everything. In retrospect, mother saw her as "a tough kid to raise," but this was said with some rather obvious pride.

Eileen started to kindergarten when she was four years old and continued there for two years. She never seemed to get along with the children and was in constant conflict with them.

When Eileen gave her first Rorschach, she was in the first grade of a different school from the one where she had attended kindergarten. She was six years, eight months of age and presented an unkempt appearance as she came in to meet the examiner. Her dress was mussed, she was missing a front tooth, and her long straight hair was poorly combed. During the intelligence test, she was most cooperative and conforming, but during the presentation of the Rorschach cards, she became restless—almost hyperactive.

Eileen's preoccupation with religious matters was evidenced in her drawing of God and an angel up in the sky. God had a white beard and golden halo. The angel was dressed in a multicolored striped garb and the portion of her wings that stuck above her head looked more like horns than wings. On the ground below the sky were two houses and a small child. The child figure was completely filled in with black crayon. Eileen, no doubt, saw herself as a sort of "sinner" being watched constantly by supernatural beings, and was obviously insecure and frightened.

She used her left hand consistently in the test situation, and was able to print her name in small, fairly neat print, with both capital and small letters appropriately placed. Although she was conforming and cooperative in the Binet examination, she was constantly distracted by outside noises, and the resulting I.Q. of 95 was considered an inadequate measure of her potential ability.

Following is Eileen's Rorschach protocol at the six year level:

Eileen's Rorschach Protocol at the Six Year Level

Performance	Inquiry
I 15″ It is upside down?	
1. A pumpkin.	1. There's feet, arms, his hair, his head, his hat.
55″	
II 4″ 1. Two little dogs.	1. Standing together.
2. What are these? (What do you think?) Red chickens	2. (upper red)
3. What's this? Q. Water.	3. Cause it's red. Q. See it coming out of the body.
10″	
Have you any gold stars to give me?	
III 5″ 1. Animals.	1. Horses. Q. In the water. Q. Standing on stones in the water.
29″	
IV 4″ 1. A man—his feet, arms, head, body. Water.	1. Q. He's a fat man. Q. At the bathroom. Here is where the water comes out of him.
31″	
V 8″ 1. A fly—his legs, wings, arms, head, body.	1. Flying.
30″	
VI 7″ 1. A angel—that's all. (upper D).	1. On top of a pole with wings out. Q. She's going to start to fly.
24″	
VII 4″ 1. Two little doggies togedder.	1. On something. Q. Maybe they're on the sidewalk.

Performance	Inquiry
25″ Is the eighth grade up- stairs?	
VIII 5″ 1. Animals. 20″ 2. Tree—leaf—leaf-	1. Climbing up the tree. 2. Pink and orange tree.
IX 5″ 1. Animals (orange). 18″	1. Climbing up something.
X 4″ 1. Colors. 12″	1. Blue, green, brown, yellow, red, orange.

Following is the "blind" interpretation of this record:

"At the age of six years, eight months, Eileen seems to show a developmental lag in terms of ego functions of control as well as in intellectual activities such as planning and concentration. She appears to give vent to considerable fantasy in a rather inhibited manner. While she is quite outgoing in her interpersonal relationships, aggressive feelings are somewhat repressed. Consistent with the tendency to immaturity, is a tendency to regress in the face of requirements of an emotional relationship to her environment.

"There are balancing features, however, in the Rorschach, showing that Eileen is seeking an adjustment with reality. The quality of her responses in general, is good, and the content suggests she perceives her world as do most children.

"One would infer that Eileen relates to her peers rather well, perhaps in an obedient manner. It would appear that a similar compliant adjustment is made to the parents but that the relationship to the parents is colored by a certain amount of reserve.

"One wonders about this girl's identifications. She gives a rather frank picture of a man at the bathroom and there is in general a phallic interest related to water. This may indicate a certain masculine identification, possibly including penis envy. The naiveness in the material suggests hysterical quality in her personality. If Eileen were to have now or have had a symptom in the past year or so, it might be bedwetting."

During the year between the first and second Rorschachs, a baby brother was born. Eileen was enthusiastic about his arrival and enjoyed him as a tiny baby. However, a few months after his birth, Eileen developed a severe case of the measles. At the same time, the baby was hospitalized with pneumonia. When he came home from the hospital, mother felt that she could not jeopardize the baby's convalescence by trying to care for both children and so a family friend came daily to care for Eileen. This plan was extended because of Eileen's severe rash and the friend took Eileen into her home where she stayed for a month. Father came to visit Eileen daily, but mother's contact with her was by telephone. Eileen was furious with mother and complained bitterly, but did not receive attention from her.

Shortly after this experience, when she was seven years, eight months Eileen gave her second Rorschach. She was obviously pleased to see me and, although she was a bit restless in the test situation, she kept herself to the assigned tasks. She did not enjoy the Rorschach cards but was delighted when I asked her to draw. Her drawings again showed religious preoccupation, guilt feelings, and a considerable amount of fantasy life. The Goodenough Draw-a-Man was quite detailed and suggested superior ability. This rating, while much higher than the Binet I.Q., earned the previous year, may be more indicative of her potentialities. Her teacher thought of Eileen as an average pupil, but it was more than likely that emotional factors were causing a repression of her intellectual ability at this time.

Eileen gave the following Rorschach responses at this time:

Eileen's Rorschach Protocol at the Seven Year Level

Performance	Inquiry
I 5″ 1. A cat's face (laughs). 9″	1. Ears, eyes, nose, mouth.
II 5″ 1. Two dog heads—ears. 8″	1. Fighting. Q. Hitting each other's head.
III 5″ 1. Two tigers (laughs). Ears, eyes, nose, mouth, 15″ feet, ears.	1. Looking at each other.
IV 5″ 1. A bear—feet, legs, head, 27″ stomach (laughs), tail.	1. Looking the other way.
V 2″ 1. Bird, wings, feet, head, 20″ ears, tail.	1. Flying the other way.
VI 9″ 1. Bear, feet, head, tail, leg, 29″ stomach, tail.	a. Bird. Q. Looking this way. 1. Cause he has arms and legs.
VII 3″ 1. Dog, ears, tail, eyes, feet, 22″ legs.	1. Two dogs. Q. Looking at each other.
VIII What was this? 11″ 1. Bears, feet, legs, ears, 47″ tail, mouth, eyes, nose.	1. Tigers. Q. Walking.

	Performance	Inquiry

IX   5″ 1. Bear   (giggles),   mouth,   1. (Orange). Q. Looking over
            legs, paws, head, feet,   something to another bear.
            leg, mouth, eyes, nose,
      40″   tail.

X   3″ 1. Fly, legs, head, nose,   1. (Blue). Q. Flying.
      25″   eyes, tail.

Following is the "blind" interpretation of this record:

"At the age of seven years, eight months, the latency period seems to be in full swing. Eileen shows the effects of considerable repression. She has pulled in her reins, putting more distance in her relationships and not expressing her impulses as openly. The repression which is sufficient to produce a certain rigidity, is not always successful. This is indicated by a certain drop in the accuracy of her perceptions, as well as the content taking on a more active aggressive tone. Denial and projection as an occasional defense, are brought into play. At this age, with the marked repression present together with a goodly number of popular responses and a more practical way of dealing with the environment, one wonders about the possibility of an over-compliance to adult authority figures.

"The interest in animals and the kind perceived, together with the marked detailing of body parts, suggests the continuation of a rather masculine identification. It is possible that in her relationship to peers, she is now giving vent to some of the repressed hostility which may not find expression in adult relationships."

Eileen's relationship with father was always better than with mother. There were continued clashes between mother and daughter, with Eileen refusing to do anything around the house. Mother frequently resorted to whippings; Eileen, when she did not get her way, resorted to sulking and pouting. Father, a kind, tolerant man who "would do anything for his family," got a better and more cooperative response from Eileen without severe punishment.

When I saw her for the third time, at the age of eight years and eight months, Eileen was as unkempt as ever in appearance but her facial features had increased in attractiveness. She was again restless in the test situation and showed few of the inhibitions characteristic of the children in her particular rigidly controlled school. During the administration of the Monroe Diagnostic Reading Examination, she was fairly cooperative, but it was evident that she was bored and she asked several times if she could not draw for me instead. She apparently wanted to "put her best foot forward" by drawing, since I had praised her for this on previous occasions. Her academic achievement was barely average. It was obvious that she lacked interest in school work and presumably was not working up to capacity.

Following is Eileen's Rorschach record at this time:

Eileen's Rorschach Protocol at the Eight Year Level

Performance		Inquiry
I 3″ 1. Cat's head, ears, eyes.		1. (W)
24″		
II 20″ I don't know.		
34″ 1. Cat's body, tail.		1. Front, back, side (S), stomach.
III 4″ 1. Two ducks. Their eyes.		1. Legs.
16″		a. In the water.
IV 4″ 1. Cat—its eyes, whiskers.		1. Legs, arms, tail.
24″		
V 1″ 1. Butterfly. Legs, arms.		1. In the air flying.
21″		
VI 7″ 1. Duck, eyes, wings, feet,		1. In the air flying. W
29″ arms.		
VII 3″ 1. Dogs, tails, ears, face,		1. On something.
30″ eyes.		a. On a stone.
VIII 11″ I don't know the names		
of these animals, oh		
60″ 1. Bears, eyes, feet, arms.		1. Legs, arms, eyes.
IX 12″ 1. Smoke, colored smoke.		1. Pink, green, orange, smoke.
20″		
X 4″ 1. Bears. (upper gray).		1. and 3. Squeezing on a pole.
2. Smoke.		2. Fuzzy smoke, pink, orange and blue and green. (W)
25″ 3. Pole (top D).		

Following is the "blind" interpretation of the above record:

"At the age of eight years, eight months, there is a loosening of the rigidity which appeared the previous year. However, at the same time, there are signs that with this loosening, Eileen is now more disturbed. Her repressive efforts are not as successful as they were and an occasional error in judgment is possible.

"The anxiety provoking material of Card II of a sexual-aggressive nature continues to present difficulty. This difficulty is also shown on Cards III and IV. In general, this anxiety is shown in the earlier Rorschachs by her responses of delay, isolation, and shock, but these devices now appear inadequate and, as a result, perceptual inaccuracies occur in the present record. There is a rather masculine or phallic connotation to most of the animals perceived on these cards.

"Another of Eileen's areas of difficulty shown in all three Rorschachs is her inability to establish warm, allocentric emotional relationships. Cards VII, IX, and X show progressive difficulty fraught with anxiety. The continued absence of human movement and human responses especially at this age, suggests that the difficulty in interpersonal relationships is not of a transitory nature.

"The continuing effects of repression is demonstrated by the lack of the expected increase in the total number of responses as well as the absence of organizational activities which were apparent on the first record."

When mother was asked about Eileen's sex information, she maintained that this child had never been interested, and added, "She's as innocent as the birds." One had the impression, however, that mother handled sex education in a rather rough way, perhaps making allusion to more mature aspects of sexual activities than a child could comprehend.

Eileen continued to have poor peer relationships, to sulk and pout at home, and to act in an infantile manner with her younger siblings. She looked to her father for warmth and comfort. The girl still referred to the incident when brother was a baby and mother sent her to a neighbor's during her illness with measles. She did only average school work, but this was of no concern to her mother, who was satisfied if Eileen just passed from one grade to the next.

At the age of nine years, eight months, Eileen showed a great need to talk during the testing period. She dramatized many of her statements and actions. Her initial approach to the Grace Arthur Performance Scale, administered at this time, was one of resistance and pretended fright, but with frequent reassurance from the examiner, she became quite enthusiastic. As on the Binet, she earned an average intellectual rating, but there was again every indication that she had a higher potential than the results indicated. She again expressed great disappointment when there was no time left to draw since she liked "to draw better than anything else."

Her Rorschach protocol, obtained at this time, follows:

Eileen's Rorschach Protocol at the Nine Year Level

Performance	Inquiry

I   3″   1. Cat's face. Q. I see its   1. Eyes, mouth, nose, ears. Q.
   27″   ears.   Looks kinda angry.

II   4″   1. Two elephants squirting   1. Arms, ears are up here.
   13″   2. Water or something.   2. (upper red).

III   2″   1. Giraffes—two of them   a. In some pond. Q. I see
          (laughs). That's all I   water.
          could see.
   12″   1. (Contd.) Their heads.

IV   3″   1. Back of a cat and upper   1. Kinda furry and here's the
          part of its face and part   top of its head and here's its
   16″   of its ears.   tail.
          Where do you get that
          stuff?

V   9″   1. A bird? Its wings.   1. Wings, ears, legs. Q. Flying.
   18″

VI   18″   (Hesitates)
        1. Looks like a giraffe.   1. His neck looks long. Here's
                             his head. Walking on some
                             land.

   24″   That's all I see.

VII   2″   1. Two dogs. Tails, ears.   1. Ears, tails, legs and arms.
                             Standing on something as
   13″   though they were statues.

VIII   7″   1. Is this an animal? Oh,   1. Here. Q. Faces. Q. In some
          yea, some kind of bear.   park or something. Q. Walk-
          Two bears—their legs   ing around in the zoo or
   24″   and arms.   something.

IX   4″   1. Two witches, their hats.   1. Hands. Q. Flying. Q. Going
   16″   That's all I can see.   up.

X   8″   1. Two crabs.   1. Under the water. I don't see
                             water. Under the water.

        2. Two snakes.   2. (Points to red).
   22″   That's all.

Following is the "blind" interpretation of this record:

"At the age of nine years, eight months, as was the case at seven years, eight months, we get a pulling in of the reins, perhaps now related to prepubertal changes taking place in Eileen. She now shows a developing sensitivity to her environment and a tendency to move to more adult fantasy, both of which arouse some anxiety. On Card IV, where she becomes aware of the shading detail, perceptual accuracy is not good, and furthermore she tends to project by asking, 'Where do you get that stuff?' Likewise, there is a tendency to project the anxieties she experiences from inner sources, continuing to see a cat's face on Card I, and adding that it looks kind of angry. However, it appears she is doing a good job of handling her anxieties, for the over-all picture is not as rigid as it had been on the second record, and the perceptual accuracy is maintained. She continues to have difficulties establishing a give-and-take emotional relationship to her environment but relatively speaking, she handles such factors better than she ever has. Some of the anxiety on Card X indicated by the need to place popular crabs under water may be related to her general phallic interest, as shown by the snakes perceived on the same card. This notion is enhanced by her shock to Card VI, the rather poor response, a giraffe, and the emphasis on its long neck. The elephants on Card II show this same basic fantasy.

"Eileen's first human-like response in several records is the popular witch on Card IX. In the second record she saw a bear in the same area and on the third record she had even more difficulty. It is possible that all of this is related and indicating an inadequate relationship to mother, and thus a poor foundation for a good feminine identification. However, as was mentioned earlier, the over-all picture of this record is an approach toward maturity."

A year later, when Eileen gave her fifth Rorschach, she had become more attractive than at any previous time; but, although her dress was clean and attractive, she still had an unkempt look about her and her hair gave no indication that it had been combed or brushed for quite some time. She again talked continuously and dramatically; she asked many questions about the test as well as saying she wished she could come to see the examiner every day instead of going to school. She mentioned many times what a good time she was having and again wanted to know if there would be time for her to draw. Her performance on the WISC, given at this time, earned her an average rating.

She gave the following Rorschach responses:

Eileen's Rorschach Protocol at the Ten Year Level

Performance	Inquiry
I 4″ 1. Looks like a face—with eyes and ears there, big	1. Dog's face. (WS)

Performance	*Inquiry*

Performance

things right here and nose right here and that's
24″   all I see.

II   2″ 1. Two elephants. These things I don't know what you call them. Ears over here and feet down here and eyes right here.

2. Two seals above and two legs of the seal.
31″   That's all I see there.

III   I don't know what you call them things.
10″ 1. I see two eyes, and legs, arms and a nose and a mouth. WS
2. And a bow or something right there.
41″   That's all I see there.

IV   3″ 1. A bear? The legs and the feet, the head, ears, the eyes.
That's all I see.

32″

V   I don't know what you call this here.
8″   1. A bird—the legs—the
23″   face—the wings.

VI   4″ 1. The face of this queer animal, the back, the
23″   legs. That's all.

VII 1″ 1. Two dogs (D). Their eyes, ears, tail, face, their
21″   nose.

VIII 7″ 1. Bears, their legs, their
27″   face, the back.

IX   4″ 1. That looks like clouds. Colored clouds and a line going right down the
16″   center of them.

X   3″ 1. Two dogs.

Inquiry

1. In the zoo. Q. Wall down the center and they both are against the wall. Q. About kissing each other.

2. In the water. Q. Seals usually are in water. (upper red)

1. Animal—I know what it is but I just forgot the name. Q. In the zoo.
2. A hair bow.

1. In the zoo lying down. (Lower D is not part of bear).
a. Looks like some sort of a long face with two eyes right here.

1. Flying. Q. A pigeon.

1. Lying down like the bear (referring to IV).

1. Right in the back yard of somebody's house.

1. In the zoo. Q. Going back toward the wall.

1. Yellow, green, pink clouds. (W)

1. Looks like they are fighting. (upper gray)

Performance	Inquiry
2. Pink things right down here. I don't know any 29″ of the other things.	2. Clouds. Q. Uneven and clouds are uneven.

The "blind" interpretation of this record was made by the same psychologist who interpreted Eileen's other Rorschachs:

"At the age of ten years, eight months, Eileen is again attempting to establish an emotional relationship with the environment, doing an ever so slightly better job than her attempt at the age of eight. The continued emphasis on a whole approach, her failure to develop more adult-like perceptions, together with the lack of human movement responses, all point to the basic problem this girl has in getting closely involved with her environment. Nevertheless, the basic form quality together with sufficient popular responses, all point toward an adequate contact with reality.

"The repressive efforts are generally more successful in the sense that where they occur (as on Cards II and IV), they are of the variety to produce blanks in her associations rather than perceptual inaccuracies. On Card II she sees elephants in a kissing position, yet cannot name their trunks. On Card IV, although she characteristically details body parts, she omits the phallic area by not seeing any tail on her bear. Yet she uses the same tail area in her next response. She is not as successful in Card III, one which has generally given her trouble, being unable to recall the animal's name, and not giving a very good response. Apparently, the connotations of the animals and water are still quite disturbing to Eileen. Consistent with the repression shown content-wise, is that shown on the Rorschach profile. Unlike the responses at age nine years, eight months, when she dealt with her inner impulses, Eileen now appears to be repressed in this area."

Eileen's battles with her mother continued. On one occasion, when mother tried to force her to carry out a request, Eileen slapped her; however, most of the time the child simply resorted to sulking and pouting. Eileen expressed her greatest hostility through silence.

It was only during her last year of elementary school that Eileen ever studied. She apparently liked her teacher and was most anxious to please her.

When I saw her in the testing situation, she acted quite differently from on our previous contacts. She was subdued and lacked spontaneity; she actually appeared dull and frightened throughout the interview. In contrast to her childish appearance on previous occasions, Eileen was dressed at this time in adolescent fashion.

She told me that her chief worry was about getting her school work done because "my teacher isn't very happy when I do something wrong." She also worried about being late to school. She said that she got angry when her sisters take her possessions or wear her clothes. When I inquired about her knowledge of menstruation, Eileen said she had never heard of such a thing either at home or at school.

Eileen's human figure drawings further emphasized the clinical impression of constriction tightly and somewhat suddenly imposed. Her drawings were stylized, almost catatonic portrayals of a nine-year-old girl and an eight-year-old boy, both stiffly looking straight forward with legs tight together, arms close to sides, and detailed fingers close together. There was noted contrast to earlier years when her figures were uninhibited in their actions.

Following is her final Rorschach record:

Eileen's Rorschach Protocol at the Eleven Year Level

Performance	Inquiry
I 4″ Λ1. Looks like a cat's face —ears, the eyes and the mouth and the nose.	1. No response. Q. Alive. Q. Mouth sort of open.
26″ That's about all.	
II 2″ 1. Two elephants' trunks.	1. Trunks are together. Q. Right here.
2. Looks like two seals 29″ above. That's all.	2. Jumping or standing up.
(Laughs).	
III 14″ 1. Looks like two . . . le's see . . . giraffes or something and	1. Standing up.
2. A puddle beneath them.	2. Shines. (lower center D).
38″ 1. (Contd.) Legs. That's all.	
Ummm . . .	
IV 12″ 1. Bear . . . face. That's about all.	1. Like it's laying down. Q. Dead. Looks like it's flat. Fur side. Q. Just the fur.
30″	
V 2″ 1. Looks like a fly— 22″ wings, legs and head.	1. Here's the legs. Q. Looks like when it's flying.

Performance	Inquiry
Performance	*Inquiry*

Performance

What does it look like?

VI 11″ 1. Looks like a dog or something. Legs, face.

    28″ That's all.

VII 1″ 1. Two doggies (laughs). Ears, face, legs. That's all.

    24″

VIII 3″ 1. Two panthers . . . legs, face. I don't know what that in between there is. That's all.

    22″

Oh, boy.

IX 3″ 1. Clouds . . . (center D).
2. Rainbow.

    17″ That's all.

X 3″ 1. Looks like two dogs fighting.
2. Flies.
3. Spiders . . . umm. (P).

    27″ That's all.

Inquiry

1. Legs, neck, face. Q. Looks like it's dead—flat. Q. Only the fur.

1. Looks like they are standing up.

1. Looks like they are walking.

1. The white—shaded like,
2. Different colors. (W)

1. Here. (upper gray).
2. They are brown.
3. Up here. Q. Like they are in a cobweb.

The final comments of the interpreter follows:

"At eleven years, nine months, Eileen's Rorschach resembles that of an adjusting person in its gross structural features except there is the glaring absence of any human movement or human responses. Since repression has been and still is the vastly predominant mode of defense, it is quite possible that the large amount of animal movement represents the reservoir of potential creative fantasy in this child. There are several lines of evidence pointing to this possibility. For one, the content of her many animal movement responses suggests that really she is dealing with human-like fantasy. The dogs standing together, elephants kissing, and so forth, suggest that repression is operating and the fantasies are not being expressed in more human-like form. Also, there is and has been an immature, naive, childlike quality to the Rorschach throughout the series and this is still present on the sixth record. Reactions to repressive efforts are in evidence, as shown by the appearance of more shock reactions than ever before in this record, despite its structural normalcy.

"The phallic water interest present on earlier Rorschachs persists on Cards II and III. The corresponding lack of development of a more feminine-sounding content still is apparent, suggesting a masculine orientation.

"In reviewing my interpretations above, certain characteristics stand out in all six records. The marked absence of popular human movements or human responses suggests a severe gap in Eileen's ability to see herself in a developing adult role. Implicit in this, especially in conjunction with her general difficulty in handling color, is the anxiety in relationship to the people in her environment. This phenomenon appears to be related to the marked repressive measures rather than any basic schizophrenic process.

"One of the major factors which the repression has had to deal with is the considerable interest in masculine sexuality, possibly related to phallic urination fantasies, a form of penis envy. However, since aggressive feelings are subject to repressive measures, this envy is not apt to be expressed in an over-aggressiveness as far as relationships are concerned. It is more likely to find expression in some hysterical symptom.

"Another characteristic present throughout the first five records was the lag in the developing of the typical practical approach to her environment. The low interest in detail might be related to the tendency to avoid involvement in her environment.

"As an adult, while there is the possibility of some hysterical symptom, a hysterical dramatic acting out does not seem likely. Instead, a compliant person who does not apply too much energy in the pursuit of her need satisfaction appears in the making."

In a review of the historical material it is apparent that Eileen was an impulsive, affect-hungry child upon whom the restraints of her religious and school standards gradually imposed a constriction that by age eleven years and eight months had reached a dramatically sudden peak. Her naturally dramatic, almost hysterical personality might not be able to endure these restraints permanently—certainly not without considerable reenforcement. There were indications that her identification problems were concerned with age as well as sex: she did not want to grow up into a woman. Her dependency needs had been grossly unfulfilled and she had no satisfactory female figure with whom to identify unless it be the young woman who was currently her teacher. There seemed to be much guilt and masochism in Eileen's behavior of sulking and pouting.

I saw Eileen for the last time around her fourteenth birthday, toward the end of her eighth grade school year. She was then very quiet, in a repressed sort of way. In fact, she was almost submissive in the test situation, and was at all times cooperative. She received a slightly superior rating on a repetition of the Binet, given to her at this interview. One can only suppose that the marked variations in her intelligence ratings at different ages reflect the marked effects that her anxieties had on her performance; and suggest that this girl, under less emotional strain throughout her youth, might have functioned at a much more advanced level intellectually.

After the test session, she told me that she planned to be a nun and was entering the preparatory school the following year. Father mentioned to me that he felt she might change her mind, but mother reported, a year later, that she felt Eileen was as sincere as it was possible for her to be and had finished her first year successfully. Mother hoped Eileen would become a nun, but her motivation for this seemed to lie in the security this would give mother that the girl would then be responsible to someone other than mother.

Eileen did not respond to my invitation to come in for an interview at seventeen years of age. There is some doubt that she received my message. However, a report from mother indicated that she has done very well in preparatory school, and has definitely decided to continue. In mother's words, "Eileen has at last found herself."

One might suspect that what Eileen has actually found is a substitute for the accepting maternal figure that was lacking in her childhood. Perhaps she now has a source of emotional help that enables her to feel a sense of security and, therefore, make better use of her potentialities.

XII : DANNY

DANNY WAS BORN INTO a lower middle class family living in a deteriorated section of the city. Father is a hard-working skilled laborer with a steady work record; and mother, a tense but fairly attractive woman, is a meticulous housekeeper and mother. Mother talks often of her younger carefree days when she entered dancing contests and dreamed of being a professional dancer. She had to go to work after finishing eighth grade, and has always regretted her lack of opportunity for "bettering" herself. She married in her early twenties and, soon after marriage, a son was born. In describing him, mother calls him the "quiet type." Judging from this and other references, she seemed to be describing a child of limited intelligence, slow in movement, but stolid and dependable like father. This boy was six years old when Danny was born.

Danny's birth was difficult and mother was initially disappointed that he was not a girl. But her account of this second son's early childhood took on a real sparkle in contrast to that concerning the older boy. She described Danny as having been a very pretty baby, always pleasant, cheerful and active and seeming to need little sleep. Mother breastfed him for three months, but her milk diminished as she began to resume her household tasks. Danny was then given a bottle until he was ten months old, when, according to mother, "he wanted to sit at the table and be with other people." He walked at thirteen months and began to talk soon after. As to toilet training, mother said that Danny was "easy to break," and he was fully trained by about eighteen months of age.

In recalling his motor development, mother dwelled proudly on Danny's early rhythmic bouncing in response to music and related this to inherited characteristics from her. It was at this point that she began to transfer her dreams of a dancing career to Danny. Father did not share these dreams, and although he was never critical of mother, he began early in Danny's life to take out his irritation on the child.

198

Danny's constant verbalizing and excessive physical activity became increasingly annoying to father and brother as the young child developed; when father reprimanded him for this, Danny often resorted to tears. Although this interaction continued for a number of years between them, Danny was always very fond of father and cherished his approval. As a young child, he talked in his sleep and sometimes had nightmares. This continued until Danny was nearly twelve years old and was probably related to an identification struggle which is reflected in his Rorschachs through the years.

Danny started to kindergarten at the age of five and remained in the same school through the eighth grade. He enjoyed this early school experience and got along well with the children. After school, however, he generally played with younger children.

At the time that Danny gave his first Rorschach, at six and a half years of age, he was a slender little boy with delicate facial features in a heart-shaped face. He seemed to be attractive in a "pretty" or effeminate way. Although he was pleasant and cooperative in the test situation and indicated an obvious desire to put his best foot forward, there was an underlying tension evidenced in a slight stuttering and an exaggerated hesitancy in responding to some of the test items. These manifestations of anxiety became less noticeable as he became more comfortable with the test material. His responses to the test items also suggested that he had feelings of inadequacy, but the results of the intelligence test showed a fairly consistent performance and indicated that Danny had average intelligence.

His responses to the Rorschach cards at the six year level were as follows:

Danny's Rorschach Protocol at the Six Year Level

Performance	Inquiry
I 8″ 1. This looks like a butterfly—a tail.	1. His head, body, feet. I never saw anything like this.
II 25″ 1. This red and this looks like a man's head.	1. That's his ribs. Here are bones. (W)
2. This is mouth, ears, tail	2. He's in the picture.
2′25″ of a bull.	
III 8″ 1. Looks like a . . . looks like a . . . looks like a funny man—here's his	1. He's in the picture. They're black men—having a little fire. (P)
1′35″ hands and neck.	

Performance	*Inquiry*
IV 7″ 1. Looks like an ape— here's his hands, feet, and that's his head.	1. He looks real ugly and he had big feet.
1′15″ 2. Here's a head (lower D).	2. This is a bull's head.
V 2″ 1. Looks like a butterfly. Here's his ears, wings; there's his feet like them little things on him— 45″ tips of his wings.	1. He's in the picture.
VI 25″ 1. Here's his ear and here's his other one, and here's 1′30″ his body.	1. This is his body—a deer. Q. In the picture.
VII V3″ 1. That sounds like a . . . like a . . . here's his head, hands, feet and 26″ this white is his body.	1. It looks like a man if it has its head on. (W)
VIII 9″ 1. This looks like two cats.	1. Whenever he's going up in in part of a guy's head.
2. This looks like his body, 29″ his head, and his ribs.	2. Of a guy.
IX 7″ 1. This looks like a head and this (red).	1. Eyes, whiskers, mouth, nose.
2. This looks like the heart and here's all of his belly right in here. 32″	2. Here's ribs—all of the body. Q. Up in a graveyard. Some of us were in a graveyard and saw bones and a body they were digging up.
X 7″ 1. Looks like a bunny— here's his ears, eyes.	1. Right here.
2. These two look like bones—part of head and all of the body here. Here's a thing in his heart (wishbone area). Here's part of his feet 40″ here.	2. W. A man.

The "blind" interpretation of the above record follows:

"In this protocol is pictured a practical, somewhat stereotyped and timid boy, who is struggling against a feminine identification, with some evidence that the struggle may not be in vain. He is also trying to adopt adult standards of conformity with elements of immaturity breaking through when he is not able to achieve the conformity he values. The 'head' theme in this record suggests feelings of mental inadequacy. His peer relations appear to be within average limits. Rorschach factors related to parental relationships are prominently displayed in the protocol. His relationship to mother seems deficient in that she is having a confused and so less positive impact on his personality development than father. Relationship to father is good, despite the excessive demands he makes on the boy. Castration fear, with resulting conflicts and anxiety is manifested in Danny's reaction to these demands. There are further indications of psychosomatic reactions to such conflicts."

It was shortly before this testing session that mother had enrolled him in a tap dancing class. She always accompanied Danny to and from his lessons, and began to live vicariously in his progress. She was now making the active transfer of her dreams of a dancing career to Danny. Father continued to disapprove of these activities for his son, but mother was determined to carry out her plans. Much of father's disapproval was directed toward Danny's talkativeness and other traits which he considered feminine. The boy often responded to these criticisms with a "squeamish stomach"; at other times he burst into tears. Mother thought that Danny was more sensitive to father's criticism than to hers because "he knows father means it."

Danny had changed little in appearance when he was seen for the second time at seven years and eight months of age. There was little manifestation of anxiety at this time, and he appeared more confident than at the previous contact. His second grade teacher thought of him as an average boy with no outstanding positive or negative characteristics so far as classroom behavior and achievement were concerned.

His drawing of a man was a large, partially front view and partially side view figure with five buttons down the front of the trunk. The face was drawn in profile above a massive neck. Arms were extended away from the body and feet were in a walking position. The unusual portrayal of trousers, which was really half skirt, suggested a continued conflict about feminine identification tendencies. Scored according to the Goodenough instructions, the drawing indicated a slightly higher intelligence rating than on the Binet examination.

Danny's responses to the Rorschach cards at this age were as follows:

Danny's Rorschach Protocol at the Seven Year Level

Performance	Inquiry
I 6″ 1. A bat or a bird. 20″	1. Wings here. He's up in the air—he's flying. Here's his tail.
II 15″ 1. Looks like a bug or a crab. 26″	1. Tail (red), head (upper d). Here's his wings—no that would be his body. (Doubtful about parts.)
III 5″ 1. A man. 20″	1. Both look like a man—feet, body, head, and neck. Q. A fire, putting something on a fire.
IV 2″ 1. An ape. W 19″	1. Head, feet, body, hand. Q. Looks like he's walking.
V 2″ 1. A bat. 10″	1. Wings—here's his head and things—here's his tail. Q. Flying.
VI 6″ 1. A bug. 10″	1. Whiskers. It looks like a cat —legs, body. Q. Hanging on a wall.
VII 22″ 1. Looks like a spider. 31″	1. Head, ears—it looks like two spiders crawling up a wall.
VIII 5″ 1. Rats crawling up 2. A tree or something and 7″ up a hill.	1. Two rats here and here. 2. Tree, hills over here.
IX 15″ 1. An ant it looks like 17″	1. One of them bugs—them bitey spiders—Here's his things—whiskers, body, tail.
X 4″ 1. Looks like crabs on each side. 2. Crabs at the tops. 10″ 3. Here are baby crabs.	1. Here and here. 2. These look like they are hitched onto this. 3. (brown area).

The "blind" interpretation of the above record follows:

"From the above protocol we see integration taking place, with a continuation of the stereotypy noted at the six year level. Danny seems cautious, self-critical and hesitant to let himself go; but this constriction operates chiefly in relation to impulsiveness. He is not withdrawn but tends to check any expression of emotion—"mother" qualities—in favor of practicality and literalness, or "father" qualities.

There is evidence of 'regression' occasionally to more immature behavior. He sees mother as an ever-encompassing figure, and is still struggling to free himself for a truly masculine identification. At present, his main defenses against his conflictual feelings are those of repression and/or denial."

Danny continued to be overconforming both at school and at home. Mother's supervision of his out-of-school activities was all-pervasive. She spoke with pride of his progress in dancing and of his public performances. Danny enjoyed putting on shows in the back yard, using the younger children in the neighborhood as actors. Mother seemed to encourage this as well as his other less masculine activities, such as decorating the house for holidays and for special occasions.

His excessive talking at mealtimes seemed to create his greatest conflict with father, who desired to "eat in peace." Meals often ended with Danny in tears as his father warned and threatened him to be quiet. This seemed to be the only thing which upset Danny at this time but unfortunately, he responded to father's criticisms with an increased need to talk, even to gesturing with his hands.

When seen by the author at the age of eight and a half, Danny was more spontaneous than on the two previous occasions. He described in detail an auto-sled accident that had occurred several months before, going into detail about the number of stitches and the number of days he was hospitalized. There was still a small scar on his face from this accident. Though somewhat unkempt and not very clean, Danny was still a very attractive child, and was pleasant and quite persistent in the test situation. His talkativeness was the major overt sign of anxiety displayed on this occasion.

His performance on the school achievement tests indicated that he was doing at least average work for his third grade placement. He was evidently achieving up to his capacity at this time.

Rorschach responses were as follows:

Danny's Rorschach Protocol at the Eight Year Level

Performance	*Inquiry*
I 2″ 1. A bat.	1. Here's his wings and that's his body and here's his face.
30″	Q. Flying.
II 2″ 1. Looks like two little bugs on top.	1. Looks like a red face and white fur

Performance	Inquiry
2. One like a black thing.	2. They are doing something like giants holding their hands together.
3. Down here is red horns, 30″ and that. (lower red).	3. Of some kind of animal—Q. Black part is the animal.

III 2″ 1. That looks like two men
2. With a bow tie in the middle.
1. (Contd.) And they are holding
3. Two balls and
28″ 4. There's fire in back of them.

1. Here and here.
2. A necktie.

3. Here and here.
4. Red.

IV 4″ 1. This looks like a monster with feet, arms and
18″ there's his face.

1. Legs walking along the ground.

V 5″ 1. This looks like a real bat. Here's his two things— his wings—and here's his
15″ back legs.

1. A black bat flying.

VI 5″ 1. That looks like a killed animal—ears, mouth, four legs, and back—like
15″ the skin of an animal.

1. Fur.

VII 15″ 1. That looks like girls.
2. Two lions standing up— this way it looks like animals. They are on their heads—standing on that
31″ thing down here.

1. Looks like girls dancing.
2. Here are the lions.

VIII 3″ 1. That looks like two rats climbing up like on a
19″ tree.

a. Flowers are the bottom color.

IX 8″ 1. That looks like a tree with some light red leaves and that on it.
2. This way looks like
24″ there's a crab.

1. Here is the tree.

2. The whole thing looks like a crab.

X 7″ 1. Looks like there's all kinds of bugs around this design here. There's bugs and that—all kinds
20″ of bugs.

1. (W)

Following is the "blind" interpretation of the above:

"There seems to have been some 'loosening up' during the year between this and the last Rorschach. Any 'withdrawal' that Danny may be showing at this time is in regard to his spontaneity and impulsiveness. He seems to have relative freedom and 'affect' in thinking about himself and in learning to perceive life. Interpersonal relationships have improved. His relationship to mother is not as uncomfortable—at least he does not think of her as so encompassing as before. Father is a frightening figure, but one with whom he is trying to identify, despite the close maternal bind which mother attempts to foster."

Danny continued during this period with his dancing lessons, with mother accompanying him to and fro. He was now spending more time with his age group, playing with the boys in the vacant lot. He had become interested in a community house program and spent much time there with boys and girls of his age. Father, while still irritated when Danny persisted in his constant talking around the house, was not so blatant in his criticism. The older brother had little in common with Danny but the two boys did share ownership and interest in a dog at this time. Danny's teachers spoke of him as a "good boy who does well in his work and is always pleasant and obliging."

When Danny was tested a year later, he had grown taller but was still quite effeminate in looks and actions. There seemed to be increased tension at this time, evidenced in frowning as he worked hurriedly on test items, a tendency to stutter, and a need to talk continuously. It was obvious that the timing on the performance test disturbed him, but he was persistent and responded favorably to praise. The results of this test indicated average ability with non-verbal material, and were consistent with the results of the earlier Binet examination.

His responses to the Rorschach cards were as follows:

Danny's Rorschach Protocol at the Nine Year Level

Performance	Inquiry
I (Turns head to one side and slants the card).	
28″ 1. This looks like a bird or some kind of bat—a bat with curved ears and that—and looks like	1. Feet; these look like the wings. Q. It's laying down like it's dead and that.

Performance	*Inquiry*

(smiles) in the middle it
is shaped like—

2. On the edge it looks like
a bear,

2. Face and head—there's his
arms—they look like they are
standing up speaking or
something.

1. (Contd.) down at the
bottom like—it's like a
1'50"   piece of—like his feet.

1. (Contd.) bat's foot.

II 8" 1. That looks like little
dwarfs up on top of the
black things—looks like
they are surprised to see
each other.

1. See the dwarfs down to the
waist.

2. Two big bears are holding hands together.

2. Here and here.

1. (Contd.) And dwarfs on
top.

3. And down at the bottom
looks like a fire or something.

3. A red fire.

III 8" 1. Looks like two men here
and they are lifting up
their hats.

2. In the middle looks like
a seat.

3. And a bow in front.

3. On the back of the seat—
decoration maybe.

4. This looks like some-
thing hanging up on a
49"   hook or something.

4. Looks like it's hanging and
maybe it's way back there.

IV 8" 1. This looks like an ape—
a big ape. You can see
feet sticking out and here
are the hands and face—
looks real funny.

1. Feet and hands and he's sitting on a

2. Down below looks like
he's sitting on a log or
40"   something.

2. Log there.

V 4" 1. This is another that
looks like a bat—looks
exactly like it—wings,
head, and down at the
bottom, legs.

1. Flying in the air—looks like
the kind that catches all kinds
of insects.

31"   He's a real bat.

Performance	Inquiry

VI 4″ 1. This looks like a cat skin —from like a cat. His skin is off and hung on a wall. See his whiskers 33″ and his hair up there?

1. Fur of a cat.

VII 7″ 1. Looks like two girls are hitched together and they are wondering what happened. Feet are hitched together and hands are 26″ going both ways.

1. Wondering what happened. Wind came and blew their hair up.

VIII 10″ 1. This looks like rats climbing up

1. Rats are trying to get away from it (the fire)—four feet right here and both the same color.

2. A tree.
3. There's a fire below with 35″ smoke coming out.

IX   Could you turn it upside down?
16″V1. This looks like some kind of an animal or something and he has a big head, arms and feet, and at the end of his feet, looks like he has spurs or something. He has eyes and his 48″ nose.

1. Looks like he's standing up, or against a wall, maybe.

X   7″ 1. This looks like two crabs on each side and
2. Other is little baby down below, and
3. In the middle is the blue thing and that looks like the crack of a water pipe.
4. Worms in a pond.
5. And on the top looks like—bone sticking up.
6. Middle two little yellow balls and they look like 60″ seed the crabs eat.

1. Out of the water—getting food—grass or something.
2. (brown) crab holding on side of wall.
3. Water goes in here.
   a. Yellow things are fish.
4. Green worms.
5. (upper gray).
6. (wishbone).

Following is the "blind" interpretation of the above record: "In these Rorschach responses, Danny reflected a continued conforming and somewhat cautious attitude with more feelings of inadequacy than were formerly noted. He seems to be a timid soul in relation to authority figures and adults, apologetic, as well as over-conformative. Identification is with the male figure but his human movement responses are passive and inhibited. He is in the midst of a struggle to free himself from what he feels is an unexplainable bind with his mother. He is finding it increasingly difficult to accept freely and naturally mother's set of values. The relationship with father is becoming better clarified with suggestions of the over-demanding impact of over-adult standards for his age and temperament, and of practical value stress, conformity and castration fear. These contrasting influences of mother and father set up a conflict in him which results in considerable anxiety."

Danny's activities had changed little during the intervening year. He spent considerable time at the community house, participating in shows and clubs. He continued his dancing classes, and, at mother's suggestion, had added a dramatic course. He continued to make average grades in school, but there was little time for normal after-school activities or socializing. What little relaxation he got came from watching TV. Mother was so wrapped up in Danny's successes in local dance programs that she was unable to consider any need or desire Danny himself might have for less routinized interpersonal relationships. Father was not so critical of Danny's dancing aspirations as he once was, although he was certainly not as enthusiastic about them as mother.

Danny was given the Wechsler Intelligence Scale for Children, as well as the Rorschach, when he was seen next at the age of ten years and nine months. He showed some confusion and inadequacy on the verbal scale and achieved much better with the performance items. It was evident that emotional factors were affecting his functioning in the academic area, with indications that his potential ability was probably high average. He was most cooperative in the test situation but was obviously distressed at his recognized failures.

Following are his Rorschach responses at this time:

Danny's Rorschach Protocol at the Ten Year Level

Performance	Inquiry
I 8" 1. Looks something like . . . some kind of bird with tail down here and open wings.	1. Looks like he's flying.

Performance	*Inquiry*
V2. Now this looks like some kind of animal . . . like a giant. W	2. Points growing out of his legs. Here's his arms—here's his head (lower d). Don't look like much of a head. Q. Standing up.
3. This looks like two kinds of dogs on the side. Can't make anything 94″ else.	3. Looks like they are looking at something, up in the tree.

II 6″

1. Looks like a kind of a big face with hat on (upper red).
    1. Looks like he's standing on gorilla's head.

2. Looks like two gorillas holding hands.
    2. Here and here.

3. This way it looks like some kind of a big bird with head up here (d) and a big mouth (red).
    3. Laying down on the gorilla. Q. Dead. (W)

V4. This looks like a bug —a real big bug. That's all I can make 65″ of that one.
    4. I forgot—oh, this is it, head here (red) and this is the side (black). Q. Flying.

III 5″

1. This looks like two men holding
    1. Here and here.

2. A big ball.

3. A real big bow in the middle.
    3. One of them bow ties.

4. With some kind of a bug back on the side of him.
    4. Here and here.

V5. Now it looks like a gorilla holding his hands up. That's all I can make 55″ out of that one too.
    5. Belly (red), head (lower D) —eyes darker than the other parts.

IV 4″

1. This looks like a real giant with real big feet (smiles).
    1. Looks like he's standing up— tail here.

V2. Now it looks like a bear—some kind of a . . . rug. That's all I can make 45″ out of that.
    2. Like a rug spread out.

V 2″

1. This one looks like a bat, and when I turn it upside down
    1. Looks like it's flying with face down.

Performance	Inquiry
V2. It looks like a pheasant —some kind of a big pheasant.	2. Has wings like that—laying down dead.
3. A bug in the middle.	
4. Two crocodiles on each side here. That's all I can make out of 43″ that one.	

VI 4″

1. This looks like a dog —all stuff out of it— like a rug laying.	1. Fur.
V2. Looks like a real big gorilla. W	2. Arms out here and there's his legs—can't see no head.
V3. Looks like there's two little gorillas on each side with their legs down at the bottom. That's all I can make 41″ out of that one.	3. Looks like they are stuck together.

VII 5″

1. That looks like two people looking back at each other.	1. Women—have hand up.
V2. Upside down it looks like a big gorilla with his arms out. That's all I can make 35″ out of this one.	2. Arms, leg, body in here. (WS)

VIII 4″

1. This looks like two rats climbing up	
2. A tree.	2. Green up there and have them things like a tree.
3. Underneath there's a flame.	3. Same color as flame.
V4. Now it looks like birds on top (lower d). That's all I can make 29″ out of this one.	4. Arms or wings and here's his head.

IX 5″

1. This looks like two big bugs and they are fighting at each other.	1. (orange)
2. Some kind of blood all over ground down here.	1. (red)
3. Now it looks like it's tree (red) with	

Performance	Inquiry
4. Some kind of animal down there in the middle.	4. Strange head and body (S) and arms here (orange)
37″	
X 6″ 1. Looks like a big—a little bunny in the middle.	1. Bunny head.
2. Two crabs up here.	2. (outer blue).
3. Bugs in the side here.	3. (brown).
4. Two bugs holding up	4. (upper gray).
5. A real big pipe.	
6. A bug (inner blue) holding onto the	6. Looks like little ants or something.
7. Wall or something.	7. (red area)
8. These bugs (upper green) are fighting with the crabs here. That's all I can make	
56″ of this one.	

The "blind" interpretation of the above record is as follows:

"Danny's Rorschach responses at this time show his continued struggle to free himself from mother's seeming determination to feminize him. There are obvious strides toward masculine identification but not without concomitant anxiety. He feels more comfortable with father than previously but still senses his disapproval of Danny's inadequacy as a male. Danny again brings in the 'head' theme, indicating resurgence of feelings of mental inferiority along with his masculine inferiority. He continued to use denial as his main defense against this anxiety and is no doubt showing some obsessive or phobic trends. Peer relationships are still within normal limits and he probably feels more comfortable with girls than with boys."

Danny's after-school hours and Saturdays were filled with dancing lessons, which now included modern dance as well as tap and ballet. He was constantly busy practicing for programs and personal appearances at hospital, church, and community affairs. Mother saw him as always in a hurry at home; he bolted down his food at mealtimes so that he could talk between bites and still manage to keep up with the family tempo of eating. The conflict with father at mealtimes remained a source of anxiety; but, in other ways, father had become more sympathetic with Danny. This was evidenced in the pride with which he told of Danny's standing up to the neighborhood bully, even though Danny had lost the fight and came home crying.

It was during this year that Danny made his first inquiries about sex. These were directed to father who, according to mother, has handled all sex instruction. Mother could not be specific about this, but one got the impression that father's comments were mostly warnings against the overtures of male strangers. It was in this connection that mother commented on the stereotype of male ballet dancers as being effeminate and cited a dancer who had participated in a show with Danny. In viewing this dancer, Danny declared that "if ballet makes me like that, I'll quit."

Danny was absent from school on the day of my last yearly visit there. He had a cold as well as some sort of hernia complication. Mother was not specific when questioned later about the extent of surgery or kind of hernia, since her concern centered chiefly around the temporary limitations placed on Danny's dancing.

I returned to the school a few days later and was able to interview Danny at that time. He expressed his delight at seeing me, saying that he had been afraid I would not return. He seemed quite immature in comparison with the other children in the study, and had the alertness and eagerness of a younger child. Danny was still small and feminine in appearance although he was almost twelve years old at this time. In talking about things that concerned him, he mentioned worrying about presents at birthday and Christmas time, about his mother giving him "heck" when he loses money, and about getting beaten in a fight. He does not want to fight, but gets angry when someone calls him names and, if they start the quarrel, he hits or throws stones. Danny added, somewhat apologetically, that sometimes he "goes in and tells on them."

His first human figure drawing on this occasion was a girl. She was an angel about ten years old. The sex and age of this figure suggested a failure to have made an identification either as to his maleness or his growing up. Black gloved hands on the figure were suggestive of masturbation concern, with accompanying guilt feelings. It seemed apparent that Danny attempted to deny his concern about sex matters by identifying with a sinless, sexless creature like an angel. His drawing of a boy was a stiff figure with prominent ears and eyes, a conforming smile, and a general appearance of holding himself in check. Buttons down the front of the body suggested his feelings of insecurity in this male role. The boy, like the girl, was ten years old.

Danny's Rorschach at age eleven was as follows:

Danny's Rorschach Protocol at the Eleven Year Level

Performance	Inquiry

I 4″ 1. Sorta like a bat and, let's see.   1. This looks like he

V2. Upside down it looks like a big gorilla with a little head. W   2. Looks like he's standing up.

<3. On its side it looks like two bears.   3. Looks like the two are in the woods. Q. Looks like they are running away.

38″ That's all I can make of that.

II 1″ 1. That looks like two bugs are fighting on top of a   1. (upper red) Looks like a bug with a real high hat on.

2. Fire or something like that.   2. Because it was red.

3. And a . . . it looks like two big animals, wild animals are holding hands together like gorillas and (whispers) let's see it upside down.   3. Legs, hands—I guess their heads are up here.

V4. It looks like a bird— looks like a bird too. That's all I can make of   4. (W)

30″ that one too.

III 3″ 1. That looks like two people holding   1. Looks like men.

2. A ball.

3. In the middle looks like a bow tie.   3. Just the shape.

4. On the side it looks like two bugs going at their heads.   4. Looks like they are fighting for their hat.

V5. Upside down it looks like a big wild animal with a bow in the middle of him.   5. Head, arms, and a bow in the middle.

That's all I can make out

43″ of that one.

IV Phew! (rubs his head).

3″ 1. That one looks like a big gorilla with feet and head and arms on the side.   1. Looks like he's laying down.

2. Looks like a bear all laid   2. The fur side.

Performance	*Inquiry*

Performance

out—the skin—like a rug. That's all I can make out
36″ of that one too.

V   3″ 1. That one looks like a bat.

2. And upside down it looks like a bird with a beak—looks like he's going after an insect or something.

3. On the side it looks like an alligator. That's all I can make out
32″ of that one too.

VI 3″ 1. That one looks like a wolf and it's made of a rug—and a . . . what do that look like now?

2. Upside down it looks like two animals with legs together, arms sticking out and them heads. That's all I can get on
32″ that one.

VII 3″ 1. That looks like two people—looks like they are going this way—they are turned around looking at each other.

V2. Upside down it looks like a dog's face.

V3. Looks like two girls dancing—they look like a lion, though (laughs). That's all I can make out
37″ of that one.

VIII 3″ 1. This looks like two rats

2. Climbing this tree.

3. Looks like there's fire underneath.

V4. Upside down these two rats look like a big ani-
34″ mal is going after them.

Inquiry

1. Like his wings in here and looks like he's flying.
2. His beak is open.

3. Part of his body—his head here—looks like he's swimming in the water.

1. Fur side.

1. Women.

3. They look like a lion—I was just thinking about it.

4. I forgot what animal it was— I saw it some place. (upper D).

Performance	Inquiry
IX 7" 1. That looks like two bugs feeding off of a little thing in the middle.	1. (upper D).
2. Upside down looks like an animal that has a big head, arms and legs. That's all I can make out.	2. Looks like he's standing up and got a mighty big head on him. (W)
31"	

X 6" 1. This one looks like a rabbit in the middle here.	1. Just his head here.
2. Looks like two bugs eating	2. (upper D).
3. A tube.	3. Tube in somebody's throat or something.
4. And two more bugs climbing up on the side of a	4. (inner blue).
5. Wall.	5. It's going up slant. (red)

Following is the "blind" interpretation of the above record:

"In this record is seen all the elements of personality that have been present in Danny's Rorschachs through the years. A generally well-integrated person, Danny is somewhat over-adult in his need to conform but immaturity continues to break through when he is not able to achieve the conformity he values. The partially incorporated restrictions which hamper his freedom of functioning seem to stem chiefly from a set of values taken over from the paternal figure, making it difficult to accept freely his mother's values. He continues to be cautious and self-critical, but not really withdrawn. This conflict between these 'mother' and 'father' qualities—softness, sentiment, expressions of emotion, on the one hand, must be constantly checked since he regards as more acceptable the 'father' qualities of hardheadedness, literalness, practicality and the like. There is occasional infantile regression as an inevitable consequence of this role identification struggle. Peer relationships seem to be good, but with some anxiety in relation to males. He probably feels more comfortable and acceptable with girls. He is often uncertain here as in other areas, however. He continues to be a timid person and may never become a forceful man. As an adult, he will probably function well enough, continuing to use denial, but other defenses, such as reaction formation, compensation and repression, will have been introduced along the path to maturity. As a child, Danny's developing techniques have been similar to these but with more phobic elements and regressive 'poor' judgment or impulsiveness."

Danny did not take dancing lessons for a year after his operation. He continued to engage in dramatic programs at the community house and had more time for his school work and extra-curricular activities there. Relationships at home were improving. He seemed to be more acceptable to both father and brother, with a minimum of friction in that relationship. It was during the end of the "inactive" period that Danny received a dramatic scholarship from a national group work organization.

Danny was seen again on his thirteenth birthday. At that time he was interviewed by an experienced child psychiatrist, who gave the following report:

"This is a well-developed, handsome, neat, well-dressed boy, small for his age and delicate. He is the younger of two male siblings in a lower middle class family. According to the boy, his father, a skilled laborer, is tall, thin, quiet but outgoing; mother is small and Danny thinks he resembles her. She is jolly, vivacious—almost too much so. Older brother, five years his senior, is like father, not so quick as Danny. Father is Protestant, and mother and sons are Catholic. There is little conflict about this.

"This boy is a well-compensated hysterical character. It is interesting that the well-sublimated exhibitionistic complex is outspokenly symbolized in his two ambitions—to be a dancing star (or teacher) and to be a biologist. At present, the conflict is easily reconcilable. His attitude toward his identification with mother seems at present to be relatively without conflict so that he may never have trouble with his heterosexual relationships. For example, he has little or no anxiety about his smallness, prettiness, gracefulness, and stage ambitions interfering with his masculine self-esteem. They have rather been integrated and he is, at least at present, able to maintain first-class peer relations with both sexes and to be a happy boy with these as attributes, not handicaps.

"There are signs of narcissistic preoccupation—such as looking over his body for blemishes, muscle-building activities, and so forth, which indicate some vulnerability—also some strong indications of castration fear in the dream life and in his worry about his health. But these seem presently very well compensated.

"Prognosis is good unless he is too stupid or too untalented to realize any of his needs for narcissistic gratification through sublimation after mother's vicarious gratification and her pleasure no longer suffices as reward."

Danny received the same dramatic scholarship for three consecutive years. "The only dancer to receive such an award, and the only boy to get it three times in a row," according to mother. During these years Danny's days were filled with lessons, dances and drama, with practice and with performances. While mother was not so actively accompanying him, her interest and enthusiasm were still high. She was living vicariously in his activity and success. It was difficult for her to talk about him except in the area of dancing. For example, when an attempt was made to find out about his interest in sex, she was vague and perhaps guarded in discussing this area of his development. As noted before, he asked no questions during his early years, and what little sex information he later received came from father. Mother saw Danny at fifteen as "normally" interested in girls. He attends dances and parties where they are and occasionally calls a girl classmate for a casual meeting but does not really date. "His thoughts of sex aren't that far along," mother says, meaning that girls are not yet seen as sexualized creatures. It was in this connection that mother spoke of Danny's pride in displaying his muscles and physique—flexing his arms and asking maternal grandmother to "look at my biceps," adding, "He is not modest like his brother."

At seventeen years of age Danny accepted my invitation to come to my office for a visit. On this occasion, he was a good-looking boy, slender for his age, with a muscular, wiry build. His pleasant, sensitive face had a scrubbed appearance and his carefully combed dark hair glistened with some sort of hair preparation. In contrast to the grooming of his face and hair, his fingernails were dirty and his hands rough, as if used to physical work. Danny talked in a dramatic fashion, with some rolling of his large, brown eyes, shaking of his head and flashing of smiles to emphasize his statements. He gave the over-all impression of an engaging, pleasing personality with an undercurrent of anxiety and a need to please, as well as a need to relate to people in a positive way.

He was at the time a junior in high school, doing average work. He has to study hard to keep up the average rating. A very verbal young man, he soon plunged into his favorite topic of conversation— his dancing lessons and his participation in dancing programs since he was six years old. He described in detail his current busy schedule of rehearsals and engagements in such a way that there was some question as to whether he was boasting or complaining about these activities. The more he talked, the more apparent it became that he really felt two ways about his dancing and any career it might lead to. In terms of his actual dancing ability, he did not think too highly of it, tending to consider himself average in this regard and at the time had no great hope or ambition of rising to the top in the field. In fact, he seemed to be more impressed with the ten years of hard work that lay behind him than any great anticipation of future developments from his dancing. He had a model of what he might become in terms of some of the dancing masters under whom he has studied and indicated that he has thought of dancing professionally for awhile and then perhaps starting a dance studio because "you can make quite a lot of money that way."

Danny said he did not like the "long-haired" dance but was unable to verbalize the reasons for this objection. In fact, he became uncomfortable in talking about the feelings involved in interpretative dancing, saying that he was much more comfortable when engaged in the muscular activities of the more mechanical choreography in such performances as musical operettas. He also reminded himself that when he started to dance many of his friends used to tease him about being a sissy because of his interest in dancing, but that this gradually died away as he never responded to it. Currently his group of friends accepted this activity without comment and made no further derogatory comments about it. His father, who at first seemed to be uninterested in his dancing, was becoming as interested as mother has always been, and urged him to continue the exercises and lessons. Danny described how his mother, during the first five years of his dancing career, worked very hard at taking him around for his lessons and almost physically exhausted herself in this process. Since then, however, he had taken more interest and initiative in getting himself around to these different activities. He spoke with affection about his older brother, who was recently discharged from the army and is now working as a welder. He remembered how he used to fight with this brother but said their relationship is currently much better.

Danny seems to have made a good masculine identification, despite the fact that he tends to relate to people in a rather small-boy fashion. He will probably continue in this type of relationship in his heterosexual adjustment, wanting in marriage a mother to continue to fuss over him. He is comfortable in his relationship with girls and is interested in getting married and having children "when the right one comes along." He says that he hopes to marry a girl who is very much in love with him and will not be unfaithful to him. Danny talked about such plans in a stereotyped fashion without any deep conviction or much affect.

Danny spoke proudly of the many adults who have sponsored and helped him through the years—his teacher, his counselor at the community house, his priest. He has been recommended for scholarships and invited to participate in programs that involve taking long trips to other cities. Danny has enjoyed all this recognition and is quite comfortable in his role as a "protege" and protected one.

Danny's Rorschachs through the years have shown a realism and stability that have stood him in good stead as mother's ambitions were transferred to and realized in him. That he would be able eventually to achieve a comfortable masculine identification was never a question when only the Rorschach responses were considered. The anatomy responses in Danny's record reflected a body preoccupation that was interpreted as indicative of psychosomatic symptoms. In his case, as in that of Larry's, one might speculate whether this type of response also covered up an interest in sex that was never brought out into the open. It is undoubtedly fortunate for Danny that this pleasure and preoccupation with his body appearance and motor skills find expression in the exhibitionism of dancing and dramatics, a sublimation that is wholly egosyntonic. This muscular agility represents an exotic discharge mechanism as well as a defense against anxiety. The gratification enjoyed through this sublimation has enabled Danny to maintain his self-respect and achieve a masculine identity in the face of the vicarious identification which his mother has shown towards him. While comfortable in his ability to relate to female figures, Danny still has difficulty in his relationship with men and tends to withdraw or submit rather than to be directly competitive. He is likely to remain highly oriented to the wishes of others throughout life and may require constant approval and acceptance by others.

It would seem that as Danny has grown up, he has drifted away from mother's domination and that at the present time he has some mixed feelings about his wish to continue in dancing as a personal future career. Lacking introspection, he will no doubt continue to pay for his adjustment with a rather stereotyped, conventional, unquestioning way of looking at the world.

XIII : ANNA

RELATIVELY LITTLE WAS KNOWN of Anna's life before she was chosen as a participant in the Rorschach study of six-year-old first graders. It was later ascertained that her mother had died of cancer nearly a year before this initial contact; but, apparently prior to this, the family, which had consisted of mother, father, and four children, had experienced a fairly normal happy home life.

Mother was described as "a gentle person who gave genuine affection to her children"; and father, a skilled carpenter, was a "good provider and affectionate father," despite his occasional drinking sprees. Mother's illness had been first diagnosed shortly after the birth of her youngest child, and she became steadily more incapacitated until her death a few months later. Anna, the second child, was in kindergarten at this time. Besides the baby sister, there was a brother five years older than Anna and a sister two years younger.

After mother's death, father tried to maintain a home for the family, and a maternal aunt and her husband did what they could to help out. However, father's drinking soon began to increase and, as a result, the aunt and uncle, who had three children of their own, were expected to assume more and more responsibility for the motherless family. At the time of the first Rorschach, the children were living temporarily with aunt and uncle.

Anna, at the age of six years and eight months, was an unkempt, stoop-shouldered little girl who was apathetic and unhappy-looking. She held her mouth open slightly which gave her a dull appearance and she seemed to be completely lacking in childish spontaneity. The first grade teacher spoke of her as "quiet, always obedient, rather slow, but sure. She does good work, is earnest, but not too grasping."

Although she was compliant and cooperative in the test situation, Anna showed no particular interest in what she was doing. On the Binet intelligence test, she earned a barely average rating; but, be-

220

cause of her obviously "flattened" affect, it was speculated that she might have greater ability than the test results indicated.

Her responses to the Rorschach cards at this time were as follows:

Anna's Rorschach Protocol at the Six Year Level

Performance	Inquiry
I 5" 1. A map—here's little 80" holes in it.	1. Has curves in it—holes shows how it's made out of paper.

II 6" 1. This looks like blood and this here is blood.
         2. This looks like a map— (Perseveration) little
   55"   things across it.
	1. It has red stuff in.

III 5" 1. This looks like a map. (Perseveration). 27" 2. This looks like blood.	2. Where somebody got killed.
IV 4" 1. A map. (Perseveration). 30"	
V 2" 1. A map. (Perseveration). Has there here up here 27" and these down there.	1. (Runs finger around edges).

VI 4"   (Urged to see something besides maps.)
         1. A map and has these little white things.
  33"
	1. (Again runs finger around edges). Q. Part of paper.

VII 2" 1. A map and has this here. (Points to lower center). 32" That's all that's on it.	1. Part of the map.
VIII 3" 1. Blood. Here's these here and has these hanging 40" down.	1. Part of where it's dripping. Q. It's all different colors.
IX 3" 1. This is blood. Has this 35" down here—has these.	1. It's dripping. That's all blood from where you get killed.
X 4" 1. That's blood. Has this here on it and this and 40" this here.	1. Red and other colors. Q. Where it's dripping.

Following is the "blind" interpretation of the above record:

"In this first Rorschach record there is little to give a picture of a unique personality. There are only two types of response on the whole record, giving the impression of a panicky anxiety, interspersed with massive emotional discharge. This record appears to be a traumatic one, in that fearfulness and violence characterize all the responses, and no other response appears possible for this girl even when specifically urged to give a different kind of response. There are no adequate defenses against discharge of affect, no signs of any sort of identification, and no indication that this girl at this time can mobilize enough ego strength to cope with the kind of problem presented by the Rorschach. On the last three cards the response of 'blood dripping' occurs, and the notion of dripping is added to the simple blood responses given earlier. The presence of m in a record that is completely lacking in human and animal movement suggests that fantasy is repressed and that this is more likely to be a traumatic record than a schizophrenic one. The impression is that something drastic has happened to this child, and she has not had time or experience sufficient to enable recovery to begin. One would expect a behavioral picture of generalized fearfulness, inability to enter new situations, extreme emotional lability, withdrawal from warm human contacts, and in general an inability to function either intellectually or socially at a level in keeping with her chronological and intellectual development. Because of the suggestion that this is a traumatic reaction the prognosis at this point would have to be guarded until some evidence of recoverability can be obtained. Within this one record there is no sign of recoverability, and one may assume that the trauma, whatever it is, has grossly affected every aspect of her functioning, making her at this point an extremely unhappy and frightened little child without the means or the outside help to respond adaptively in new situations."

As has been noted, the above Rorschach was given at a time of increasing environmental stress, shortly after inter-family conflicts had arisen because of father's excessive drinking. A few months later, after a period of caring for Anna and her siblings in their home, the aunt and uncle took the initiative in getting help from the Juvenile Court in placing the children. The baby was adopted and the three other children were placed in an institution for dependent and neglected children. The court worker described Anna and her siblings as "alert, friendly, and enjoying the companionship of their cousins and aunt and uncle." It was with evident reluctance that Anna left the home of these maternal relatives.

This move to the institution came just before the beginning of a new school year, and Anna was enrolled in a nearby public school.

It was here that I saw Anna for the second time. She looked better cared for than on the previous occasion, but there was still a definite stoop to her shoulders and her expression was sober. Her second grade teacher saw Anna as an extremely shy child, slightly retarded in school achievement, somewhat slow in motor activity, with considerable daydreaming.

In response to my request to draw a man, Anna drew a figure consisting of a leaning body, symmetrical, with one shoulder higher than the other; legs which appeared to be only a division of the trunk; club-like feet; short arms extending outward from the body; and a round pumpkin like head. There was much erasing and redrawing. Goodenough scoring indicated average intellectual ability.

Anna's Rorschach responses at this age were as follows:

Anna's Rorschach Protocol at the Seven Year Level

Performance	Inquiry
I 35" 1. Wing.	1. Wing of a bird—a bird that flies over the sea—just the wings.
40"	
II 12" 1. Has blood on it.	a. Like a design with
15"	1. Blood on it.
III 7" 1. Some man and he has	1. Body, leg, head, neck. Q. Looks like he's dancing.
10" 2. Blood on him.	
IV 70" (Encouraged). 1. Looks like another wing	1. Bird isn't there.
72" off a bird.	
V 3" 1. Looks like a butterfly	1. And that's his head. Q. Looks like he's flying.
7" and his tails on it.	
VI 7" 1. Looks like a wolf. (Had to be told to lay it	1. Head, body. Q. Looks like he's dead.
37" down).	
VII (Encouraged) 57" 1. Looks like a design— like has a butterfly on it.	1. Like somebody made him out of paper.
VIII 4" 1. Looks like another design	
7" 2. With bears on it.	2. On a design.
IX 16" 1. This looks like another design.	
33" 2. Another butterfly on it.	2. On another piece of paper.

Performance	Inquiry
X 20″ 1. This looks like another design	
55″ 2. With sea animals on it.	2. They look like crabs or something. Q. In the designs.

Following is the "blind" interpretation of the above record:

"In the second record several important changes have occurred, mostly in the direction of recovery, but with many indications that this is still a very disturbed and frightened child. One of the most striking changes is in the length of reaction times. Whereas the first record had reaction times varying from two seconds to six seconds, this second record has reaction times ranging from three seconds to seventy seconds. On this second record it is striking that the two most lengthy RT's occur to Cards IV and VII, the so-called father and mother cards respectively. This fact may be a clue to the nature of the trauma noted in the record of a year previous. Tentatively it is suggested that the trauma involved the sudden loss—very likely a literal loss, in view of the traumatic nature of the earlier record—of both parents. However, this is a rather drastic interpretation, based on the knowledge of two consecutive records. From the second record alone only a much more conservative hypothesis would seem justified. This would take somewhat the form that this child has extreme difficulty in relating to both parents, and has repressed some frightening feelings with regard to them. However, the quality of unreality to the responses on Cards IV and VII—in one case the bird isn't there and in the other case the butterfly looks like somebody made him out of paper—suggest that there is an unreal quality about this girl's feelings about the parents, a notion that would fit in with the idea that the parents literally have been lost. Signs of recovery include the presence of a human response at this point, a wider variety of content, and the ability to give form responses that are at least compatible with the form of the cards. There are three possible populars on this record, a fact indicating that this girl has progressed in the direction of being able to perceive the environment as other people perceive it. The presence of two "blood" responses indicates that emotional control is still poorly established, and massive affective outbursts still interrupt her efforts at intellectual control. There is still a definite timidity about coping with the environment, as indicated by some perseveration, and by the presence of vague responses as well as partial animal responses (wing of a bird). However, the improvement over the previous record is definitely noticeable, and one can say that at this point the girl has accomplished the ability to delay the expression of emotionality, although not to parcel it out in socially acceptable ways. She has progressed somewhat towards being able to look at the environment and respond to it. However, she still appears only minimally able to relate to people (there is one *M* response) and has still closed off, by repression, the crucial relationships to parents or parent figures. It is felt that this is probably still a very isolated child, and because of the violence (blood) juxtaposed with the repressed responses to parent cards, it is suggested that this child may at this point be possibly phobic or have nightmares. Prognosis is decidedly improved, however, as compared with the first record. The defense of repression appears to be the primary one at this point, a fact which represents an improvement over the last record where there appeared to be no evidence of good defense. Despite the fearfulness of entering new situations, there are signs that this child is reaching out to the environment and responding to it however tentatively. There is some expectation, although by no means a certainty, that peer relationships may be somewhat better for this child than her relationships with parent figures at this point. This is implied in the human movement response to Card III, indicating that some relationship with people is possible even though the parent cards evoke the repressive responses noted. It is felt that this child very likely has feelings of unreality about both herself and the environment, and to this point has rather weak identification."

Little information could be obtained about Anna's first year in the institution. No immediate reaction to placement was observed by the personnel. Father's visits were infrequent, and Anna became increasingly dependent on her older brother. She was obedient and conforming with the institution personnel, and there was no difficulty in regard to the school situation.

Anna was living in the same institution and attending the same school when she was seen again at the age of eight years and eight months. On this occasion, there was a slight twitching, an almost choreiform body movement, apparent. Although she still expressed little spontaneity, Anna was able to answer direct questions without hesitation. She seemed to enjoy talking about her family: her father lived in a room not far from the institution, and she and her siblings had visited the baby sister in her adoptive home. Anna had a bad cold at this time but it did not seem to affect her test results adversely. She was most persistent and cooperative in the testing situation.

Both her reading and her spelling scores on the Monroe Diagnostic Reading Examination were within the average range for her third grade placement, but Anna's arithmetic grade showed a year's retardation. She expressed a preference for drawing above all other school subjects.

She gave the following Rorschach responses at this time:

Anna's Rorschach Protocol at the Eight Year Level

Performance	Inquiry
I 10″ 1. Looks like a bear when 20″ he's cut open.	1. Q. Fur side. (Cut open). Both sides shown.
II 2″ 1. Looks like two men dancing.	
2. And that's somebody cut off their head.	2. Looks like blood up there— blood from their head coming. Q. Feet was cut off and it's bleeding.
18″	
III 4″ 1. Two men taking something	
2. Out of a fire and	
16″ 3. Their bow came off.	3. Bow on them.
IV 8″ 1. Looks like wolf cut when he's hanging up on the 19″ wall.	1. Fur side. That looks like head.
V 3″ 1. Looks like a butterfly 12″ when he's flying.	1. When he's flying.
VI 3″ 1. Looks like a fox when they killed him and he's 11″ hanging up on the wall.	1. Fur side.
VII 8″ 1. Looks like two dogs hanging up on the line 13″ or something.	1. They killed him and he's hanging up like that.
VIII 3″ 1. Looks like two bears climbing 13″ 2. Up a mountain.	1. The kind that lives in the woods.
IX 6″ 1. Looks like goats climbing up the wall.	1. Walking together.
2. Some men are in behind 22″ them.	2. Hand, head, feet. Watching so they won't run away.

Performance	Inquiry
X 4″ 1. Looks like water and	1. All around is water.
2. Crabs in it.	2. Swimming around.
3. Looks like a little girl.	3. Nose, mouth. Q. Face (lower
She's looking in it.	orange).
4. Looks like there's a snail	4. Looks like he's crawling out
91″ in there (green).	of shell into water.

Following is the "blind" interpretation of the above record:

"This record represents a very marked improvement over the previous one and one may anticipate later developments by saying that between the ages of seven years, nine months and eight years, eight months have occurred the greatest improvement that this girl has shown in the entire course of the developmental study. Attention immediately focuses on Cards IV and VII, both of which show at this time good formal responses, without strikingly long reaction times, indicating that identification with parent figures has now become possible, although the responses themselves to these cards indicate still that there is tremendous anxiety associated with perceptions of parents. In one case the response is a wolf cut up and in the other case, two dogs hanging on the line—'they killed him.' These responses of violence are in contrast to the other responses to human figures which include men dancing and men taking something out of a fire as well as other non-violent human response. Nevertheless, some expression of the fearfulness associated with the thought of the parents is now possible to this child, and the fearfulness does not extend to the non-parental cards, indicating that this girl now has areas of good functioning. Eight of the ten cards yield responses now that show definite improvement as compared with the responses given the previous year. The presence of inanimate movement responses (hanging up) on Cards IV, VI, and VII are somewhat offset by the presence of no less than four good human movement responses, and five animal movement responses. These indications imply that although there is still a good deal of repressed fantasy surrounding the parents, the capacity for fantasy has been restimulated, interpersonal relationships are now possible for this child, and the qualitative aspects of the responses indicate that fantasy can even be enjoyable. The fact that one of the human responses is of 'a little girl' indicates some acceptance of her feminine role and the establishment of an identity. Human figures are seen in relation to each other, generally in cooperative activity, suggesting that peer relationships have decidedly improved. Nevertheless her feeling about interpersonal relationships can be described as hopeful but distrustful. The hopefulness is inferred from the presence of climbing responses, particularly one in which two figures are seen as walking together, juxtaposed with 'watching so they won't run away.' From these responses it is suggested that this child may have formed some new relationships which are extremely important to her, which enable her to express feelings towards people, which give her a great deal of satisfaction, but towards which she has fears that they will be lost. Concurrent with the increase of fantasy and interpersonal interactions there is a decrease in the uncontrolled color responses. There still is one blood response, but aside from that, emotional responsiveness is fairly well shut off at this point. The child is afraid of her emotionality, tends to stifle it, just as she is afraid that her new relationships are very tenuous. It seems likely that in her thinking, there is a relationship between massive emotional outbursts and loss of love. It appears that strong emotional control is exerted at this point for fear that if it is not these new relationships will be lost. On the whole the record is an optimistic one, and is possibly best characterized as an emergent one —of a child who is now testing out new relationships, her ability to get along with people and trust them, and testing also their stability. This is summarized in her last response on the record which is a snail 'crawling out of the shell into the water.' This appears to be what she is doing herself at this point, and generally speaking, prognosis is good. Dangerpoints still reside in the inadequate emotional control, the repressed fantasies about the parents, and the potentiality for a violent regressive setback if another trauma touching on these problems should occur. However, barring unexpected setbacks, one may look forward at this point to increasing socialization, especially with peers, and the concurrent emergency of improved reaction to parental figures coinciding with ability to express emotionality in a controlled way. One would expect these things either to emerge together or to remain submerged together."

There is again very little known about Anna's activities and behavior during the year between this Rorschach and the previous one. The institution personnel simply stated that she continued to be conforming, and that she never complained as some of the children did. Despite the fact that father's visits were highly irregular, Anna never criticized him for his negligence. One got the impression of a highly repressed child who did not dare to show her feelings overtly. Her anxiety did express itself in her tics and jerky body movements, however.

Except for being taller, Anna had changed little in appearance by the time of our next meeting. Her stooped shoulders straightened slightly and the sad, somewhat dull expression on her face brightened visibly when she recognized me. She was again cooperative in the test situation and, at the end of the hour, waited expectantly for me to ask her questions. When I inquired about her family, she said that she and her siblings had been to visit the little sister recently. Anna was defensive when I asked about her father. She said that he had been to see them two Sundays "in a row," but the institution personnel reported later that he had not been there for several months.

Anna achieved a low average rating, with a wide scatter of scores on the Grace Arthur Performance Scale given at this time. It seemed that her anxiety was still affecting her functioning ability.

She gave the following responses to the Rorschach cards:

Anna's Rorschach Protocol at the Nine Year Level

Performance	Inquiry
I 5″ 1. Legs, skin, his tail, head, 33″ his mouth.	1. Of a bear. Q. (Is this part of him?) Yes, they cut him open.
II 3″ 1. Two men—dancing. 23″ 2. Blood.	2. Blood up there. 1. Don't have no head, hands, feet.
III 5″ 1. They're fixing 2. A fire.	1. Two men. 2. There's the fire (gray). 1. (Contd.) & 5. Putting a pot on it.

3. A bow.
      4. Some blood.
  22″ 5. Pots on the fire.
	3. Necktie bow.

IV 5″ 1. Wolf's head, tail, his legs. 23″	1. Hanging on a wall. Q. Dead. Fur side.
V 4″ 1. Wings, head, feet. 11″	1. Butterfly in a case where they keep dead insects.
VI 1. Head, feet, skin. 14″	1. Wolf, hanging on a wall. Q. This is fur side.
VII 9″ 1. Dogs dancing. 15″ 2. A butterfly.	1. (Upper ⅔). 2. Flying around.

	Performance	*Inquiry*
VIII 5″	1. Two dogs climbing	
	2. A hill—rocks on the hill.	
21″	3. A butterfly.	3. Got a skinny body.
IX 4″	1. A garden.	1. Whole thing around there. Q. Because of carrots and apples.
	2. Apples.	2. Round and red.
	3. Carrots.	3. Orange and shaped like a carrot.
X 8″	1. Ocean.	1. Fishes and that. The ocean. Q. (Not same if black.)
	2. Worms.	2. Kind that make their home under the ground.
	3. Crabs.	3. In the ocean.
26″	4. Fish.	4. Orange fish (outer orange).

The "blind" interpretation of this record follows:

"In many ways this record is very similar to the one of the previous year, but the differences are interesting and striking. The primary changes are as follows: improvement in the concept in response to the mother card. Whereas previously only dead and unreal things had been seen on Card VII, at this time Anna can see dogs dancing and a butterfly flying around, both indicating in their good form quality and animal movement that the concept of the mother has diminished in anxiety, and some identification has taken place, especially as suggested by the feminine butterfly concept. The father figure has not improved, and the focus of this girl's anxiety seems to be fairly specific to relationships with men at this point. On two occasions where she sees men she also sees blood, a fact indicating that her perception of men is one that still provokes a tremendous emotional response from her. However, at other points in the record, there are indications that emotionality can emerge with more freedom and better control than previously. This is indicated by the two good FC responses on Card IX, followed by a controlled color response (orange fish) on Card X. These responses indicate not only that an effort at emotional control is being made, but that some genuine ability to integrate emotionality with intellectual achievement has been accomplished. Clear differentiation between the sexes appears to be related to the differentiation in perception of mother and father, and male sexuality emerges at this point as a somewhat frightening thing, indicated by the long reaction time to Card VI, followed by a response which is a popular and essentially the same response she

had given on previous years, but which is given at this point frag-
mentarily. Fragmentary responses also occurred to Cards I and V
and since such responses have not occurred in the previous year, it
may be hypothesized that the increased freedom of emotional expression and increased feminine identification have been accomplished at
the expense of some regression in regard to timidity about entering
situations, and possibly a generalized increase of manifest anxiety.
The presence of several food and near food responses, such as a pot
on the fire, apples, and carrots, suggests that this girl is now able to
express some of her dependency needs, but the general context of
the record suggests that she is relatively comfortable in her dependency on a mother figure, but is extremely threatened by the need for
dependency on a male figure. The fact that this child at age nine is
approaching puberty may supply reason for increased anxiety with
regard to relations to men; and, actually, the striking thing about the
record is not so much this anxiety as the fact that the relation with
the mother figure seems to have undergone tremendous improvement
in the course of the year. In a way, this record also reflects less feeling of pressure to relate to people than was shown in the previous
record. The presence of only two *M* responses on this record as contrasted with four on the previous one, taken with the emergence of
good color responses, indicates that relationships with people have
improved enough that the need to conjure up such responses on the
cards was diminished. The increased ease of handling color and the
ability to use human movement, as well as the emerging feminine
identification, suggests that peer relationships also may have improved."

It was during the year preceding the above Rorschach that father
was hospitalized with both legs broken. Anna, with her sister, visited
him faithfully, but never expressed her feelings about him to any of
the staff. Though still quiet and shy she was beginning to make
friends with the other girls in her unit. She was still dependent on
her brother, but she seemed to like school and her teacher said she
did average work there.

By the age of ten years and seven months, Anna had developed a
rather husky build and walked with a slight boyish swagger. It seemed
as if she might have been trying to identify with her brother, to whom
she had been so attached through the years. She was more alert than
I had yet seen her and showed more interest in the test materials
than she had on any previous occasion. However, she sat with shoul-

ders as stooped as ever and her fingernails were badly bitten. She spoke affectionately about her younger sister and was even more defensive of father than she had been at the preceding interview.

The results of the Wechsler Intelligence Scale for Children showed a wide discrepancy between verbal and performance scores; the former was low average while the latter was high average. This resulted in a full-scale average rating. The outstanding characteristic shown on this test was the unusual sensitivity to social situations.

Anna's Rorschach responses at this age were as follows:

Anna's Rorschach Protocol at the Ten Year Level

Performance	Inquiry
I 6″ 1. Two little elfs.	1. Looks like they are dancing.
2. Design in the middle.	2. On the wall.
3. And a fox.	3. Up there—just his head
26″	(outer d).
II 4″ 1. Two little elfs.	1. Dancing too. Arms, feet, have no head.
2. Blood.	2. On the wall.
3. Design at the bottom.	3. Butterfly. Q. Swallow tail.
21″ That's all.	
III 2″ 1. Two men cooking some-	a. There's the pot.
thing.	
2. Bow tie in the middle.	2. Bow tie.
3. And design on the side.	3. Looks like a girl. Q. Hair. Head.
	a. That's the bird's tail and
12″	up there's the body.
IV 5″ 1. A wolf.	1. His head.
2. Man's feet.	2. Down here.
3. A flower and that's all.	3. Up here. Q. I don't know.
16″	Q. This and leaves like.
V 2″ 1. A butterfly—	1. Flying. Same as moth. (without upper d.)
	Looks like he's flying.
2. A moth.	
13″ And that's all.	
VI 6″ 1. A fox. Two feet and	1. Dead. Q. Skin split up. Q.
18″ that's all.	Fur, feet and head.
VII 2″ 1. Two girls dancing.	1. (Upper D).
2. Butterfly at the bottom.	2. Looks like he's flying.
3. Two dogs and that's all.	3. (Same as girls.) Looks like
15″	they are jumping.

Performance	Inquiry
VIII 2″ 1. Two bears going up	
2. The hill and a	2. (Gray.)
3. Butterfly and	3. Different colors.
19″ 4. Water on the hill.	4. It's the color of water.
IX 4″ 1. A crab.	1. There. Here. Q. Pinchers.
2. A bear.	2. Head and tail. Q. Climbing up the—just climbing.
18″ 3. Tomato.	3. A row of them. Q. Round and red.
X 3″ 1. A crab and a	1. Pinchers and legs. Q. In the water. Q. Looks like he's swimming a little bit.
2. Snail and	2. (Brown) Looks like he's crawling along.
3. Water.	3. (Inner blue). Color of it.
4. Dog.	4. (Yellow) Looks like feet. His head and tail. Q. Looks like he's crawling along.
5. Flowers.	5. (Gray). Stem and that's the ground. Q. Flower didn't
26″	come out yet.

The "blind" interpretation of this record is as follows:

"Anna at this point appears to have gone in the direction of coming to terms with the extreme anxiety-producing nature of her perceptions of male figures. The primary defense mechanism in this regard appears to be a counterphobic one, as indicated principally by the perception of 'two little elfs' where she had seen men before. Her feminine identification seems to have matured considerably in the last year, and Anna appears to be quite secure in it at this time. In fact, it appears that one of the attempts that she has of handling her fears of men is to feminize them, because she seems to know that the perception of women is a benign one. Therefore, on Cards III and IV, where she sees masculine figures, she follows them immediately with feminine ones, apparently neutralizing the anxiety of the male perceptions in this way. She still cannot tolerate the clear perception of men, but can reduce anxiety by transforming the perceptions into harmless mythical creatures or into women. The fact that that technique does actually lower the anxiety is indicated by the fact that for the first time in any of her records she sees 'man's feet,' the first frankly male perception that she has yet given. The record on the whole appears fairly normal at this time, with some tendencies towards exceptional emotional lability, as indicated by the presence still of uncontrolled color responses, which are not only blood this time, and by the surprising contrast between the M and FM responses, in that the latter appear in many cases more constricted than the former. The human responses are most frequently of people dancing, a rather exhibitionistic perception, whereas the FM responses include such things as crawling along, climbing, and generally reflecting slow and difficult progress. Such a contrast raises a question of whether this girl may be acting more outgoing, sociable, and generally enthusiastic about things than she really feels. The counterphobic indications play into this idea, and suggest a kind of emotional lability that may result in an hysterical personality structure."

Anna was getting along well with her peers and had formed a fairly close relationship with one of the counselors at this time. She seemed less dependent on her brother and on good terms with her sister. Father had not visited the children very often during the past year and was intoxicated on his last visit. Anna was glad to see him, and despite the fact that she was obviously embarrassed about his condition, she made no comment about it to any of the personnel.

When I saw Anna again she had grown much taller and seemed more stoop-shouldered than ever. She was initially glad to see me but her facial expression soon returned to an unhappy, lifeless gaze. She still lacked spontaneity and, for the first time, she was reluctant to talk about her family. However, I was finally able to obtain the following information from her: she had not seen her younger sister for some time; her brother, who was now fifteen, had been sent to a home for delinquent boys because "he was going to hit the superintendent." She also said that her father still lived in the neighborhood and came to see her and her sister every Sunday. The superintendent denied this last statement later, and said that father came very infrequently and was generally drunk when he did come.

Anna's human figure drawings were of a boy and girl each five or six years old. The boy was drawn first, with exaggerated shoulders on which there were many erasures. The shoulder exaggeration was no doubt a reflection of her body preoccupation since the institution personnel had been persistent in trying to correct her posture. It is interesting, though, that the age of these figures was that of Anna at the time of her mother's death.

Anna was at first reluctant to talk about her worries but after a little prodding she stated with sincerity that her greatest concerns were that her brother might not come back to the home and that her father might stop coming to see them. She was also able to express her anger at the counselor when she made Anna do her work "over again," and at the younger children when they were noisy (since "the counselor depends on the older kids to keep them quiet.")

She liked school and the teachers' reports were favorable. They saw her as a conscientious average student, conforming and somewhat shy, but not as withdrawn as she had been when she was younger.

Her responses to the Rorschach cards at the age of eleven years and eight months were as follows:

Anna's Rorschach Protocol at the Eleven Year Level

Performance	Inquiry
I 5" 1. Two elves.	1. They are just dancing.
2. Bear skin.	2. Flat on the . . . Q. Fur side.
15" That's all.	Q. Black.
II 2" 1. Two men dancing and	1. Dancing around. Q. Their hands—holding them. Q. Heads—they're red.
2. A heart.	2. From an animal. Q. Shaped like one. Q. It's red.
15" 1. (Contd.) Head of men.	
III 2" 1. Two men playing with a	1. Dancing.
2. Pot.	
3. Bow tie.	3. Wear on a suit.
13" 4. Squirrel.	4. Running (sees him sideways).
IV 4" 1. Two feet and a . . . head	1. Wolf. Q. Looks like a rug. Q. Fur side. Q. On the floor.
15" and tail.	
V 4" 1. A bat and feet.	1. Looks like he's flying. Feet of the bat.
10"	
VI 2" 1. A wolfskin. Two heads.	1. Fur side—rug. Two heads of wolf.
10"	
VII 3" 1. Two girls and	1. They're dancing.
2. A butterfly.	2. He looks like he's getting ready to fly.
9"	
VIII 4" 1. Two bears climbing	1. Red bears (never saw a red bear).
12" 2. A . . . mountain.	2. Different colored mountains.
IX 6" 1. Two men (green) and	1. Looks like they are ready to

Performance	Inquiry
	climb the mountain. Head, arms.
2. Some fruit.	2. Down here—looks like apples. Q. They're red.
13″	
X 3″ 1. Two crabs. (outer blue).	1. In the water. Q. They are going to swim.
2. A worm.	2. Green. Q. No. They just look like they are crawling along.
3. Two men (inner blue).	3. (Sees them upside down). Q. Looks like they are ready
17″	to jump off the mountain.

The "blind" interpretation is as follows:

"This is by far the healthiest record of the series, combining as it does, good human perceptions of both men and women, good efforts at emotional control sometimes achieved and sometimes not, the continuation of the firm feminine identification and the willingness to take a chance on dealing with emotionally stimulating parts of the card even when there is no certainty of the degree of control available. At some times the responses to color are forced (red bears), at other times they are relatively uncontrolled (different colored mountains) and at still other times good control is achieved (a red heart). There is still a good deal of anxiety attached to the perception of men, but at least they can now clearly be perceived. The anxiety is inferred from the perception first, of two men ready to climb the mountain and then two men who look like they are ready to jump off the mountain. Where in previous years Anna had perceived blood, people without hands, etc., at this point she is able to see whole men, with red heads. It is felt that this girl will still have a major problem in relating to men, that there is tremendous anxiety attached to her perception of them, and only with women does she feel really comfortable. There is a good deal of hostility implied in the kind of anxiety that now accompanies the male perceptions (jumping off the mountain, for example), and there appears to be little doubt that in forming heterosexual relationships this girl would be very timid and potentially easily frightened away or, in the case of a passive man, potentially very destructive. However, it should be emphasized that the possibilities for heterosexual relationships have improved greatly in the course of these years, and on this most recent Rorschach possibilities are much better than they would have been judging from any of the previous ones. The counterphobic defense appears somewhat relaxed at this point but still present again in the dancing figures contrasted with the animals crawling and also in the elves. Nevertheless, it is felt that at this point this is a girl who is responsive both to internal stimuli in the form of free fantasy and to external stimuli, and who is able to empathize and form good emotional relationships with people, but much more easily with women than with men. Peer relationships, particularly with girls, are probably quite good at this point, and with boys probably less so, although she seems to be reaching out for them. The defenses of repression, isolation and counterphobic reaction have predominated in the course of these records, with isolation apparently less active at this time, and the general level of defensiveness lower than in the past, as indicated by the variably controlled channels of emotional expression. At this point it is felt that the prognosis is favorable with regard to peer relationships, and relationships to adult women. The prognosis with regard to heterosexual relationships is quite guarded, and in time of stress this girl may resort to hysterical modes of response to a perceived sexual threat. It is felt that at this time her intellectual capacities are being reasonably well used, but it was noted in the past that fragmentation of responses has occurred during times of particular emotional involvement, and one of the effects of a crisis situation may be a deterioration of intellectual performance."

Anna continued to live in the institution, which takes care of about seventy-five dependent boys and girls, ages ranging from five to eighteen. It was during the period between twelve and thirteen years of age that the superintendent described Anna as going through an "I don't care" period. This was evidenced in part by her stooped posture, which continued to bring many comments from personnel, who hoped to correct the condition and thus improve her appearance. Since they got no results by talking, the superintendent sent her to a hospital for a physical checkup and a shoulder-strap type brace was prescribed. Anna was quite irregular about wearing this at first, and this reluctance was cited as further evidence of Anna's passive way of defying.

On the day before her thirteenth birthday, Anna accepted an invitation to come in to see me. She had grown taller and plumper, and her face was more animated than I had ever seen it before. She spoke enthusiastically about her junior high school experience, and also volunteered the fact that the next day was her birthday. Her brother, who now lives with father, was coming to take her out, either to a show or to her aunt's.

In talking to the director of the institution, I learned that they considered Anna to be getting along well. Their only concerns were about her stooped shoulders, which did seem to be gradually improving, and her recent flashes of hot temper. These two phenomena might well have been two sides of the same coin.

The child psychiatrist who interviewed Anna at that time gave the following report:

"Anna is a well-developed, attractive, thirteen-year-old. She is friendly but not spontaneous. However, she relates adequately and can get warmed up a little when talking about school or the institution in which she lives. It was quite a while before I realized from the content of the interview that she was an institutional child. It was certainly not possible to distinguish her as such from anything in her behavior or attitudes.

"Anna's mother died before she was six. For a year she lived with a maternal aunt, and thenceforth has lived in a children's institution. There is an older brother, eighteen, who lived in the home until rebelliousness led to his commitment to a training school. There is a younger sister, eleven, who has always been with Anna, and still a younger sister, eight, whom she sees rarely. She is in an adoptive home.

"Anna feels closest to her older brother, with whom she is identified. The father is pictured as a loving protector despite the fact that as she recounts it, Anna seems to have had little protection from him. I suppose the need to deny and repress so much in this particular relationship is one of the things that makes Anna so constricted. It sometimes seems as if she has to appear dull so that her secrets of self-deception will not leak out.

"The surprising thing about this child is that she is so well-preserved after six institutional years and much conflict with father. She paints a very favorable picture of the institution and its staff. While she is constricted, she gives little evidence of any major pathology and, in fact, has unusually good school performance as well. She likes her teachers—especially the women.

"It seems to me that this child has not been damaged much except that she is a little dulled—flattened. Her personality development, passive and mildly inhibited though it may be, gives her nevertheless a good prognosis for adaptation, especially if she finds, say in marriage, a supportive mother-in-law or some other kind of controlling force.

"I see nothing to indicate that she is or will be sick in the sense that ordinary expected events are likely to stimulate her hostility and make her incompatible. Her attachments are gone, but not that gone. However, I would not look for her to be able to do well with people who are active in interpersonal relations and who need much in return."

At this time, when Anna was thirteen years of age, she was moved to the junior-senior section in the institution and thus separated from her younger sister, who remained with the younger girls in the intermediate division.

During the years that followed, Anna and her sister continued to live in the institution. Brother, after leaving the training school, was making unsuccessful attempts to reform father. At the same time he was trying to add some variety to the lives of his sisters by visiting them faithfully and taking them out as often as they were allowed to go. Brother had told both the girls, as well as the personnel at the institution, that his ambition and goal in life is to make a home for his sisters. Anna never verbalized to the staff her enthusiasm about her brother's attention, but her pride and pleasure were obvious when he visited.

Anna was considered by the institution personnel to be a mature girl when compared with the other children in their care. Her placement there has been one of the longest—few children stay longer than four or five years. She got along fairly well with her group, always being the follower. She "will go along with anyone who comes along in the way of making friends." Infrequent outbursts of temper were noted around puberty and have continued through adolescence. She also had "blue" spells when she went to her room and cried, but she could never talk with anyone about this.

By way of reviewing the dynamics of Anna's personality development through the years, let us summarize the manner in which the Rorschach records highlight her psychosexual changes:

During her sixth year Anna was exposed to the shock of the death of her mother as well as the irresponsibility of an alcoholic father. The main reason why she was able to recuperate as well as she did from these events perhaps lies in the fact that the mother was "a warm, gentle person who gave genuine affection." The developmental Rorschach studies show beautifully the initial "traumatic" response with paucity of production except regarding "dripping blood" and death. One would wonder if Anna had witnessed or heard vividly described some hemorrhagic or operative event associated with her mother's terminal cancerous illness. In later tests the idea of people being "cut" is frequent and possibly reflects Anna's fearfulness of physical injury in herself.

By Anna's seventh year there are some initial signs of recovery in her ability to view her environment more as others might. One would postulate that in the home and school she was beginning to be supplied with support in the form of mother-substitutes. Completely abandoned by mother through death, partially abandoned by father, and by the maternal aunt, who did not follow through in providing a home for her, it is understandable that Anna's recovery was slow and incomplete.

It is interesting to trace the emergence of a feminine identification with the first mention at eight years of a "little girl." Combined with her becoming more comfortable with a female role, we see a developing anxiety in regard to male figures which she attempts to cover up in various ways, utilizing counterphobic mechanisms (describes men as harmless mythical "elfs") by juxtaposition of females in her associations and most noticeably in her defensiveness regarding her own father. It is in covering her undoubted ambivalence to father that her greatest vulnerability seems to lie. She denies his neglect and tends to idealize this inadequate parental figure in an unrealistic manner. Her older brother seems also to have fallen into the trap of unduly optimistic hopes of reforming his father.

By eight years, Anna gives a perfect pictorial representation of herself as a "snail crawling out of its shell." She begins to have some meaningful relationships with women and with peers, as well as demonstrating a capacity for fantasy of an enjoyable character.

At nine years, we see a great improvement in her relationship to the mother figure and we can only guess that some warm teacher or supervisor has taken Anna "under her wing" and satiated some of her hunger for affection. Meanwhile, the "father card" remains as a "wolf," one of the most frightening concepts in children's fantasies.

At ten years, Anna is able to describe a man's feet as her first acknowledgment of male anatomy but would seem to have a long way to go before accepting a male in entirety. Very noteworthy, at this point too, is the discrepancy between her somewhat exhibitionistic human responses of people dancing and animal movement responses of things crawling along, climbing, etc. These raise the question in the examiner's mind as to whether she is acting more outgoing than she really feels, and suggest that her emotional lability may result in an hysterical personality.

Similarly, I suspect that Anna's outward demeanor may mask the extent of her underlying immaturity in regard to her psychosexual relationships with males. I feel that in this area Anna still must do some "slow climbing" before she is ready to "dance," and that she needs careful protection during this period of adjustment. From a practical viewpoint, it might be unwise for Anna to leave the institution immediately to go to the insecurity of the father. Her brother too has demonstrated extreme rebelliousness and might not be a suitable guardian at this point for the girl. She seems unprepared for complete freedom and might well suffer from "going along with anyone" to be traumatized by sexual experiences or unwise choice of mate.

Anna seems to have some sparks of spontaneity which, given sufficient time, might well be carefully fanned into more vivacious group participation and heterosexual relationships. Given support and encouragement, some integration of her damaged self-concept might ensue with resulting inward initiation of change so that we could look forward to the day that Anna's "shoulder brace" would be unnecessary and that she would hold herself erect with a new self-esteem.

When she was seventeen and a half years old and about to enter her senior year in high school, Anna accepted my invitation to come to the Center for an interview. She was an attractive adolescent—tall and blond—but still appeared to be generally unpoised. Her stooped shoulders and reticence of speech helped to create this impression.

Although she found it difficult to talk freely, she was able to respond to direct questions. There have been family changes. Brother, who is in basic training for the Marines, was married just two weeks before. And then, just two days before this interview, father had been found dead, apparently from a heart attack. In fact, Anna had just come from the funeral home. She spoke of this without affect, but said that her sister was "pretty broken up," since father had always favored her. The final comment about father was, "He's in good hands now."

Anna had a boy friend at this time and had visited in his home and liked his mother very much. He was in the Marines and she heard from him every day. They were not engaged yet, but considered themselves "going steady." She hoped to marry him after his discharge from military service.

Anna said that she wanted a home and family more than anything else in the world. But, in the meantime, she planned to finish high school, where she was taking the commercial course, and then get a job as typist. She used to think about college, but gave up those plans because she knew she could not get through.

In reminiscing, Anna felt that she had been well treated at the institution, despite the fact that she had always been less favored than her siblings. She always wished she could have been in a foster home because "there'd be only one of us then." It was obvious that Anna had resented her anonymity at the institution, and her most cherished ambition was to be a "famous person—well known." In expressing the feeling that she had never had a home of her own or anyone to really care about her, Anna demonstrated her greatest affect.

Anna's very modest ambitions—to be a typist, and eventually, a mother—are probably within her grasp. This wish for a family of her own is probably the most important theme of her life. The fact that she can verbalize her resentment of regimentation and her wish for something better gives us the indication that her blandness is a defense that is consciously used. She is concrete in her thinking and appears to be defending against depression. Her Rorschachs give evidence of an active wish-fulfilling fantasy life, but she keeps a sharp rein on her emotions and disapproves strongly when they show.

XIV : AMY

THE LAST STUDY TO BE PRESENTED, the case history of Amy, requires a special introduction. Amy was not a member of the original sample of 160 children chosen for intensive Rorschach analysis; however, her case material is so illuminating that its inclusion in this book on the use of the Rorschach to study child development is essential.

Amy is the niece of a clinical psychologist. Even before her birth, her arrival was anticipated with pleasure and emotional involvement by this unmarried older sister of Amy's mother. As one will readily note in surveying the case material that follows, the relationship that Amy has had since birth with aunt as well as parents has been close; and, while a certain amount of objectivity is always sacrificed when observer is also participant in the recorded events, the rich material that has resulted more than compensates for this less-than-perfect scientific circumstance.

The excellent combination of close interest and scientific training on the part of the aunt has yielded a wealth of data in this case which is rarely available to the research psychologist. Amy's aunt is almost totally responsible for the historical and anecdotal material from which this case was written, and her records of Amy's development have been scrupulously kept—with many verbatim statements recorded—throughout Amy's sixteen years. Her fondness for the child is obvious to the reader in her choice of events to record; but so is her quick understanding of those events which are pertinent to Amy's psychologic development. The scientific accuracy with which anecdotes and case material connected to the child's physical, intellectual, and psychosexual development have been retained is a rare find. The author is unaware of any other material in the literature that even approximates this depth and quality.

The Rorschach records on Amy begin when she was two years old—four years earlier than the age at which the children in the study were first seen. The reader is no doubt aware by this time, as was the

243

author, that it is of great value to have records from this early period when the origins of many personality factors already present in the records of six-year-olds are just beginning to display themselves. The psychologist aunt was aware of how important an immediate start on recorded depth data is to future personality analysis; and nine of the ten Rorschach records to be presented in this final chapter were obtained by her during her frequent visits with the child and her family throughout these years. The author is deeply indebted to the aunt for having this information available by the time it was sought in connection with her own research.

One final note is required here. The interpretations of Amy's records were made by the author and are not "blind" in the sense that we discussed earlier in connection with the first ten cases. The interpretative technique varies somewhat as well; however, the basic orientation is Freudian as is that of the previous interpreters. The author was not only aware of many of the events in Amy's life but was personally acquainted with all members of her family when the Rorschach analyses were made, and is most grateful to all of them for their cooperation during the collection of the data and for allowing this material to be published.

Amy is a child of very high intelligence, reared in a middle income family who live in a small industrial town. Her mother is a dynamic, youthful-appearing woman in her thirties, a college graduate who, before her marriage, had a short career as a hospital dietician. Amy's father is a few years older than mother, had one year of college, and is now chief receiving clerk in a local steel mill. At the time of their marriage, father was a widower who had three sons by his first wife. The youngest of Amy's step-brothers was nine years old when she was born, and all three boys spent much of their time with their maternal grandmother after their mother's death. The parents have always been compatible and the home a fairly congenial one. Amy's step-brothers are fond and proud of her, and she has always been devoted to them.

Following is Amy's first Rorschach, obtained at the age of two years and four months:

Amy's Rorschach Protocol at the Two Year Level

Performance	Inquiry	Scoring	
I 1. An airplane.	1. W.	W F	obj
2. Shoes.	2. (Wing detail).	D F	obj

Performance	Inquiry	Scoring
II 1. Dogs barking. No more guys.	1. (Popular).	D FM A P
III 1. Dogs.	1. (Usual).	D F A
IV 1. Black Max (neighborhood cocker). See his black hair (rubs hand over blot).		W Fc,FC' A
V 1. A big rabbit.	1. (Center D).	D F A
VI 1. A giraffe.	1. (W). He has a long neck.	W F A
VII 1. Dogs walking.	1. (Upper ⅔).	D FM A
VIII 1. Dogs coming up.	1. (Popular).	D FM A P
IX 1. I don't know.	1. Refused.	— — —
X 1. Giraffes (red).	1. They have long necks.	D F A

It may be difficult for even an experienced clinician to accept the fact that the responses above are those of a twenty-eight months old child, since all published studies report that the Rorschach of the average two-year-old consists of perseverated whole responses of somewhat vague form. That a child of this age is able to give this number of clearly-conceived responses is the first indication of her precocity. Even the possibility that enrivonmental stimulation may have developed her attentive and perceptive powers does not invalidate the very early presence of such ability. The considerable amount of large detail of good form indicates an early emergence of a matter of fact realistic approach to the world about her, and the high F% gives evidence of conscious thinking and ego development well advanced for her age level.

Since the capacity to give movement, even animal movement, is rare before four years of age, Amy's free use of movement in her responses shows the early beginning of her response to inner promptings and feelings—indicating the potentials for a rich fantasy life. In contrast to this early use of movement, color shyness is noted at this time: the colored areas on Cards II and III were avoided; Card IX was refused; and only the most obvious areas were used in the other all-color cards. This lack of color responses in a two-year-old is not unusual, but such responses, though sometimes crude, usually emerge simultaneously with movement responses. This capacity for establishing emotional contact with others appears to be slow in developing when compared with such advanced assets as ability to differentiate herself from the rest of the environment, to perceive reality objectively and to respond to her inner feelings. From the Fc response on Card IV, it is evident that Amy is precociously aware of social implications, since texture is rarely perceived at the preschool level. Because of this unusual sensitivity, as well as the other evidences of precocity, it is possible that the absence of color responses in Amy's record could point to the beginning of a neurotic disorder in a basically introversive personality. If it can be said that interpersonal relationships are causing anxiety at such an early age, Amy seems to be using the mechanism of denial and flight into fantasy to offset it.

The variety of content instead of the usual perseveration of a two-year-old indicates a wide spread of interests most unusual at this age. The presence of the two adult populars in this record suggests a very early attempt to adapt to communal thinking.

Since relationships within the family group, as evidenced by responses to Cards IV and VII, the so-called father and mother cards respectively, appear warm and satisfying, it is possible that she feels no need to seek satisfaction from outside sources at the present time and that her shyness may be, as yet, no problem to her. She sees mother as the more active of the parents. While there is the indication of a good relation with both parents, the texture response on Card IV suggests that she feels closer and more affectionate towards father than towards mother at this particular time. In a child of this high intelligence and sensitivity, such relationships suggests the beginning of an oedipal involvement. In her use of phallic areas and symbols, Amy shows an awareness of sex differences and of some preoccupation that could be related to castration fears.

Amy's ability to handle the first card and her manner of dealing with it, seeing such divergent things as an "airplane" and a "shoe" at the age of two, reveals a very early tendency to encompass opposite poles of experience, the distant vision as well as the concrete near-at-hand reality, the inner and the outer worlds, without onesidedness. She is already open and perceptive, accepting experiences without retreating to "safe limits." She is already a child who views the unfamiliar aspects of experience with a sensitive alertness and a definite quickening of interest.

Amy's early developmental history substantiates the general acceleration noted in this Rorschach record. There were no feeding problems, although she showed food preferences early; and, by the time she was a year old, she insisted upon feeding herself. Toilet training too was accomplished rapidly, with no apparent effort; by eight months she used the potty for bowel movement and urination during the day. It was a year later before she was trained for night-time as well.

In regard to her motor development, Amy was pulled to a sitting position at twenty-six days and showed no head lag at that time. She sat alone at five months and shortly thereafter moved around by sliding over the floor in a sitting position. She never crawled but began to walk before she was a year old and was walking well by thirteen months. By the third month she was using her hands to pick up and play actively with toys; her finger movements were skillful enough at eight months that she was able to turn pages in a book.

Amy enjoyed story-telling and nursery rhymes at a very early age. She could point out the nursery illustrations in her book when she was ten months old; and her first word, "see," spoken at nine months, was used for the next two or three months to call attention to things. She was using short sentences at eighteen months although difficulty in pronouncing her "r's" and "l's" persisted for nearly two years. At twenty-seven months Amy began "writing" letters in scribble and thought aloud as she did so. The first of these was directed to her aunt and was copied down by her mother:

"Two allow (yellow) airplanes are flying around Amy's house. Skippy (her puppy) is a good boy, p'ays with Amy, Mommy, Daddy. Mommy no stay Amy's house—go down street—buy ice-cream, buy one book, but no other book. Dat's all, Aunt Meeme."

There were many incidents to show Amy's awareness of the feelings of people around her. These began to occur very early. At the time of the first Rorschach, an aged relative at the family home for Sunday dinner, blew his nose without wiping it clean. Amy's family were apprehensive that she would notice and make some remark about his appearance. When the old man had left, Amy said, "Did you see that big b'ack boo on Uncle Frank's nose? I felt like to laugh but I didn't." The very early appearance of texture response on the Rorschach evidently reflects this sensitivity to feelings of others, which is very unusual at this age.

Amy's parents felt that her chief problem at this time was shyness with strangers. She was very talkative with her own family but would not talk to people she did not know well. She objected to visiting in the homes of other people, and even in the safety of her mother's presence she would whisper, "Et's go to Amy's house." Her avoidance of color and her rejection of one of the all-color cards reflect this reluctance to respond overtly to her environment.

She had already asked her first questions about babies at this age. All of these were answered, as were later ones, as simply and factually as possible. It was at about this time, twenty-eight months of age, that Amy first noticed her mother's pubic hair. She had always been permitted to go in and out of the bathroom while either parent was bathing but showed shock one afternoon when she came upon mother emerging from the bathtub. She ran from the bathroom crying and was unable to verbalize her difficulty. A few days later, when her aunt was visiting, Amy came into her room while she was dressing and said, "I want to see you without any clothes on." She was allowed to do so and commented, "You look just like Mommy. Daddy is the prettiest." (At five years of age, she recalled the episode with, "I'll never forget the first time I saw all that brown hair on Mommy. I was so shocked and disappointed that I cried.") She was obviously disturbed as well as disappointed to discover that even growing up did not promise the acquisition of the desired penis.

In comparing the social history of Amy's first two years of life with the Rorschach picture taken at twenty-eight months of age, the similarity between the two is striking. The developmental picture of superior intelligence with all the details that involves of responding to inner feelings more readily than to outside stimuli, of sensitivity to social situations, of warm family relationships, of the possibility of an incipient oedipal involvement and of an early expression of castration fear—is apparent in both.

Thirteen months later Amy gave the following Rorschach:

Amy's Rorschach Protocol at the Three Year Level

Performance	Inquiry	Scoring	
I 1. A Japanese boy. (Center D). (Note the influence of VJ Day on this and next response).	1. Here's his head and here's his feet. He's just standing waiting for something to happen. Maybe he heard a bomb.	D M	H
II 2. Japanse little girls.	1. They're looking at each other and	W M	H

Performance	Inquiry	Scoring
	touchin' each other. They got high hair.	
III 1. Two big ducks.	1. They're jumpin'. (Why ducks?) Because of their beaks.	D FM A
2. That's a butterfly, of course. Just these two red things and they're nothing.	2. It has a middle and two wings.	D F A P
IV I can't speak about that one.		
1. Oh, yes, it looks like Santa Claus on his way to town.	1. W. He's sittin' on his sleigh seat. Here's his eyes and here's his beard and his big feet. Doesn't he have little arms? Such skimpy arms.	W M H
V 1. Another big butterfly.	1. It's just standing still.	W F A P
VI 1. A turtle. See its big head comin' out of its shell. Here is its water it's swimmin' in.	1. W.	W FM A
VII V1. A clown. W	1. Here's his head. He's standin' with his feet spread out.	W M- H
VIII 1. An octopus. D 2. Those are lions comin' up on the octopus.	1. (Upper D).	D F A D FM A P
IX 1. Those are cherries.	1. Because they're pink.	D CF A
2. We live here and Dorie lives here.	2. It's just the grass in our yards.	D CF N
X 1. Mosquitoes.	1. (Outside yellow).	D F A

Performance	*Inquiry*	*Scoring*		
2. Butterfly.	2. (Center blue). Don't you see—it has wings and a little front middle.	D	F	A
3. Ants.	3. (Inner yellow)	D	F	A
4. Cobweb.	4. (Top gray). It's got threads.	D	F	obj
5. Here are spiders making the web.	5. (Outer blue).	D	FM	A P

This second record, taken at three years and five months of age shows that considerable growth and change in personality has taken place during the thirteen month interval since the first record. There are the same indices of superior intelligence as were noted in the first record. The appearance of human movement and the increase in number of responses, in the variety of locations, determinants and content—all point to a growth in intelligence. Her outlook has grown more realistic, as shown by the increase in D%, and she is more discriminating, as noted by her more elaborate description of concepts.

The appearance of four human movement responses at this early age shows a ready access to a rich fantasy life. That her external surroundings have become more stimulating to her during the past year is seen in her responsiveness to the color areas which were ignored the year before. Some apprehension in this relationship to her environment seems likely, in view of the first response given in this record, "A Japanese boy, just standing waiting for something to happen. Maybe he heard a bomb."

The 4M, an unusual amount for this age, may be reflecting a kind of pseudo-maturity which results from an attempt to understand adult relationships that are disturbing to her. A similar overproduction of M was noted in the records of six-year-olds in the longitudinal study whose parents were having marital problems.

The color responses themselves suggest an egocentric reaction which is not uncommon at this age. In her struggle for adjustment to this increase of environmental stimuli, the sensitivity to social situations noted in the first Rorschach has been pushed into the background. Since this egocentricity seems to have supplanted, to a degree, her former unusual social sensitivity, Amy is no doubt reacting to her environment more in keeping with her age level than was the case a year ago. A certain amount of aggressiveness is noted, particularly in the kind of animals she chooses. She appears to be more apt to resort to temper tantrums and other kinds of non-conformity than was the case a year ago.

Despite these more normal childlike reactions to her environment, she has grown in ability to adapt herself to adult thinking, as shown in the increase in number of populars.

There are signs of negativism which seem to be directed toward parents, mother in particular. Amy reversed Card VII, the so-called mother card, and called it "a clown with feet spread apart." This M minus response here further emphasizes her confusion in relation to mother. There was a tendency to point out father's limitations, as noted in her response to Card IV, the so-called father card, but he is seen as a much more benevolent figure than mother, a "Santa Claus." Amy is no doubt experiencing an oedipal struggle, the incipiency of which was noted in the first record. Sex preoccupation is not as evident as was noted a year ago. Information in this regard is apparently being better assimilated at this time.

From this record, it can be seen that Amy is not only working on her relationships at home but, as has already been suggested, she has ventured "abroad." She is less retiring than a year ago but is struggling somewhat apprehensively with her social relationships. Her defenses, however, seem adequate to take care of any anxiety that may arise.

Amy's behavior during the year between the first and second Rorschachs highlights some of the new developments found in this protocol. It was during this interval between two and a half and three and a half years of age that Amy became interested in coloring books and was able to color within lines very successfully. As a matter of fact, by the time of the second Rorschach, she was challenged by pictures with stripes, dots, broom handles, small flowers, and other details that required skill at keeping within lines. Shortly after her third birthday she asked to be taught to read. She brought nursery rhyme books, pointed to the words one by one and said, "What do these words say?" Her family refused to cooperate in this venture, however. Evidently she was not discouraged by their refusal, since it was later discovered that she had taught herself to read.

Early in this interval before her third birthday, Amy began to have imaginary companions. She demanded they be given a place in the family, at the same time recognizing, "Of course, they are 'imagerary.'" Her favorite companion was a little black fox, which she had allegedly brought up from the basement and they would play on the living-room floor, rolling over one another and romping about the room. When she began, a few months later, to play with a five-year-old girl next door, the imaginary companions disappeared. Amy was still too shy to go to the other child's home but was very happy to play with her in her own home.

She was at this time quite realistic in appraising her own behavior. At Christmas, before she was three years old, when she was asked what Santa Claus was going to bring her, she would name the toys she wanted and add, "and ashes and switches." A kindly neighbor who had asked the questions reassured her that she would receive only toys, since good children get toys and bad ones "ashes and switches," but Amy patiently explained, "I'll get toys *and* ashes and switches because sometimes I'm good and sometimes I'm bad."

During this period, around the age of three, Amy showed more rivalry than at any time before or since. If her father and mother were dancing to radio music, she would try to get between them and would demand that her father dance with her. This jealousy went beyond parent relationships. Her aunt mentioned a cute child elsewhere and Amy asked, "Was she nicer'n me?" It was around this time also that she told her aunt that she was glad the aunt had not married. "If you were married, you would have a little girl," and added with eyes flashing, "and I would fight with her." It was not difficult for her thus to express her feelings of aggression—at least in her home and family relationships.

Only six months intervened between the second and third records.

Amy's Rorschach Protocol at the Four Year Level

Performance	Inquiry	Scoring		
I 1. It could be a man in the middle.	1. He's standing up and holding his hands up.	D	M	H
	a. The whole thing is a pumpkin face —see its eyes and mouth.	(WS	F	obj)
2. This could be a clown with a tassel on his cap. It could be two clowns, one on each side. It	2. They're standing very straight with their arms out. That's what the mess is—ju st arms.	D	M	H

Performance	Inquiry	Scoring		
would be better if it didn't have so much mess around.	I didn't know what it was at first.			
II 1. The two little red things look like socks.	1. They have feet and this looks like heel and toe. (T.L. Would still be socks if gray).	D	F	obj
2. Elephants.	2. They have trunks. They're shaking hands with their trunks.	W	M	A P
III 1. Two gooses.	1. Because of their beaks and they stand like geese. They're both lady geese and	D	F	A
	a. Here's two fishes ready to bite their tails.	(D	FM	A)
		D	F	A P
2. A butterfly or	2. (Why a butterfly?) They have wings. (How do you see it?) Just a butterfly.			
3. A hairbow. You can say whichever you want. It looks like both.	3. The parts that stick out are like loops. (T.L. Would be butterfly and bow if gray).	D	F	obj P
V4. These look like monkeys.	4. They have long tails and their heads are bent down looking at their tails.	D	FM	A
IV 1. A man with a mean look.	1. He's jumping up and banging his big feet against the ground. (Why mean?) He's not pretty. Here's his head and his arms and his feet, and I guess this must be his penis.	W	M,m	H

Performance	*Inquiry*	*Scoring*		
2. A stove	2. It doesn't look so much like a stove now, but I thought it was the right shape.	D	F	obj
V 1. A butterfly with big wings.	1. (What makes you think of a butterfly?) The wings and the feelers. (How do you see it?) It's standing still in the air. I could catch it. I could catch any butterflies if they weren't so fast. If I had wings I could do better.	W	F	A P
VI 1. A caterpillar with	1. It's the shape of a caterpillar.	D	F	A
2. Sunshine behind it.	2. Sunshine because lighter and darker.	D	cF	N
3. Funny bottle of ink.	3. Ink because it's dark.	Dr	FC'	obj
4. Two heads and two arms. It's a baby with two heads and two arms.	4. We saw a baby like that in *Life Magazine*. It's lying and staring waiting for its mommy and daddy to cut one head off so it won't die.	W	M-	H
VII 1. Two clowns.	1. They're talking to each other.	W	M	H
2. Butterfly.	2. It's got wings. It looks like the dead butterfly we saw outside of your apartment house.	D	F	A
VIII 1. Two pink tigers climbing up both sides of a	1. Here and here.	D	FM,F/C	A P
2. Christmas tree.	2. (What made you think of a tree?)	D	FC	pl

Performance	Inquiry	Scoring
	The big tall top and the three colors. If it didn't have that pointed top it wouldn't look like a tree so much.	
IX V1. A dog, a big dog.	1. Here are its eyes and mouth and its ears, of course. It has a green jacket on. It's sitting on its haunches.	W FM,FC A
X 1. Monkeys climbing up	1. (Upper gray)	D FM A
2. A tree.	2. It's shaped like a tree and the monkeys are climbing it.	D F pl
3. Two pink clowns.	3. They're looking at each other. They have a butterfly in their mouths. One wing is in each clown's mouth.	D M,FC H (D F A)
4. Two green caterpillars.	4. Here.	D FC A P
5. Clouds of an orange color. Lots of color that don't look like much. There's too many pictures on here for me to say them all.	5. The shape, and clouds are sometimes that color.	D KF,CF Cl

In the third protocol, Amy's superior intelligence continues to be demonstrated in all the areas pointed out in the two previous records. There is the added factor here of trying to achieve beyond capacity. Twenty-five responses for a four-year-old is most unusual. The protocol also contains statements to confirm this need to show her ability: Human movement has increased, she delineates form more in detail, her D% has increased, content is more varied. In addition, conformity to group thinking, as indicated by five populars, is beyond what could be expected of a child who was not yet four years old.

Amy was still functioning in an introversive frame of reference, but there is evidence of a continued struggle toward more outgoing behavior. The use of color in this record suggests increased maturity in handling outside contacts, as evidenced by the FC responses. These obvious attempts at conformity are not always successful, however, since some of the color responses are forced.

It is in this record that she introduced her dog on Card IX. This response comes on the card to which she was unable to associate at age two and on which six months ago she saw grass in a playmate's yard; it seems significant, especially when she continued to cling to this dog concept through the years. It seems possible that this is the remnant of her "imaginary" companions that she felt called upon to abandon when she began to venture outside the home.

Amy's aggressiveness at this time is no doubt shown in overt behavior—temper tantrums, for example. Even though such outbursts might arouse some anxiety within her, she seems capable of adequately handling such feelings. The sensitivity that was noted in the first record and repressed in the second does not reappear in this record. Little c has been again superseded by color responses in her struggle to adjust to her environmental stimuli.

A slight note of depression is seen both in her use of achromatic color and in content. That this depressive trend is connected with increasing sex information and an accompanying confusion, is suggested by her responses to Card VI, the so-called sex card. Instead of the more age-appropriate response of a "turtle" given in the previous record, she gives four responses, three of which are original and one of which is a K. The last response of "a two-headed baby" with its M minus quality, denotes added feelings of anxiety. One has the impression that this child is at present overstimulated with her increasing knowledge in the area of sex, and is in the throes of trying to assimilate this latest information without success, as yet.

Father is seen as a definitely mean figure with a futilely, aggressive manner. One can see another figure being equated with mother— perhaps the aunt, at whose apartment she saw the "butterfly" on the same card. The equating of these two figures seems to arouse some anxiety in Amy.

During the six months interval preceding the above Rorschach, Amy's family had noted that she had a tendency to set her sights too high; she also seemed to be unable to accept help in attaining her goals. An example of this was reported in which she insisted upon wrapping the Christmas gifts she was sending. She would accept no help and yet could not be reassured that they were all right since it was not difficult for her to realize that they were "te'ible." Amy pounded her heels on the floor in a rage when she had tried desperately, but unsuccessfully to make a perfect performance of gift wrapping. This is just one of a number of such incidents and tantrums that she and her family suffered through during this period.

By her fourth birthday, Amy's speech difficulty which had been connected with "r's" and "l's" had straightened out. It was about this time she made another assault in the subject of reading. She would ask, for example, "What does T—I—M—E spell? I think it would be 'time' because it's on the front of *Time Magazine.*" She was still discouraged in the matter of learning to read but the family cooperated to the extent of spelling words for her when she took up letter writing again. She printed her words in capitals.

During the six months interval between the second and third Rorschachs Amy continued to play with the little girl next door but was still too shy to play with more than one child at a time or to visit the homes of other children.

At this time the aunt first sensed mother's resentment toward her as a rival for Amy's affection. While this was never an open issue, there is no doubt that Amy sensed the situation early and handled it in a mature fashion. Amy continued to seek and receive sex information. One cannot help note that Amy was probably surfeited with knowledge in the sex area, while denied satisfaction in the area of learning to read.

There was an interval of one year between the third and fourth Rorschachs.

Amy's Rorschach Protocol at the Five Year Level

Performance	Inquiry	Scoring	
I 1. A funny man.	1. WS. It's just his face. Has big ears and here are his eyes and his mouth. If it were rounder it would be a Jack-O-Lantern.	WS F	Hd

Performance	Inquiry	Scoring		
	a. These tiny spots could be bees buzzing around.	(dd	FM	A)
II 1. Two elephants putting their trunks together.		W	FM	A P
2. This could be a butterfly between their legs.	2. It has wings like a butterfly and it's red. It's sitting perched on the elephants' knees.	D	FM,FC	A
3. Caps on top of the elephants' heads.	3. They look like stocking caps because they're so long. They could be any color.	D	F	obj
III 1. A ribbon bow.	1. Shape and color.	D	FC	obj P
	a. These could be two ducks (D)	(D	F	A)
V2. Two little China boys going along holding	2. China because they have such round heads.	W	M	H
3. Sticks.	(China-Chinese).	D	F	obj
4. Fourth of July fire crackers. (outer red).	4. They're so funny shaped and red, and they're falling from the air. (Outer red).	D	FC,m	obj
IV 1. A giant jumping up and down.	1. W. Because he's so huge and has such big feet.	W	M	H
V 1. A bug with big wings.	1. W (Points out parts). It's just standing still.	W	F	A P
VI V1. A fur coat. See its sleeves.	1. Because it's wooly (feels it). It isn't really wooly but it looks it.	W	Fc	obj
V2. Some grass down below.	2. (Wing detail). It's curled up like grass.	D	cF	N
3. There's a coat rack.	3. (Dark detail in center)	D	F	obj

	Performance	Inquiry	Scoring		

VII V1. Two kids lean-   1. W. (Points out   W M,cF   H
      ing together and   parts). Their hair
      dancing.   is fuzzy.

VIII 1. Some woman   1. W. Her hair is   W M-,Fc   H
      with a big fluffy   mussy and hides
      skirt and jacket. her face. She's
      That's her hair.   standing like a
      (Points to   queen.
      gray).

    2. Two pink sheep   2. Sheep aren't really   D FM,F/C A P
      crawling up   pink but these are.
      over something.

IX V1. A pink dog   1. He's standing with W M,FC   A
      wearing overalls his feet far apart.
      and a green   He's a story dog
      jacket.   with arms and legs
                like people. He's
                standing on his
                hind feet, with his
                hands on his hips.
                He could talk, I
                suppose.

X 1. There's so much   1. It's a king that be- W M-,FC   H
      here, I couldn't longs to that
      name it all. A   queen before.
      great big man.   (Why a king?) Be-
      There's a big   cause he's dressed
      blue bow on his up so much. Other
      stomach, and he men would wear
      has a tall hat   red on their neck-
      and big blue   tie, but they
      gloves and little wouldn't wear red
      green socks.   otherwise, and
                he's got a red
                coat. He's stand-
                ing all spread out.

    2. A carrot on   2. Shape and color.   D FC   fd
      each side.

The fourth Rorschach, given near Amy's fifth birthday, shows many changes during the preceding year. She is no longer putting forth the effort to achieve at a maximum but is still struggling in her attempt to find a more satisfactory adjustment to her environment. She is adopting a somewhat superficial intellectualized approach to emotional contacts, as shown in her forced FC's. Though she is permitting herself less emotional freedom than would be expected from her age level, she can at times let herself go emotionally. The social sensitivity noted in the first record is again apparent and in full force, as evidenced by the *c* responses.

The relationship with parents seems to be of a more relaxed nature than a year ago. Mother is seen as a peer and the two are mutually dependent "kids dancing." Increasing feminine identification is apparent in her use and description of clothes—caps, fur coats, fluffy skirt and jacket, and others. Father is seen as an aggressive authoritative figure. In addition, Amy seems to be more than ever aware of the maleness of the father figure. In fact, the response of "jumping up and down," which appears at this age for the second time, is evidently connected with Amy's understanding and/or fantasy about the sex act.

Her own relationship with each parent is realistic and not particularly disturbing to her. However, one might suspect from the large number of human movement responses, some of which are poor in form, that she is trying without too much success to assume a more adult role than she is capable of in understanding the relationship between the two of them. As was noted earlier, a similar high production of M was found among children in the longitudinal study whose parents were having some marital adjustment difficulties about which the children were not only aware, but greatly concerned. Any altercations that Amy's parents may be having at this time are making Amy uncomfortable and she seems to be struggling to understand what is going on between them. Preoccupation with sex information is still present, and, whereas there has been some successful integration of this, there are indications that sex and aggression are being correlated in these integrative efforts. Her feelings about male figures could be such that she is already approaching the so-called "latency" period, in which girls characteristically play with girls and boys with boys.

According to the above record, Amy, at the age of five, shows in her Rorschach an awareness of social interactions, especially between parents, and has learned to apply a superficial control to her feelings in this regard. Her struggle to maintain this intellectual control and to integrate the multiplicity of stimuli, from without as well as from within herself, occasionally breaks through. She is fast assuming a feminine identification, with indications that she is already in the latency period.

It was in the year preceding this Rorschach that Amy began to use subtle ways of expressing her aggressive feelings, as evidenced by an incident that occurred just before her fifth birthday. Amy came from the back yard into the kitchen where her mother was baking pies. She was wearing a one-piece snowsuit which was so tight at the ankles that her shoes were likely to come off with it, and which she did not like to remove herself. When her mother said she was busy and could not help with it, Amy attempted to wait her out. She pulled the zipper down to her waist, pulled her arms out and meandered about the kitchen with the sleeves dragging on the floor. Her mother finally put her foot down saying, "Now you go take that snowsuit off and stop dragging it through the flour. Imagine! A great big girl like you can't take off her own snowsuit!" Amy recognized that further protest was useless and obeyed with apparent good grace. However, at the dinner table that evening, she rehearsed the events of the day to her father, as was her custom. She included the story of the altercation with her mother, ending it with, "And do you know what, Daddy? When I'm a big girl and I bake pies, Mommy will say to me, 'A big girl like you can't bake a couple of pies without spilling flour all over the kitchen floor.' "

On another occasion, when an older child told her she had dirty spots on her face, she promptly replied, "You have dirty spots, too, but they're on your personality."

Amy seldom had temper tantrums now but still showed occasional outbursts, usually arising from her continued, but not wholly successful, struggle toward independent action. She found it difficult to accept help in any of her undertakings.

Shyness was lessening but was still evident. She would play with several children at a time now and enjoyed having parties at her home; but she would not go to parties at the homes of other children. Not only did she play exclusively with little girls, but when she played house, no husband was even mentioned and all of her dolls had to be girls. She announced at one point that, if she had any boy babies when she grew up, she would give them to her mother to bring up for her. On one occasion, when she pressed her aunt into service to play dolls, one of the conversational questions put to Amy was, "And how is your husband, Mrs. Jones?" "Oh, didn't you know?", Amy said. "He died." When sympathy was expressed, Amy said, "Oh, that's all right. He drank himself to death but he left me very well off."

It was also just before her fifth birthday that she expressed her awareness and acceptance of the "flash" quarrels her parents sometimes had. She had mentioned casually to her mother that her father sometimes started quarrels and quickly added, "Of course, if he starts them, Mommy, you always finish them." When her mother expressed contrition, Amy said, "That's all right, Mommy. Everybody gets into scraps sometimes. We all know nobody means them."

At six years of age, slightly more than a year after the fourth Rorschach, Amy gave the following:

Amy's Rorschach Protocol at the Six Year Level

	Performance	Inquiry	Scoring	
I	1. A butterfly.	1. It's flying.	W FM	A P
	2. A man making funny faces like Dad does sometimes. He's being funny.	2. (Center figure).	D M	H
II	1. Two leaves joined together.	1. Just the shape. (All the black).	W F	pl
	2. Two eagles saying hello to each other.	2. (Upper red).	D M	A
	3. A butterfly down here.	3. It has wings and it's flying.	D FM	A
III	1. A butterfly.	1. It has wings and it's flying.	D FM	A P
	2. Two sea lions.	2. (Outer red). They're swimming.	D FM	A
	3. Two men saying "Howdy" and tipping their hats.		W M	H P
IV	1. A great big man, a giant.	1. He's making ready to jump.	W M	H
	2. A tree stump behind him.		D F	obj
	3. A dog jumping.		W FM	A
V	1. A bat.	1. He has his wings spread ready to take off.	W FM	A P
	2. Some frogs' legs.	2. (Lower d).	d F	Ad

	Performance		Inquiry		Scoring	
VI	1. A snake.	1.	It's crawling along. (Center dark detail).	D	FM	A
	2. A butterfly under it.	2.	Its wings are fluttering.	D	FM	A
	V3. A tree with	3.	It looks more like a tree than something else in shape.	W	F	pl
	V4. Two puppy dogs sticking their heads from behind it.			d	FM	Ad
	V5. A little piece of grass in the sun.	5.	It's lighter and darker.	D	cF	N
VII	1. Two elf men on	1.	They're talking to each other. Elves because of caps.	W	M	(H)
	2. A big silken ribbon.	2.	Silk because it looks "feely."	D	cF	obj
VIII	1. Two pink monkeys climbing	1.	Monkeys aren't pink really.	D	FM,F/C	A P
	2. A beautifully-colored Christmas tree.	2.	Shape and colors.	D	FC	pl
IX	1. This is my dog! He has huge ears and orange trousers and a green jacket.	1.	He's standing on his hind legs and has hands on hips. He's like dogs in funny books, dressed up as a man.	W	M,FC	A
X	1. Two lobsters.	1.	(Outer green). Shape.	D	F	A
	V2. Two pink men. They're bakers dressed in pink.	2.	They have baker hats on and they're putting something in the oven.	D	M,FC	H
	3. Two little men.	3.	(Upper gray) They're tipping their hats.	D	M	H
	4. Butterfly.	4.	(Inner blue) Just the shape.	D	F	A
	5. Two beautiful dogs.	5.	(Inner yellow) Just their shape.	D	F	A

Performance	Inquiry	Scoring	
6. Two baby ele-phants.	6. (Upper gray) They're climbing something.	D FM D CF	A N
7. Little patches of grass.	7. (Lower green) Just because it's green.		

This fifth Rorschach portrays an unusually rich fantasy life. Amy is constantly alert to the amenities of interpersonal relationships but the struggle in this regard does not arouse the same anxiety that was noted in former years. Although she can conform to adult standards of thinking, there is a certain amount of superficiality to her conformity. This is fortunate, since it leaves her free to act at times like a spontaneous child.

The relationship with each parent is comfortable, though somewhat over-adult, as noted in her response to the father and mother cards. She and mother appear as peers in a feminine, somewhat make-believe world. Father is masculine, aggressive, and a little foolish —"making funny faces." There is a continued interest in sex and, specifically, in the relationship between mother and father. This concern with the process of procreation is seen in her response to the last card, "two pink men—they're bakers, dressed in pink, have bakers' hats and they're putting something in the oven." That she is aware of the sex act is further suggested by the sequence of the snake and butterfly on Card VI.

Amy's productive capacity has again assumed a high level, no doubt due to the solution of some of these relationship problems. There seems to be a concomitant increase in independent thought and action, with a very realistic approach to all kinds of environmental stimulation, whether from without or within. In fact, this is an amazingly mature Rorschach to be given by a child barely six years of age.

At the time of this fifth Rorschach, Amy's parents were still ignoring her attempts to learn to read. Amy had evidently solved any problems she might have had in this regard by teaching herself, since it was discovered a few months later, when she entered first grade, that she could read well.

Amy had been in attendance at Sunday School for some time, but it was shortly before the above Rorschach that she decided she was not going any more. "They tell you such silly stories and expect you to believe them. Now that story about those people that got chased out of the place where they lived because they ate one little apple from the wrong tree. No *person* would punish people for a little mistake like that, and you know *God* wouldn't. You know, Mama, that story just plain stinks." A few months later she cornered her aunt with the direct question, "Now tell me the truth, Aunt Mimi, *do* people *really* go to heaven when they die?"

During this year, Amy's shyness almost disappeared. She went willingly on errands to other houses and was happy to attend children's parties. Amy knew this was a victory for her, and was proud of it. When a neighbor mentioned concern over the extreme shyness of her little grandson, Amy told her not to worry: "He'll be all right. I used to be just like that and I'm not at all any more."

It was also evident from Amy's verbalizations and behavior that she continued to be interested in and concerned with sex. On one occasion she indicated her awareness of the sexual relations between parents by implying that she knew what happened when parents retire after an evening in which father has shown amorous advances to mother. She was reluctant to go to sleep at her early bedtime during this period. Although her oedipal feelings were apparently pretty well under control, the fact remained that mother, still Amy's rival, had a relationship denied to Amy. (It was in this interval too that she reminisced about her traumatic feelings three years before in regard to seeing her mother's pubic hair.)

Amy had been taught to discuss sex only with members of her immediate family. On one occasion, she told her aunt about a pregnancy in the neighborhood and ended it with, "Sh-sh, Uncle Frank is in the next room." When Amy was asked if she thought he did not know the facts of life, she replied, "He does, but he doesn't know that I do."

At the author's request, Amy was given the following Rorschach at an age that corresponded to those of the children in the longitudinal study described earlier.

Amy's Rorschach Protocol at the Age of Six Years, Eight Months

	Performance	Inquiry	Scoring		
I	1. A face.	1. (WS) It's a Halloween mask. Here are its eyes and nose and mouth.	WS	F	obj
	2. A bat.	2. (W) There are its wings. It's flying.	W	FM	A P

Performance	Inquiry	Scoring

3. Two little animals looking at each other over bumps.
  3. I can't say what kind of animals. They could be little men. You can see just their heads.
  d M   Hd

II 1. Two little bugs looking at each other.
  1. (Upper red).
  D FM   A

2. A butterfly.
  2. Q. It has very fancy wings and here are its legs and its body and it's flying. Q. Well, it's red, too.
  D FM,FC A

3. Two elephants sitting trunk to trunk.
  3. (All the black).
  W FM   A P

III 1. Two men tipping hats to each other.
  1. (All the black).
  W M   H P

2. Two little bugs.
  2. (Outer red).
  D F   A

3. A bow tie.
  3. It's shaped like a bow and it's red.
  D FC obj P

V4. Little choir boys standing back to back,
  4. The hats become the colored boys' heads and the other men's legs are the candles and the colored boys' legs are the other guy's heads. (What makes you think of *colored* boys?) The color and they have fuzzy hair.
  W M,FC' FcH

5. Holding candles.
    D F   obj

IV 1. A big giant sitting
  1. (W) He has huge legs and a little head and teeny arms.
  W M   H

V2. On a tree stump.
    D F   obj

V3. Two women beside a great big
  3. They're standing with their hands
  D M,cF H

Performance	Inquiry	Scoring

| | tree with a lot of hair sticking out. | touching the tree. You can't see their legs but they have lots of fluffy hair. | | | |

V 1. A bat with big wings.

1. It has a little body and big wings and here are its feet. It's ready to start flying.

W FM A P

VI 1. Two men back to back.

1. They have their hands out as if they're tipping their hats to ladies but you can't see much hat or the ladies.

W M H

V2. Little patch of grass.

2. ("Wings"). The way it's sticking in tufts.

D cF N

Λ3. An enormous candle holder with a candle in it and a light.

3. The long thing's the candle. Now the grass becomes sparkling light. Q. It's light and dark.

W F,cF obj

VII 1. Two little elves talking to each other.

1. (Upper ⅔). They're standing on something, I guess, but I don't know what.

W M (H)

V2. Oh, boy! What funny-looking elephants!

2. (Same as 1). Here are their trunks. They're standing on their hind legs balancing something. They're circus elephants.

W FM A

VIII 1. Two buffaloes climbing up a

1. & 2. Tree because of its shape. Buffaloes are brown but you can't say brown buffaloes because the color is pink.

D FM,F/C A P

Performance	Inquiry	Scoring		
2. Beautiful colored trees.		D	FC	pl
IX 1. Little elephants with pointed caps on.	1. (Orange detail). They're sitting on something stretching their hands out.	D	M	H
V2. A dog with green jacket and orange pants and great big ears.	2. He's a story book dog standing on his hind legs with his hands on his hips. I've seen this dog ever since I was four years old.	W	M,FC	A
X 1. Two cooks holding a	1. (Pink figures.) Cooks, because of their big hats.	D	M	H
2. Cake they baked.	2. The cake is being taken from the oven.	D	F	fd
3. Carrots.	3. (Outer brown details). Shape and color.	D	FC	fd
4. Birds.	4. (Inner yellow) Shape and birds could be that color.	D	FC	A
5. The blue things are spiders.	5. (Outer blue). They have lots of legs.	D	F	A P
6. Two little elves.	6. (Pink figures). They're eating something between them.	D	M	(H)
7. Little bugs looking at each other.	7. (Top gray).	D	FM	A

This record, taken at six years and eight months, again brings into relief Amy's basic introversiveness. Her affect control is still somewhat forced and very mature for her age, as evidenced by her color responses. Her fantasy involvement, as shown in her movement responses, is pronounced. At the same time, she is able to think like other people and to act conformingly and comfortably in their presence. Her intelligence is functioning at the usually high level—a large number of good form responses. Sensitivity to social situations is also at a high functioning level. Sex still holds a fascination for her and there is every indication that her curiosity is being satisfied, but with some degree of anxiety connected with it.

There have been some changes in her relationship to her parents, as shown by the responses on Cards IV and VII. She still feels on a par with mother, but is beginning to think of her as somewhat masculine and dominant. The father figure offers no threat to her—in fact, a desire to establish a closer relationship with him is noted. References to men and boys are more common, with the added inference that her interest in the other sex has taken a sort of romantic turn.

In general, Amy seems to be functioning as a mature, independent, sensitive little girl with an effectively operating method of defense. That she has insecure feelings at times, perhaps when her independence is taxed, is shown by an increase in food responses. The lack of overwhelming anxiety signs, however, attest to the adequate handling of such feelings.

At the time this record was obtained, Amy had been in first grade for about two months. Her mother went with her on the first day to give registration information and, after this was done, joined other parents standing about the room. In a few minutes Amy left her seat to walk over to her mother and said, "You can go home now, Mama. I don't need you for anything." Later reports from the teacher were to the effect that, because Amy could already read, she was being given extra work, that she was liked by her classmates and in turn seemed to enjoy them. Still later in the semester, Amy warned her mother not to expect perfect lessons in her workbooks "because the kids don't like you if you are too perfect."

At Christmas time, Amy gave up the idea of a literal Santa Claus. In retrospect, she said she would not have wanted to miss the excitement and mystery of the Santa Claus myth in her preschool years and does not think she was upset by the disillusionment. However, she thinks parents should tell their children the truth just before they start to school so that they will not hear it from other children.

Amy was not as superior in motor skills as in intellectual areas. When she found herself inferior to many of her classmates in rope jumping, and expressed her concern about this, her parents handled the situation by taking time on a Saturday morning to turn the rope for her and teach her the proper rhythm.

The seventh Rorschach was given a year after the sixth, when Amy was in the second grade.

Amy's Rorschach Protocol at the Age of Seven Years, Eight Months

	Performance	Inquiry	Scoring		
I	1. Two little elves looking at each other over a mountain.	1. The mountain has two round hills.	d	M	(H)
	2. Two great big eagles with wings spread.	2. (Upper wings on each side). They're ready to pounce.	D	FM	A
	3. Could all be a cat face.	3. WS. It's a Halloween face. Here are eyes, nose and mouth.	WS	F	obj
II	1. Two queens talking to each other.	1. (Upper red). One little face is better than the other. They have red crowns. It's just the upper halves. I can't see their legs.	D	M,FC	Hd
	2. Two little men sitting with their backs to each other.	2. They have tall peaked hats. (center d)	d	M	H
	3. Butterfly.	3. It's a good butterfly! It's standing still. It's red but I don't know what kind it is. I know it's not a Monarch and I don't know many kinds.	D	FC	A
	4. Two elephants holding trunks together.	4. (Popular).	W	FM	A P
III	1. Two butlers.	1. They're dressed in uniforms. They're	W	M,K	H P

Performance	*Inquiry*	*Scoring*	

	lifting something hot. Q. You can see steam around it. It looks misty.		
2. Big red bow tie between them.	2. Right shape and it's red.	D FC	obj P
3. Two bugs.	3. (Outer red). I don't know enough yet to know the kinds of bugs.	D F	A
V4. Two little choir boys	4. They're colored boys. Q. The color it is in and their fuzzy hair.	W M,FC'	H
5. With candles.	5. The candles are lighted, see this lighter part? They're more like torches.	D F,cF	obj
4. (C o n t d .) They're marching.			

IV	1. A giant.	1. He has especially big feet. He's leaning against a stump.	W M	H
			(D F	obj)
	2. A bat.	2. (W) Not as good as one of the other bats. I guess it's flying.	W FM	A
	V3. Two women.	3. They have long hair. It floats in the air. Here are their faces and their hands holding onto the stump.	D M,cF	H

| V | 1. A bat. | 1. Flying. | W FM | A P |
| | V2. Turned this way it's more like a butterfly. | 2. Flying. | W FM | A P |

| VI | 1. Insect with beating wings. | 1. I don't know what it is but it's not a butterfly. | D FM | A |

Performance	Inquiry	Scoring		
V2. Two funny-looking people standing back to back.	2. They're stretching their arms out in a gesture.	W	M	H
VII 1. Two little people talking to each other.	1. (Upper ⅔).	W	M	H
V2. Two little elephants rearing up.	2. (Same as 1).	W	FM	A
VIII 1. Two pink bears climbing up on	1. They look like bears. They just happened to color them pink.	D	FM,F/C	A P
2. A Christmas tree.	2. Christmas tree because of its bright colors.	D	FC	pl
IX 1. Two people facing each other.	1. (Orange). Their hats make them look like witches. Their hands are stretched out.	D	M	H
V2. A dog all dressed up standing on his hind legs. He has a green jacket and orange pants.	2. You remember my old dog! I'm sure I do.	W	M,FC	A
X 1. Two spiders.	1. (P)	D	F	A P
2. Two people in the middle.	2. They have funny little faces and stocking caps. They're smoking pipes.	D	M	H
		(D	F	obj)
3. Two mice.	3. (Gray-brown) They're the color of mice and you can see little legs.	D	FC	A
4. A boot.	4. (Outer brown) The shape.	D	F	obj
5. Green worms.	5. Shape and color.	D	FC	A P
6. Two cats.	6. (Top gray) They're climbing a little tree	(D	F	pl)

Performance	Inquiry	Scoring		
V7. Turned this way the people look like cooks.	7. They have big cooks' hats on and they're setting a tray of cookies down carrying it between them.	D	M	H
		(D	F	fd)

Amy's seventh Rorschach record, given at the age of seven years and eight months, contains most of the concepts of the preceding years; but they are handled in a slighly different manner. There is more anxiety manifest here in both determinants and content. Amy seems to be resorting more to fantasy now than at any other time. Most of her people are "funny-looking" or removed from reality, like elves, queens, giants, and witches. This is no doubt, in part, a function of her age level. Her anxious moments seem to be in connection with social contacts but this anxiety, as usual, is adequately dealt with. There is an absence of the struggle seen in this connection in some of the former records. Her sex interest still excites some concern, but this is not overwhelming. She seems again to be using her long-established sensitivity to social situations. She would no doubt give the impression of a most adequately-functioning, conforming child, who is successfully dealing with any anxiety she might be feeling.

In the second grade at this time, Amy had a teacher who was intelligent and compulsive. She demanded perfection from Amy and embarrassed her by saying, "A little girl of *your* intelligence should not make mistakes." Her use of the paddle on other children who had academic difficulties also made Amy unhappy. However, it was this teacher who stimulated her interest in science and nature study and it was during this year that Amy started her collection of stones and fossils, the first of a series of many collections.

Her attempt to understand the feelings of others is evidenced by the following incident: On one occasion she commented upon her unsuccessful effort at teaching the little girl next door how to tell time. When the aunt suggested that perhaps the child, who was two years older than Amy, might sometimes find it convenient not to know the time, Amy commented, "Maybe you are right, but do you think it could be that she doesn't like to learn from a younger child?"

During the year between this and the preceding Rorschach, Amy suffered her first illness. She had measles and recurrent bronchitis and developed an infection that resulted in a tonsillectomy. The hospital routine was described to her in advance and, when it was over, she said, "Just a breeze. It was just the way you told me it would be."

Another year intervened between the seventh and eighth Rorschachs. Amy was in the third grade at the time of the eighth record.

Amy's Rorschach Protocol at the Age of Eight Years, Eight Months

	Performance	Inquiry	Scoring		
I	1. Little gnome heads.	1. They're looking at each other over something. (Top center).	d	m	(Hd)
	2. Two eagles flying.	2. (Wing details).	D	FM	A
	3. A Halloween face.	3. (WS) Here are eyes and mouth and ears.	WS	F	obj
	4. A dog's head on each side.	4. They're shaggy like English sheep dogs.	de	Fc	Ad
	V5. Little pixies.	5. They're singing and these are their notes.	d (dd	M F	(Hd) notes)
	6. A snail out of its shell crawling up (dr).	6. dr.	dr	FM	A
	7. Two mittens. (I used to hate this but I like it now).		d	F	obj
	8. Boys' heads and faces.	8. They're singing too.	dr	M	Hd
II	1. Little queens.	1. (Upper red). They're talking to each other. They have robes and high headdresses on.	d	M	H
	2. A butterfly.	2. He's shaped like one. He's flying.	D	FM	A
	3. Two tired little men.	3. They're leaning on each other.	D	M	H
	4. Two elephants.	4. (W) They're putting their trunks together as if to say, "To your health!"	W	M	A P

Performance	Inquiry	Scoring		
V5. A man's head like on a Tobey jar.	5. Here.	d	F	Hd
III 1. Here are the butlers.	1. They're serving wine out of a fancy container.	W (D	M F	H P obj)
V2. And the colored choir boys marching along holding their	2. The boys are dark-colored and have fuzzy hair.	W	M,FC'	cFH
3. Big candles.	3. You can see the lighter flame. They're like torches.	D	F,cF	obj
4. A big bow.	4. Shape alone.	D	F	obj P
5. Two seahorses.	5. (Outer red). They have seaweed sticking on them. It's rough like seaweed.	D (D	F cF	F A N)
IV 1. A stump.	1. Shape.	D	F	obj
2. A giant with a tiny head and two big large feet. (It's silly to say both big and large. Don't put that down.)	2. He's jumping up and down. He has shaggy hair	W	M,Fc	H
V3. Old witches. Oh, boy, look how wonderful.	3. They're tied to a stake and	D	M	(H)
V4. These two women with real long hair are talking to them.	4. These women are trying to persuade the witches to be good people like them. Their hair looks fluffy.	D	M,Fc	H
V 1. A bat to begin with.	1. (W) It's flying.	W	FM	A P
2. A rabbit's head.		d	F	Ad
V3. This way it's a butterfly flying. (I don't like this one. It's too simple. At first		W	FM	A P

Performance	*Inquiry*	*Scoring*		
it seems easy but there's not much to find on it).				
VI (This is hard).				
V1. Siamese twins.	1. They're stuck to-gether back to back. I guess they're just standing wishing they were just plain twins, not Siamese.	W	M,m	H
V2. A fire at the bottom.	2. It has flames lighter and darker in color.	D	cF	Fire
3. A snake's head.	3. I guess it's the whole snake.	D	F	Ad
4. A silhouette of a little Dutch girl.	4. (dr.)	dr	F	Hd
VII 1. Two people talking.	1. They're sitting talking. (Upper ⅔).	W	M	H
2. Two dog dishes.	2. (Lower ⅓). They're shaped like Jupiter's dishes and look deep like his.	D	F	obj
	a. Taken to-gether, that bottom part could be a butterfly fly-ing.	(D	FM	A)
V3. Elephants.	3. (Upper ⅔). They're pranc-ing.	W	FM	A
VIII 1. Two bears climbing up		D	FM	A P
2. Rocks.	2. Colored rocks.	D	CF	N
3. Two butterflies, one orange and one pink. (I like the colored ones. They're prettier).	3. Shape and color. They're flying, one almost on top of the other.	D	FC,FM	A

Performance	Inquiry	Scoring		

IX 1. Two witches.

1. (Orange). They're leaning back and fighting.   D   M   H

2. Someone humpbacked, climbing up something.

2. (Green).   D   M   H

V3. I still see that dressed up dog but don't put it down. I don't like it much any more, it's kind of babyish.

W   F   A

4. A deer's head. (d)

d   F   Ad

X 1. Two fairies.

1. (Red). Drinking out of straws.   D   M   (H)
(D   F   obj)

2. The green worms eating something.

2. Shape and color.   D   FM,FC   A P

3. I'd say it's a rabbit head, except it's too small in proportion to the worms.

3. (Popular).   D   F   Ad P

4. Two big spiders.

4. Because they have so many legs.   D   F   A P

5. Two grotesque animals fighting.

5. (Upper gray).   D   FM   A

6. Little gnomes on their hands and knees. You can see just one hand down.

6. (Inner yellow)   D   M   (H)

7. A seal.

7. (Outer brown). It's shaped like a seal and seems to have flippers instead of legs.   D   F   A

8. Two rats.

8. Color mostly and shape. (Outer gray).   D   FC   A

V9. Chefs.

9. (Pink). They   D   M   H

Performance	Inquiry	Scoring		
	have chefs' caps. They're stirring dough with a long-handled stirrer.	(D	F	obj)
V10. A fancy butter-fly of some kind.	10. (Green, including rabbit's head). It's a fancy shape.	D	F-	A

This Rorschach record, given at the age of eight years and eight months, shows a marked increase in productivity, with an adultlike approach. Anxiety is at a minimum. Her social sensitivity underlies all of Amy's activities and seems to be always on tap. This girl no longer feels the need to conform, and, what conformity there is, seems to be more genuine than that shown on her earlier Rorschachs. There is none of the impulsivity that is sometimes shown in children of this age. Even aggressiveness, portrayed in occasional content and movement responses, is well controlled and is unlikely to show up in overt actions. In the repetition of references to eating, this record indicated that Amy continues to have some insecure moments with feelings of dependency. However, this dependency has increased in strength from the previous record and is accompanied by aggressive reactions. She is still struggling with dependent-independent aspects of her development.

The gradual changes to more common and less disturbed responses on Card VII, the so-called mother card, indicate that Amy is identifying with and accepting the mother figure increasingly. Her greater awareness of mother's more dominant characteristics, however, is shown in the sequence on this particular card in this record. It may be a partial source of the conflict that Amy is having relative to her dependency needs.

Sex is becoming an increasingly dynamic force in Amy's life. In spite of the ready supply of information that she has had through the years—or, perhaps because of it—it is still difficult for her to assimilate all this information to the point where it is not of such immediate concern. Only at five years of age, has Amy given any response to Card VI (the so-called sex card) that approached the popular response. The current sex concern is partially connected with father's role; and the recurring concept of "jumping up and down" connected with the father card is no doubt related, as has been noted before, to the father's part in the sex act. This points up Amy's continued concern and preoccupation in this area. The father figure is seen as aggressive but desirable. This is indicative of the adolescent stage of heterosexual interest and, in the case of Amy, suggests a continuation of her advanced psychosexual development.

The maturity and advanced development which are indicated in this Rorschach record are likewise noted in the anecdotal material available on Amy's behavior at this time. She was apparently an eager, highly productive girl who handled her anxiety with ease. The anger feelings she experienced were expressed with a finesse that even an adult might envy. Examples of her sensitivity to social situations point up this characteristic as a quite prominent aspect of her behavior at this time also. One story illustrating this follows: The family went to a street carnival and brought along a Catholic friend of Amy's. Mother wanted to treat both of them to hot dogs, but Amy declined politely for both of them. When Amy was questioned at the end of the evening about her refusal of something which she generally enjoyed, she explained that Bonnie was Catholic and could not eat meat on Friday. Amy had foregone her own treat since Bonnie could not accept with her.

Amy's interest in collections continued and she extended it to include postcards, stamps, and dolls. This was evidently an extension of her second grade teacher's influence, although by this time Amy had progressed to the third grade. Her new teacher was a rather prosaic person who seemed threatened by Amy's precocity. At first she seemed to single Amy out in class with both positive and negative comments to her; but this died down as the year progressed, as did Amy's resentment toward her. Although there was never any attempt on the part of this teacher to encourage new intellectual interests in Amy, she, like the first two teachers, was tolerant of the child's attempts to keep herself busy.

Amy at this time liked to "scribble" verses when she had extra time in class. One such verse, written hurriedly, was as follows:

> "Arabella, Arabella, my darling, my doll,
> You are the best
> By any test
> With your lovely southern drawl."

She was well liked by her peers in school as was evidenced by her receiving what Amy looked upon as a great honor. In an impromptu election and ceremony, Amy was elected May Queen by the children in her room, and a wreath of apple blossoms was placed on her head. Three boys proposed to her after school on this occasion.

At this age, Amy usually expressed her hostility in an indirect, rather intellectualized fashion. On one occasion, when her father refused to take her on a promised jaunt because it was raining, she expressed her disappointment and anger in the following poem, entitled "Bad."

BAD

The day is bad
And Dad is mad
And I feel sad
'Cause I hate my Dad.

She let no one see the poem at the time, but a few days later she showed it to her aunt and said she felt better as soon as it was written. Amy was obviously learning the art of sublimation.

All of Amy's Rorschach records up until this time had been administered by Amy's aunt. However, the ninth was obtained by the author, who met Amy and her family for the first time on the day of the testing.

Amy's Rorschach Record at the Age of Nine Years, Eight Months

	Performance	Inquiry	Scoring		
I	1. Two little elves. (Drums on card).	1. Have little pointed hats and pointed noses. Q. Yes, they are looking at each other like this (dem.) Q. Just the heads.	d	M	Hd
	2. Two eagles. (D)	2. Head, neck and wings. Sitting like this with wings back.	D	FM	A
	3. Two little mountains.	3. Here and here. (d)	d	F	Geb
	4. Head of a Scottie dog.	4. Little ears here and nose and mouth. Looking at something.	d	FM	Ad
	V5. Looks slightly like Abraham Lincoln with his beard and	5. Here and here.	d	F	Hd

		Performance		Inquiry		Scoring		
		another Abraham Lincoln.						
II	1.	Two queen bees saying hello to each other.	1.	Wearing big crowns—saying hello to each other. (dem. with waving hands).	D	M		H
	2.	Two elephants with trunks together.	2.	Whole elephants —their trunks are up together here.	W	FM		A P
	3.	Red butterfly.	3.	Just the shape.	D	FC		A
	4.	Two elves leaning against each other (d).	4.	Back to back— leaning back to back.	d	M		(H)
III	1.	Two butlers.	1.	Head, collars and legs. Q. Standing like this. (dem). Holding something.	W	M		H P
	V2.	Two little choir boys.	2.	Holding candles.	W	M		H
	3.	Bow tie.	3.	Right here is the bow tie.	D	F		obj P
	4.	Some kind of sea thing—animal.	4.	No special way. (outer red).	D	F		A
IV	1.	A giant, tiny arms and huge feet.	1.	Head—tiny head —tiny arms. Q. Standing.	W	M		H
	V2.	Two women (usual).	2.	Standing, holding onto this with their long hair blowing back. Q. Old tree (D).	D (D	M,c F	F,M	H obj)
V	1.	Butterfly of some kind. Oh, dear (looks at me). I'm afraid that's all.	1.	With his wings out like this (dem).	W	FM		A P
VI	1.	Looks like one of those things you get in something-to-do books you cut out and	1.	W.	W	F		obj

Performance	*Inquiry*	*Scoring*		
fold them to-gether.				
2. Snake's head.		D	F	Ad
3. Kind of a cloud. (wings).	3. It just seems to look like a cloud —not anything else.	D	KF	cl
4. Kind of a can-dle holder right in here. (dr).		dr	F	obj

VII	1. Two little elves. (Upper ⅓).	1. Got a high hat and something sticking out in the back. (wings).	D	F	(H)
	2. Two little dog dishes.	2. Dog dishes—you paste them to-gether.	D	F	obj
	V3. Two ducks—funny ducks.	3. Standing. Q. Their beak. (Upper ⅔).	D	FM	A
	<4. The back of a camel I believe that is all.	4. (de)	de	F	Ad

VIII	1. Two tigerish animals climb-ing up	1. He kinda looks like a tiger.	D	FM	A P
	2. Top of a Christ-mas tree.	2. Pointed at the top and almost the color of a Christ-mas tree.	D	FC	pl
	3. Butterfly.	3. Two colors—pink and orange. Q. No, just two but-terflies.	D	FC	A
	4. Dog dishes. (blue).	4. Here and here.	D	F	obj

IX	1. I believe I kinda still see that dressed up dog.	1. Legs, arms, head and ears like Jo-Jo. Q. Large, standing up and dressed in Sunday clothes.	W	M	A
	2. Kind of rough Dutch shoe (green).	2. Heel and here is a little thing. Here is the toe. Never saw one like it.	D	F	obj

Performance	Inquiry	Scoring		
3. Little elves.	3. Just standing there. Q. Their heads.	D	M	(Hd)
4. Pink cloud. 1. (Contd.) The dog doesn't look as he used to but I still see him. Boy, I like these colors.	4. Just like a sunset.	D	KF,CF	Cl
X V1. Two little elves.	1. Holding up the cooks.	D	M	(H)
V2. Two cooks (red).	2. Cooks are holding up ice-cream for a party.	D	M	H
V3. Two scoops of ice-cream.		D	F	rd
4. A . . . not a butterfly (green) a dragon fly.	4. Wings, body. Q. Just the shape.	D	F	A
5. A little face (outer orange).	5. Face, just about to shoulders. Q. Elf.	D	F	(Hd)
6. A . . . crab (blue). Guess that's all.	6. That's all. a. Two little girls sipping soda through a straw.	D (D	F M	A P H)

While the productivity in the above record is not at the heightened level noted a year ago, it is still far above that of the average child of this age. The decrease in responses could be related to the change in examiners, but there was nothing in the relationship at the time to suggest this.

There appears, further, to be a decrease in spontaneity and an accompanying increase in anxiety shown in this record. While these factors also could be related to the new examiner, they are no doubt primarily a function of Amy's personality development. In fact, many of the changes are in the direction of adolescent reactions.

The poor quality of responses on the mother card suggests anxiety regarding the mother-child relationship. That these feelings are related to mother, and this connection has been present for some time, may be seen in the "dog dish" response on the mother card which has persisted for two or three years. This strain in her relationship with mother may be related to Amy's feelings about father at this time. The accompanying sense of rivalry with mother for his affection seems to be reflected in the second response to Card IV, "Two women—holding onto this," ("this" being the phallic symbol). Her increase in references to food, indicating an increasing feeling of insecurity and dependence, may be another reflection of this strain on mother-daughter relationships. How can she depend on a mother whose relationship to father she would like to usurp? The next step in normal heterosexual development would be an active interest in boys of her own age, and it is possible that she was already showing an active interest in this area.

Environmental pressures like those just mentioned are no doubt giving Amy some bad moments at this time, but she meets these with both conformity and retreat into fantasy. As usual, when Amy is concerned about environmental stimuli she shows a decrease in sensitivity to social situations. The more evasive and poor quality responses on Card VI, the so-called sex card, suggests a preoccupation that is met with repression and evasion in the area of sex concern. There seems throughout this record to be a slight lag in Amy's functioning at this time, which may be accounted for by her struggle to meet these present environmental pressures, both external and internal. One would predict that this situation is temporary or intermittent, however, since there is little to indicate that her defenses are not sufficiently adequate to cope with her present anxieties.

The stresses noted above in the Rorschach seemed to reflect Amy's current problems at this time. She was having difficulty with an allergy to chocolate, a food of which she was particularly fond. On previous occasions, she had had a little trouble in the form of mild urticaria, but now her allergy to this favorite food had reached a climax. In her aunt's opinion, this could have been related to a family concern over a persistent low grade infection from which her mother had been suffering and which necessitated a minor (and successful) operation shortly after. Amy's allergy seemed to decrease simultaneous with mother's recovery.

Amy's school relationships at this time were the best she had experienced so far. She was in the fourth grade with an understanding and imaginative teacher. They got along well together, although Amy was frequently chided for her obvious carelessness about her school work. This teacher shared Amy's interest in her growing collection of dolls, postcards, stones, fossils and, particularly, stamps. During this year Amy learned to play the clarinet and joined the school band. She evidenced no outstanding musical talent, however, and soon abandoned this project.

Early in the year, she became enamored with a little boy in her room. He and she were the only children in their room who went to band practice. In fact, he may have been the reason for her decision to join the band. She reported at home one day that he had called to her as she started for another school building to practice, "Hey, Amy, wait up for me." "And," she added, "when he said that my knees just knocked together with excitement!"

It was during this period that she began a correspondence and frequent exchange of articles and gifts with a pen pal in Israel. She was proud of his ability to write correct English, saying, "He's not bright, he is brilliant." They continued this contact for several years.

A little more than two years intervened between the ninth and tenth Rorschachs. During this interval, the author had been invited to present Amy's Rorschachs at a meeting of the American Orthopsychiatric Association and arrangements were made for the child to come to the Center for a final Rorschach, as well as an interview with a psychiatrist. Amy was interested and wanted to come in; but mother had some resistance to the plan at the time it was made and, at the last minute, cancelled the appointment. She said that Amy would not be able to come in till a later date. Since it was necessary to have the Rorschach immediately if it was to be included in the report, the aunt agreed to get it on her next visit to the home. During a telephone conversation with Amy, who had called to tell her aunt that she would not be coming in for her appointment with the author, the aunt asked what she thought about taking the Rorschach during the coming weekend. Amy consulted with her mother and came back to the telephone to say, "I'm quoting Ma now. She says it's all right, but she thinks the whole thing is crazy." According to the aunt, when the time came for Amy to take the Rorschach, there was an initial self-consciousness, and the spontaneity of former occasions was lacking. This reaction was no doubt related to mother's frequent interruptions during the testing.

Amy's Rorschach Protocol at the Age of Eleven Years, Nine Months

Performance	Inquiry	Scoring		
I 1. Well, there are two little elves peeking at each other over the humps. (upper d).		d	M	(H)
2. Two little colored kids —look as if they are singing (d).	2. Just their head and neck. Q. They have fuzzy hair.	d	M,FC' Fc	Hd
V3. A mongrel dog turned about three-quarters away (bottom d).	3. Just the head and neck.	d	F	Ad
Λ4. A pair of windswept witches riding their brooms.	4. D.	D	M,m	H
II 1. Two little ladies in Spanish mantillas reaching to shake hands with each other.	1. This one has a pretty little face. (left). (upper red).	D	M	H
2. Of course a big butterfly.	2. It's the right shape and it's flying.	D	FM	A
3. Two elephants facing each other trunk to trunk.	3. P.	W	FM	A P
4. Two little boys in dunce caps leaning against each other (d).	4. (Center d)	d	M	H
V5. An old Philadelphia night	5. He has a jutty chin (d).	d	F	Hd

Performance	Inquiry	Scoring
w a t c h m a n on his corner.		
V6. If you look at the elephants this way they are l a u g h i n g— sitting back to back.	6. They have big chins too and long noses.	W M A

III 1. Ah, here are the waiters in a swank hotel.

1. They are lifting a fancy container and making a very formal gesture of it.

W M   H   P
(D F   obj)

2. A hair bow.

2. Just the shape.

D F   obj P

V3. Ah, my little choir boys, of c o u r s e, with their

3. They are marching along. They have fuzzy hair and very Negro profiles.

W M,Fc   H

V4. L i g h t e d torches.

4. (D).

d   cF   obj

Λ5. Little   m e n with   highspired   hats (outer red).

5. Just looking at each other.

D M   H

IV 1. A giant sitting on a

1. He has big feet and he's sitting with them in front of him.

W M   H

2. Stump.

D F   obj

3. Little   elf heads   with long noses.

3. de

de F   (Hd)

V4. They are ladies with luscious shapes and long hair —not   too luscious,   I guess. They ate too much.

4. D.

D F,cF   H

V 1. Some kind of A ustralian butterfly.

1. It has   its   wings spread out.

W FM   A   P

Performance	Inquiry	Scoring

Performance	Inquiry	Scoring			
2. Horses, legs about from the knee down. I'm certainly not productive on these all black and white cards.	2. (lower d).	d	F		Ad
VI 1. An animal's hide stretched out for drying.	1. It's like a dark-like fur and here's where its spine was.	W	FM,FC'Fc	A obj	P
2. An emblem like you would see on a flag pole.	2. (Upper D).	D	F		obj
3. It's a man's profile— here's his nose and he has a beard.		D	F		Hd
VII 1. Two elves— they have just said "boo" to each other.	1. (Upper ⅔).	W	M		(H)
V2. Two thin moth-eaten elephants standing on their hind legs.	2. (Same as 1.)	W	FM		A
3. This could be a worm in here.	3. (d)	d	F		A
VIII 1. Two pan-thers climb-ing on		D	FM		A P
2. A lot of rocks —I might have thought of any kind of animal if there hadn't been that		D	F		N

Performance	Inquiry	Scoring

Pitt Panther in the morning paper. These could have been the model for that panther.

3. That gray ought to be something. Kind of looks like my idea of the gray matter in your brain.

3. (Upper D).

D CF   At

4. I guess that could be another butterfly. (orange and red). It's not as good a butterfly as the other ones but it is pretty colors.

4. It doesn't seem to be flying like the others.

D FC   A

IX V1. (Laughs). Ah, here's the one I like! It still looks like, a tiny bit like the dressed up dog but it's not the way it used to be. It's not so much that I really see it now, but that I remember how I used to see it when I was little.

W F   A

2. Witches looking in

D M   (H)

Performance	Inquiry	Scoring			
the mirror with their hands up practicing their witching spells.					
3. It's a sand dollar. They look pretty much like that and they are that color and they are thin and tear easily.	3. (Inner d).	d	FC,Fc	A	
4. Two little tontes curled down fast asleep.	4. (Small s).	S	M	(H)	
X 1. Two choir girls coming into church Look like choir robes.	1. (Red area).	D	M	H	
2. Characters in mythology that are half men and half lion.	2. I suppose they are Greek mythology. No, they are not. (Yellow area).	D	F	(H)	
3. Two green worms.	3. Shape and color	D	FC	A	P
4. Crabs (outer blue).	4. (Popular).	D	F	A	P
5. Fighting bees.	5. (Top gray)	D	FM	A	
6. Dogs barking at the moon. (outer brown).	6. See their mouths pointed up.	D	FM	A	
7. One of those funny little airplanes. There's a picture of it in the National Geographic and they look like that.	7. (lower green)	D	F	obj	

Performance	Inquiry	Scoring		
V8. Cooks in chefs' hats grinding some kind of	8. (Red area).	D	M	H
9. Pastry machine between them.	9. (Inner blue).	D	F	obj

In the two years that intervened between the ninth and the present Rorschach, there was little change in Amy's general pattern of conformity—high P, low FM, high FC, low CF. There is still marked introversiveness and fantasy with the suggestion in the current W to M ratio that her fantasy is not always helpful in organization and production compatible with her potential ability. The lag in the constructive use of her resources is noted first in her response to Card I, where she skirts around the edges before giving even a large detail response. This is in contrast to her response to Card I in earlier years and shows a tendency to hold herself in cautious reserve rather than reaching out impulsively before she is ready. This is perhaps an aspect of her introversive makeup—a tendency to reflect and experience inwardly before meeting things head-on. An organized whole does not come until the second card. It should be noted that Amy seems aware of the kind of performance she is giving, as indicated by the remark on Card V, "I'm certainly not productive on these black and white cards." This control over her thoughts and actions is unusual for a child not yet twelve years old. She rarely yields to impulses, thinks before she acts, and has difficulty accepting aggressive urges. She attempts to intellectualize them, as can be seen in her first response to Card VIII. Her acute awareness of social implications is also an important part of her mature functioning.

However, despite these signs of maturity, this record indicates much fantasy of a childlike quality. The fairy tales or elfin qualities assigned to the majority of her human figures suggest a clinging to the childish aspects of life. There is further evidence of this in her inability to give up completely the persistent poorly-perceived "dressed-up dog" on Card IX. At the same time Amy also shows her interest in further growing up by such content as, "ladies in Spanish mantillas reaching to shake hands," "waiters in a swank hotel," and "ladies with luscious shapes and long hair." Her ambivalence about her desire, on the one hand, to be a little girl and her desire, on the other, to be grownup and sophisticated, is apparent in this record.

There are, in addition, indications that other identification problems are not entirely solved. She seems, at the present time, to be identifying with her somewhat phallic mother, and she sees the opposite sex in a servile role of waiter or "little boys with dunce caps on, leaning against one another." However, this identification is not completely satisfactory to her, as evidenced in her confusion of roles in her response to Card X. First, there are the "good" figures—"choir girls." Then men are aggressive lions—"in reality." Finally, the choir girls reversed become cooks grinding a pastry machine. This seems to indicate a confusion of good with bad, if we can interpret the last response as having sexual implications.

Sex, itself, seems more acceptable and less anxiety-producing to Amy than at any other stage of her development. She is still quite curious about it and interested in it, however, as is evident in the content she gives. Her "ladies with luscious shapes and long hair" is one instance of this. This response occurs on Card IV and seems to be further indication of a continued rivalry with mother for father's favor.

Amy's relationship with mother seems to be her most absorbing problem at the moment. She sees mother not only as a rival, but also as someone who is too watchful and dominating. Card VII response suggests that Amy would like to say "boo" to her and have the domination crumble, but must settle for more subtle (and, therefore, more self-acceptable) means of accomplishing her emancipation.

Amy is much more comfortable with father at this time. While she depicts him in the usual authoritative role, she also endows him with spritely characteristics and, as was already suggested, she appears to be competing with mother for his interest and attention.

The response to the red area of Card X of "cooks grinding some kind of pastry machine" may be viewed as a return of Amy's interest in the process of procreation, noted in this same area of the Rorschach at six years of age. In this instance, there is indication of a more mature reflection on the autonomous nature of sexuality. It should be noted, in this connection, that her responses to this red area on Card X during the latency years were: "cooks taking something from the oven," at seven years; "setting a tray of cookies down," at year eight; "stirring with a long-handled stirrer," at nine; and "holding up ice-cream for a party," at ten. These earlier responses suggest more concern with the *product* than with the *process,* and seem to indicate a satisfactory solution of the oedipal conflict. The response to this area, at the present age, is another indication of a resurgence of her interest in father and feelings of rivalry with mother for his attention; it is not an unusual situation for a daughter approaching puberty.

Amy's Rorschach responses at this time were indicative of the great strides in growing up that she had made in the two years that had just passed. Her schoolwork had been excellent, but she had felt the need to play down her academic acceleration and had kept within the bounds of what was expected of her group. She was able to size up her teachers quickly and acted accordingly with each one. To distinguish between three of them, she gave the following report to her family: "In Miss A's room, you sit like this (hands folded on the desk and a smile on your face); in Miss B's room, you sit like this (body stiff and erect, and eyes straight forward); and, in Miss C's room, you sit like this (relaxed with elbow on desk and chin resting on your palm)."

She had continued her collections, and even expanded them at intervals. Her current interest was in antique dolls. She knew the makes, prices, and sources of supply, and could immediately judge the genuineness of the claims made for dolls in antique shops. She was also an omnivorous reader. Her aunt kept her supplied with all kinds of literature, and one of her Christmas gifts was a dozen new books picked especially for her by a buyer in the book section of one of the large department stores. Since there were similar gifts two or three times a year, she never lacked for stimulating reading material.

Amy's social adjustment and interpersonal relationships also seemed good. She was instrumental in organizing a club of girls who met in the different homes. They called themselves the "Hen Club" and planned to offer their services in community activities, such as fund-raising. At first, their meetings consisted of gathering together, eating and talking, with abortive attempts at a business meeting. The first active project was Christmas caroling, directed by Amy's father.

Amy's interest in the other sex had grown by leaps and bounds. She was popular at the Friday afternoon school dances and made an effort to have the boys become interested in her. She got tips from the "American Girl" magazine and tried them out. For instance, she read that a good way to insure a boy's interest was to ask his opinion or advice or help. She tried this out by saying to one of the boys in a seat nearby her, "By the way, Fred, how many sentences did Miss A assign for our lesson tomorrow?" She was most gratified to see how easily it worked. He came over, put his arm across her shoulder and pointed the sentences out to her. She was also acting on the following advice from the same magazine: "When you are dancing with a boy you should have some conversation on tap so he won't think he's dancing with a dolly with a hole in her head."

During the two year interval, a baby was born to her oldest brother and his wife. Amy had been interested in Bobby ever since she knew he was coming; and by eighteen months of age, Bobby was as devoted to her as she was to him. They were eagerly looking forward to the birth of a second baby in the family but Amy commented that she must be careful not to let Bobby think his Amy had deserted him. This empathy was active with all ages of people. She not only sensed their feelings but acted appropriately in response to her sensitivity.

Her sex information continued to grow. When the grandfather had a prostate gland operation during that summer, Amy was interested to the point of studying a diagram of the operation. Her mother asked her what she would say when neighbors inquired about her grandfather. She answered, "Oh, I'll appear very juvenile and say, 'It's some sort of bladder trouble, I think.' " There had been no overt indication of anxiety in the sex area as there was in previous years. She was, however, eagerly looking forward to shopping for a brassiere and sweater that "will do something for me."

Amy's relationship with mother was embellished with much endearment at this time. She was compliant with mother's wishes, but managed to get most of the things she wanted.

To summarize this story of Amy's personality development, we note first that this series of Rorschachs given by her shows most clearly how children's Rorschachs not only capture the uniqueness of the individual, but also the more universal aspects of personality development. It is easy to see the imprint of individuality in each of Amy's records, and there is a consistent core running through all of them. In this case, the consistence is not confined (as with most children) to the general handling, the approach and content, but extends to the structural aspects of the Rorschach as well. For example, she shows consistent and unequivocal introversive balance on all records. Some children shift from one age to another in the experience balance, but Amy's movement-to-color ratio is never below the 2 to 1, and runs as high as 16 Movement to 1.5 Color at year eight. Moreover, the controlled type of color responses (FC) consistently exceeds the more labile CF from the age of four years on. This again represents a precocious development, since few children attain this degree of emotional control until years later. There is also a much lower F% than is usually found in children's records. Apparently her poise and self-control are built in, a part of her basic stability, not a superimposed intellectual control which stifles spontaneous expression. The preponderance of movement responses, as was noted at certain age levels, suggests an unusual capacity for identifying with people, particularly with adults, and may be related to the extent to which she has been surrounded by adults. One wonders if a nursery school experience between the ages of two and five years of age might have changed the quality of her peer relationships and of her introversive adaptation.

In viewing the completed picture of Amy's first twelve years of development, one sees a continual, steady growth toward maturity—albeit fraught with anxious moments and occasional regressive tendencies, as she passes from one developmental stage to the next. At the threshold of adolescence, she presents a more mature picture than is usually found in a child of this age. In summarizing her adjustment at this time, it can be said: first, that Amy can accept and enjoy her rich fantasy life, using it frequently in the resolution of her conflicts; second, that her emotions are so controlled and so integrated with social demands that she has no need to express them as openly or as frequently as the average child; third, that she has sufficient sensitivity to her environment to enable her to keep her reactions in line with social norms, without developing overcaution or undue anxiety; fourth, that she can participate in group attitudes without losing her individuality; fifth, that she has varied and appropriate interests; sixth, that she has had continual difficulty with an identification problem and that this conflict is evidently of some concern to her. Despite any strain that this or any other conflict exerted during the years, Amy has always been able to use her energy in a constructive way, and has shown a type of adjustment that any adult might well envy.

From the developmental picture of Amy's first twelve years, could we have foretold what sort of person she would become at her current age of sixteen? Could we have expected her to continue her steady growth with sufficient strength to solve the problems she might have encountered during the intervening five years of adolescent development, or would these beginning adolescent years have tended to work changes in her basic personality pattern? As a check on our speculative answers to these and other questions let us take a glimpse of the sixteen-year-old Amy.

Amy is now a junior in high school—a most attractive, alert edition of the current "teenager." She is well-groomed in a casual way, expressing pride in a pony-tail, second in length to only one other in the entire school. A "steady" boy friend, who is a senior and a football player in the same school, drops in the home frequently; he often stays for supper and sometimes takes Amy to a movie or a party. He has also assumed an interest in her driving lessons, which she takes at school. This is one of the very few areas of Amy's life in which father has participated in recent years. He initiated driving lessons before Amy enrolled in the driving class at school. Father, however, has been superseded by the boy friend, who is currently expressing concern that the family car does not have an automatic gear shift. Mother and father heartily approve of Amy's choice of this "boy friend," and mother is relieved that the "going steady" stage is fraught with so few complications. The only concern Amy has in this regard is that this spring was the time she had set to start wearing high-heeled shoes, and, since she has picked a fellow no taller than she is, she will have to forego the high-heeled shoes as long as she goes with him.

In her freshman year, Amy decided that she wanted to be in the high school orchestra, since the "orchestra seems to get into everything." She further decided that she would choose the violin as her instrument, since there was a dearth of violinists in the school and this choice would therefore insure her a place in the orchestra. Consequently, a month before school opened, she paid a visit to the music teacher, who was the orchestra leader, and came home with a violin. After a month of private lessons from this instructor, with two hours of conscientious daily practice, she was accepted in the school orchestra, and has remained a faithful member ever since. She has become interested in different composers and shows an increasing appreciation of music, despite her lack of any real talent. Her present aim is to become a member of the all-county orchestra during her junior year, and she expects to begin cello playing in her senior year.

As far as academic work is concerned, Amy has no difficulty at present. During her sophomore year there was some trouble with algebra. She resisted doing her homework and complained that the teacher did not know when it was correct, so why bother? Mother enrolled her in an evening TV class and saw that she covered the subject matter she was supposed to cover during that year. Amy offered no resistance to this plan on the part of the mother. Other subjects, including plane geometry, during the current year, have presented no problems. Amy predicts that she will finish third in her class. She is not interested in first or second honors, since speech-making is attached to these. She can foretell exactly what average she will make on each of her subjects, because she plans her homework and recitations accordingly.

As already suggested, not all of Amy's teachers are of the highest caliber and her response to these poor academic situations in which she had found herself has been varied. In the instance of the inadequacy of her algebra instruction, she tended to feel resigned. However, in a more recent inadequate, though totally different classroom situation, Amy has assumed the role of "crusader." An older, retired, handicapped woman, who has been called back into service, teaches a section of Junior English, in which Amy is enrolled. Immediately upon taking charge of the class, the teacher divided it according to the ability of the pupils, and told the children that she knew that those she had put on one side of the room would do well while the other group would not get along at all. Therefore, she would direct her teaching toward the brighter group. Such a blatant announcement angered Amy, and she enlisted two girls and a boy in joining forces with her to offset the teacher's position. The four crusaders have set about earnestly coaching the "goats" on the daily lessons, encouraging them to volunteer in class. They have cautioned the "sheep" not to raise their hands, since the teacher calls on only those who volunteer. The teacher, still unaware of the crusade, stands in front of the "sheep" when she talks, but when the students recite orally they stand in front of the "goats." While everybody, especially the crusaders, are enjoying the situation, Amy is not at all sure that the campaign will be successful, since the teacher has already figured out who will pass and who will fail. She and her fellow-crusaders are considering approaching the principal with their problem.

Amy continues to be an insatiable reader. Her favorite reading matter at present is *The Saturday Review,* from which she makes lists of books which her aunt continues to buy for her. She and the aunt have long conversations about world affairs and philosophical subjects; and Amy seems to save her serious questions for such occasions. This relationship is reminiscent of Amy's early years, when she cleared such questions as Santa Claus, religion, and sex in this way.

While Amy has given some consideration to the choice of a college and a subsequent vocation, she does not discuss this with her aunt. She early talked of going to the same university as her aunt and studying psychology. This mother disapproved of. Of late, Amy mentioned dress designing as a vocation and mother eagerly suggested the girls' college in which she was trained as a dietician. Amy, however, has been investigating small coeducational colleges and has consulted her aunt in this regard. One can speculate that this mother will have considerable difficulty enduring a separation from her child, since she has been unable at any time during the sixteen years of Amy's life to allow her to take weekend trips without her. The child has never visited her aunt, who maintains an apartment in the city, without being accompanied by mother.

With this type of mother, why has Amy not been smothered? How has she remained so relatively unencumbered? It appears that she has achieved an emancipation for herself not by rebelling, as most adolescents do, against a subtly controlling mother, but by superficial compliance, thus freeing herself to pursue her own interests. Another question that keeps recurring is: What prevents this child from giving full sway to her intelligence in the academic area, and why does she need to curtail and sublimate such activities? She seems to be still struggling with identity problems, being torn between the two mother figures that have meant so much to her in her life. In answer to a third question which relates to the quality and depth of this girl's friendships, one might speculate that her relationships with people can never reach the depths that a less calculating, less objective person might obtain. This concept, of course, leads to the further speculation as to her ability to find a satisfactory relationship in marriage. The answers to these questions seem to lie in the final resolution of Amy's identity problems; and time is probably the major factor necessary for this resolution.

As a final brief reflection on this story of the personality development of Amy, one senses a concurrent basic theme of the psyche in its power to manifest itself—to reach out toward fullness and maturity. There is no doubt that Amy's favorable environment cleared the way for this dynamic process; wise handling and guidance have, without a doubt, helped this child to face her fears and handle her anxiety so as not to obstruct the developmental process. It also seems quite clear, however, that this drive was part of her native endowment coming from within the girl herself and propelling her through the years.

All of this, and more, has been reflected in Amy's Rorschach responses through the years. It adds considerably to the feeling of confidence that the clinician may have already associated with the use of the Rorschach test with children, after reading the other case studies in this book. Amy's Rorschachs, however, emphasize two specific points in addition: that the technique can be used effectively with preschool children and that the core of a child's personality development may be thus revealed at an extremely early age.

PART : III

Technical Aids
to Clinicians
and Researchers

XV : PRELIMINARY COMMENTS

IN THE FIRST TWO SECTIONS of this book, we have presented material which is of great importance to those concerned with the many varied aspects of personality development. Certainly, the teacher, the student of human behavior, and the developmental psychologist as well as the researcher who is interested in developing new measurement devices can benefit greatly from an intensive study of these data on the development of "normal" children.

There is, however, a specific population for whom this book may prove of first importance, in the same way that the material has already proved essential to those who initially sought it as a much needed, but conspicuously absent, tool in their profession. We refer, of course, to the many clinicians and psychiatrists already actively engaged in therapy with children, and constantly alert to new information to help them improve the methods currently in daily use. Only through continued research, and the publication of detailed results based on that research, can we hope to increase our knowledge and potential usefulness to members of the community. Since this is, essentially, the "personalized" goal of those who enter any phase of the therapy field, it is hoped that, through publication of this book, the results of our present endeavor may extend in usefulness beyond the few individuals already reaping its rewards.

Over the past years, many general findings in terms of aids to this research have been acquired. These include means of improving the technique of blind Rorschach analysis as well as aids to the more valid interpretation of children's records as opposed to those of adults. Few students learning the techniques of Rorschach testing are taught special details of its application to developing individuals; and, therefore, if a student's special interest lies in work with children he is forced, upon completion of his formal training, either to forego the use of this valuable depth tool or to learn slowly from his own cases. Specific norms, based on the longitudinal research study, have

303

been published in *Rorschach Responses of Elementary School Children* and were referred to earlier as a means of evaluating individual responses in terms of the responses of other children the same age. However, equally important, are many pointers on the skillful use of the Rorschach, based on our learning experiences during this long period of investigation. It is hoped that they can be of value to implement skill in Rorschach administration to children, and can provide a background of interpretive information from which the clinician may benefit in his work with therapy cases.

Part III is written, therefore, as an aid to those who use the Rorschach test as a research tool or as a measurement device to assess individual cases. In it, we include statements from five of the skilled interpreters whose work is incorporated in specific cases of Part II. They have summarized many of the techniques of "blind" analysis acquired during their years of experience with children's Rorschachs. For the benefit of the reader, who may want to follow the meaning of these over-all comments in terms of specific case examples, the name of the child whose case each one has handled in Part II is included. Much can be gained from studying each method with the help of specific reference to the actual protocols.

The final chapter of this book is based on the author's many diversely-acquired general concepts of child personality analysis. The author has been fortunate to be the one most closely related to all aspects of this published material—this includes Rorschach administration, interpretation, and its interrelationship with all the other data acquired during this research. However, the information reviewed in this last chapter is based not only on the data from the 138 children followed in this study, but also on data acquired in the course of testing hundreds of children in connection with work at the Pittsburgh Child Guidance Center. As a means of final summary, this chapter covers some of the aspects of children's Rorschachs which, through years of experience, have been found of great significance.

XVI : THE INTERPRETIVE TECHNIQUES
OF FIVE SKILLED CLINICIANS

IT IS UNFORTUNATE THAT limitations of space prevent us from including statements from each of the interpreters whose work is exemplified in Part II. However, it is of great importance that some overviews of how experienced interpreters of children's Rorschachs go about their work be here included as an aid to the individual who may want help in using the Rorschach test with children. The five short statements of method included in this chapter have been written by the psychologists themselves and are reprinted verbatim to indicate the somewhat diverse, but equally efficient, means they have used to arrive at many interpretations of many protocols. It may be again noted that these interpreters are basically psychoanalytically oriented.

A. *The Comments of Adele's Interpreter:*

"In the area of clinical testing in general and the Rorschach test in particular, I feel that interpretation and analysis have more validity when the technique is looked upon as a field of behavior rather than a test that has rigid standardization, rationale or definition. The less structured the field of behavior, the more difficult it is to apply standardization, rationale or definition. This is particularly true of the Rorschach. Because of this personal bias, my approach to the interpretation and analysis of Rorschach protocols approximates a free association within a structured setting.

"The structured setting I would define as the actual Rorschach cards, or the field, together with the possible reactions to this field, or in other words, the behavior as manifested by responses, response time, comments, etc. My experience with both these factors, Rorschach and possible responses, would be further influenced by my psychological knowledge, as well as my clinical experience with behavior in general and personality theory in particular. Therefore, any 'free-associating' I do is guided and delimited by the above mentioned factors.

"It then follows that the more prior knowledge I have of the person being tested, the less opportunity I have of evaluating the behavior as manifested by responses to test items as strictly indicative of test-derived personality attributes. Prior knowledge may range from actual information about a person to subliminal cues picked up by secondary responses made by the person being tested.

"Therefore, my first step is to consider the Rorschach responses with as little prior knowledge as possible; age and sex being the only required variables. So whenever possible, I prefer a blind analysis.

"My next step is to consider the Rorschach responses and inquiry in their entirety, reading through responses and inquiry of all ten cards scoring them without pausing to consider any one card, any singular response or particular inquiry.

"This second step then leads to a number of other steps which are in no particular sequence or order but may occur as a result of their emphasis in the Rorschach protocol. There are thema or patterning of recurring percepts, or ways of responding: places where defenses are most in evidence, interpersonal relationships, sexual preoccupation or indifference, symbolic meaning of an area where initial or recurring response is directed, hostility, handling of color cards, recovery following disturbing percepts, fantasy activities, emotions, anxiety levels and type, etc.

"Once this emphasized material is noted, then I attempt to integrate it into a dynamic whole utilizing the complete test together with incorporation into the structure of the psychogram.

"When this material is combined into a report, an attempt is made to transpose the behavioral trends, feelings, defenses, etc., into everyday activities, trying to predict how the person functions, which things are stressful to him, how he handles them, what he needs to help sustain or stabilize him.

"In the series of Adele's six protocols, the Rorschach at each age level was handled discretely and then placed in a comparative continuity and an attempt made to describe a dynamic developmental sequence.

"In short, I prefer to analyze Rorschachs 'blind' knowing only sex and age. Within the structure of age and sex, I peruse the Rorschach as a whole and then free associate to the variables that strike me as being conspicuous. This material is then placed into some semblance of a pattern and qualified. Then the whole thing is incorporated with the psychogram and the behavioral trends are transposed into everyday activities as much as is possible."

B. *The Comments of Edgar's Interpreter:*

"The first thing I do is look for what might be called the 'entrance to the data.' It is a sort of first cue or clue, a general impression, a question that I ask myself as I look at the data. This may come from any source—a particular response, some behavior during testing, a preponderance or absence of a particular determinant, a reaction time, or a ratio. For example, one youngster gave away the key to his percept of the male role in his Card VI response of "a little, little wasp dragging a big leaf." The child whose Rorschach I looked at for a blind analysis in this project had the middle of the psychogram loaded, with practically nothing on either extreme. His intelligence was obviously high, from the form quality, etc., and yet the question of from where this terrific control and repression has come and why it is necessary sets one to look further in the data for answers. Another youngster may have extreme color shock, with denial of color usage, and poor form level. Again, one is set to wondering about where and why for this behavorial mode.

"After this has been gathered, I look for variations in the central theme—that is, other behavioral phenomena which are either logical or consistent with the central theme by personality theory or experience. If material, themes, or ideas come up which do not seem logical or consistent, some attempt at reconciliation of ideas is made or the validity of one or the other is questioned. Frequently, initial hypotheses are of the 'either the child is this or this' type and the secondary materials tend to validate one of these hypotheses. As an example, a child may not be able to see the usual human movement responses in Card III. One immediately wonders why. Hypotheses which leap into possibility at the beginning are psychosis, an inability to perceive people well because of lack of emotional interaction with them, or even that the possible sexual stimuli there are disturbing. When consequently, the child sees 'scarecrows,' 'statues,' or human-like animals where human responses usually occur, one is inclined to accept a paucity of good emotional interactions as the most acceptable hypothesis. In this way, a 'case' is built for the central picture of the child.

"The formal analysis procedures as such are employed only to support or refute hypotheses and are not accepted on their own merits. A high W% is not very meaningful by itself unless one knows about the F% and F+% for the reality of organizational tendencies: is it burning ambition to satisfy unfulfilled affectional drives, or is it a procedure to stave off or intellectually inspect oedipal tendencies, or is it reasonably good organized though compulsive tendencies for the previous purposes? It may be an approach to staving off a psychosis. Anything unusual or striking kicks up a 'why' or a 'how' and answers are sought.

"In this way, an attempt is made to get at a central picture or the core of the child. I like to think it is an attempt to get at the core of the child's personality, his or her essential uniqueness. Admittedly, the lack of inclusiveness and the unsystematic approach facilitates the missing of possibly important data, but I find my 'system' more exciting and more of a game than a 'cook-book' approach. In this inevitable dilemma of the clinical psychologist trying to be a scientist because he has been so trained or an artist so that he can feel less like a lab technician, I try to take a slightly more 'artistic' position and hope research interests will satisfy my compulsivities and well-indoctrinated superego."

C. The Comments of Allan's Interpreter:

"At a basic level, I approach children's Rorschach attempting to understand grossly the child's view of himself, and secondarily his view of the world, the latter of these interpretive tasks being the simpler. Regarding the former, such questions are raised as: does he view himself as deprived, hungry, poorly taken care of, and does he need to remain a small, succorant, nonthreatening figure or is he well fed, eager to grow, and to strive for a more independent status; does he view himself as put upon, manipulated, a foil for other's aggressions and extreme demands for conformity or can he assert himself with freedom and without the need to resist suggestions from another person, or to define each new situation idiosyncratically; is he accepting of his impulse life or rejecting, i.e., are warm, sensual feelings, and hot, 'angry' feelings a natural part of life or are they to be hidden or acted out without regard to their appropriateness in terms of context?

"Regarding his view of the environment, what is the over-all level of interest in it, what aspects of it are inviting and entered into freely and satisfyingly, and which not; which are threatening, and tend to curtail striving for more mature status in their anxiety-provocative aspects. Out of the interaction of these, I get some notion of the anxiety level characteristic of the child and something of his primary modes of defense. However, regarding the latter, I approach interpretation of the child's defenses with considerable humility and questioning, not believing that we can simply 'translate downward' the defensive patterns which we find in neurotic adults. Avoidance and denial appear to me to be characteristic of such a large proportion of the pre-eight year old records as to render extremely difficult, intricate teasing out of individual defensive systems. The rare early compulsive patterns, the massive repressions, I can decide about with some confidence, but this leaves at least 90% as the remainder.

"Now what about the cues? Well, I pay special attention to the first card, even the first responses to the first card, as frequently being indicative of either the parental figure with whom the child experiences the greatest conflict, the relationship of the child to his parents, and/or a condensed self-image. I also think Card X frequently pulls out especially conflictual material, particularly regarding relationships with the mother, although Card VII, I still rely on, for the most consistent reactions to the mother figure, and Card IV for attitudes towards the father. I don't have a 'peer' card but it seems to me that I use Card X, Card II and Card III, in that order, to infer attitudes here. The child's perception of the relationship between his parents, I believe, is most frequently reflected on Cards II and III, in that order, and the 'eternal triangle' Card I. I go along with the generally accepted notion of the central figure in the card most frequently being the child's own identification figure, although this is not solely the card area in which he identifies and reflects his attitudes. I pay much attention to the animal figures on Card VIII, perhaps even a little mystically, inferring a special meaning with regard to both the child's acceptance of himself and his impulses, and the amount of social anxiety which he experiences, according to the type of animal figures seen and the action in which they engage. I have a strong preference, mental healthwise, for a mammalian quadruped, preferably fur bearing here. (Beavers, bears, dogs, wolves, rodents.) Least satisfactory to me here are the amphibian creatures (lizards, salamanders, etc.) which convey for me a lack of trust of one's own feelings and impulses, evasiveness and duplicity in reflecting one's feelings, and uniformly, anxiety in relationships with both peers and authority figures. Birds and fish are figures, implying immaturity in relating to other people and, depending on the child's age, an index of difficulty of initiating relationships with people and sustaining them.

"Particularly with the records of very young children, although undoubtedly with all records, I am sensitive to something which I shall impressionistically call the 'affective tone' of the record. By this I mean very simply the relative incidence of both the 'good things and bad things,' in the child's frame of reference: percepts which suggest happiness, enjoyment, fulfillment, satisfactory nurturance, pleasure vs. those that suggest pain, discomfort, destruction, decomposition, etc. As I talk about it, the lowest common denominator of this dimension appears to be offered in the antagonistic metabolic processes of anabolism vs. catabolism. Orthodox Freudians would probably see this as a reflection of the temporary dominance of life vs. death instincts.

"Animal content, the most frequent content category in children's records, (in adults as well) is the single most important content for interpretation. As indicated above, with regard to the animals on Card VIII, I place emphasis on the place of the animal perceived in the human evolutionary scheme, and to the 'personality characteristics' of these animals. Also important, and in some records even more important, are a child's specifications of the kinds of movement engaged in by the animals, their satisfaction in doing what they are doing, whether or not they achieve their goals, and what happens to them as a result. I frequently press for quite detailed inquiry information, even approximating a TAT inquiry on some animal responses, particularly the animals on Card VIII, with boys especially.

"Early human content almost uniformly reflects attitudes toward parental figures, in my experience, except where a child content is specifically mentioned. I watch for the occurrence of human content even where no human movement occurs, as an index of interest in people and one's security in relating to them, naturally qualified by particular attitudes which are projected on them (natural, real vs. unreal, phobic, distant). However, the converse does not seem to hold, i.e., the lack of human content in children's records does not necessarily indicate a lack of interest in human relating. Particularly at the pre-school level, I think that a well adjusted child can yield a Rorschach without any human content.

"The area of popularity and usualness of the child's responses is of some utility in detecting marked disturbance, and also of some prognostic value in determining whether or not a child taken in treatment is likely to turn up with some even greater problems, i.e., even more marked signs of reality distortion in the direction of a 'damaged ego,' than was initially suspected.

"Related to this latter factor is the child's production of 'ego-alien' content: waste products, sexual organs, unusual and minute ana-

tomical details, extreme hostile-destructive orgies (not hostile interaction itself, but in particular hostile manipulation of other creatures
toward a destructive goal), infection, poisoning, decomposition. Actually one takes account of the age of the child and of the ratio of
such content to other more constructive and satisfying or even bland
content in assessing its meaning. However, as such content builds up,
one is made more wary of the potentials in the child for basic distortion and disassociation in relationships with people and the learning of a negative self-image. I certainly have no available slide rule
for precisely determining the adjustment levels reflected by combinations of these. I am impressed with the extent to which latency age
children use fantasy as a buffering defensive device in comparison
with adults. As interpreter, one expects to find more phobic objects
in the pre-oedipal and oedipal child, and to a less extent other
atypical content. Actually, with our notions about the limited experience of very young children, the appearance of certain ego-alien
contents in the early years can be a sign of unusually weak ego development and/or traumatic experience. Here the content of other
cues becomes even more important, and I believe, our knowledge of
the parents and the kinds of lives they lead (sexual exhibitionism,
open physically aggressive display) is of great importance.

"I pay relatively less attention to the psychogram in children's
Rorschach than in those of adults. In the movement area, the precocious and inflated development of human movement I fairly readily
interpret as probably index of a child's trying to gain perspective on
himself in relationship to his parents, as a result of marked parental
conflict. The absence of animal movement I can no longer accept as
an indication of the child's lack of acceptance of his impulse life and
his attempts to overcontrol it, as has been suggested by Klopfer. As
a matter of fact, some of the most impulse-oriented children that I
have seen have had very moderate animal movement levels. Actually,
I find myself moving towards a kind of 'need-tension' conceptualiza-
tion of the relative incidence of the non-pure-form determinants in
the Rorschach, much like is found in the Szondi Test, (e.g. much
texture, much need for affection). I do not have a satisfactory formulation here as yet, and shudder at the possible chaos in the interpretive task which might be introduced by such a double standard.
However, I do believe that it is something with which we are going
to have to come to grips, i.e. certain aspects of the Rorschach reflect
the individual's world as he sees it, and other aspects reflected are
those around which he experiences a higher degree of tension, and

the threatening character of the important people in one's life. However, an absence of inanimate movement unfortunately does not permit for me the opposite interpretation. Regarding the use of bright color, frankly, I have no great confidence at this point in the nature of the color responses reflecting the way the individual child experiences feelings, expresses them, or relates to other people. This comment pertains chiefly to the pre-eight year old records. The possible exception to this is the inflation of primary form color responses as an index of precocious socialization, probably indicative of reaction formation and for boys, at least, passivity in interpersonal relationships."

D. *The Comments of Eileen's Interpreter:*

"In describing my use of the Rorschach, I first want to list the mechanical steps I usually go through and then add the kind of thinking applied to the data.

"First off, if I am giving the Rorschach, I permit whatever behavioral cues and hunches or hypotheses that occur about the person or his data to 'register.' I usually jot these down at the moment. The reason I say permit them to register is that I am not actively searching through the material as I will when I score and interpret the Rorschach.

"After the administration of the Rorschach, I read through it with what I would call an impressionistic attitude—sort of seeking an over-all view of it but not asking any particular question of the data. This is followed by the formal scoring during which time more specific attention is paid to the way the patient handled a given response, its particular meaning, its relationship to the rest of the test data.

"After the formal scoring, a profile is developed and a more active integrative attempt is made at interpreting the Rorschach. At this point more generalizations about the personality are made, whereas in the previous steps more attention was given to the isolated meaning of a given response.

"Obviously one cannot isolate completely the specific and the general approach to the data. As a matter of fact, while there is the general pattern to my approach as described above, I deliberately avoid any rigid application of it, sort of giving the data meaning at any level of specificity or generalization whenever it occurs.

"In scoring and interpreting the Rorschach I utilize two frames of reference (as does everyone) which are somewhat independent.

There is what I would call the frame of reference which applies to the formal features of the test: for example, form level, originality. W and M, say something about intelligence. In other words, the various scoring categories: determinants, location, ratios, etc., in certain constellations refer among other things to a person's intelligence, emotional life and relationships with people. This is the test frame of reference.

"Just what is said about a person's intelligence, his needs, relationships with people, and the interactions of all these factors is determined by another frame of reference which deals with personality development and psychopathology. My particular model is somewhat oriented toward the Freudian theory.

"This latter frame of reference determines the kind of specific meanings attributed to particular responses and the generalizations made about the individual. However, in applying this frame of reference from the beginning contact with the person and his test data and later to the test data alone, no conscious attempt is made to force the data into some prearranged order. I mean by this that I don't have some mental check list which is used and which insures that all aspects of the personality model will be applied to the data. Rather, the previously described mechanical steps used in going over the Rorschach are geared to permit the patient's unique style of perception, of defenses, of impulse expression and their interaction to show themselves. The test data of a given individual may say a great deal about a particular drive and very little about another drive. Another record may show clearly the style of defense and relatively little about the motives for defense.

"As I apply my frame of reference to the test results, I permit myself considerable freedom to speculate and think about the possible meanings of the data. Of course along with this freedom, I exercise the responsibility of paying attention to the danger of projecting my own problems into the data. On the other hand, I still frequently use reference work in an attempt to broaden my understanding of the particular test data and to learn more about the way others use the Rorschach. This applies to a search for interpretative slants and normative data, the latter especially at the child level.

"In summary, I view the Rorschach as one sample of a person's behavior and, when I administer the test, I relate the test data to other behavioral samples of the individual which are occurring in an interaction situation, part of which includes me.

"In evaluating the data, I carry out a somewhat systematic procedure which includes impressionistic reading, formal scoring, profiling, use of reference material, all subjected to a combination of speculative and logical thinking done within a given frame of reference."

E. *The Comments of Anna's Interpreter:*

"My approach basically is from psychoanalytic theory. The things I am most interested in finding out have to do with the general level of intellectual functioning and emotional control, specific conflicts within this context, and types and adequacies of defenses employed in handling conflicts and problem areas. With regard to the Rorschach record the first thing that I do is to score it. This I do in a somewhat autistic scoring system, which combines Beck's locations with Klopfer's determinants, and a list of content categories which derive from both Beck and Klopfer and also some of my own. For populars I score both Beck and Klopfer listings. I score F plus and minus generally according to subjective criteria, but I do use Beck's norms in cases where I am uncertain. I also employ some of Rapaport's categories, such as confabulation, and the scoring of responses for form, both plus and minus, when they have good and bad features combined in a single response. With regard to determinants, I deviate from Klopfer to the extent that I do not consider some determinants to be main and others additional if they occur within a single response. I give all of the determinants of a particular response equal valence unless there is specific information to the contrary contained in the patient's verbalizations. When the record is scored I examine it in order to get an over-all picture of general disruption. I am interested here in whether the general form level is adequate, whether the patient can use such determinants as movement, shading, and color in an adequate way, whether the distribution of content seems to be diverse, constricted or bizarre, and whether there seems to be a reasonable number of popular responses. From this initial examination I can get a fairly clear immediate picture of such things as impulsivity (in terms of wild use of color, poor form, confabulation, etc.), compulsivity, flexibility or constriction in terms of number of responses, wide variety of determinants, and ability to be somewhat adventuresome in the use of determinants. I can get an idea whether there is a variety of responses with regard to quality of form, use of determinants, use of locations and contents. In general, I am likely to perceive a record that shows wide range of all of these things as more benign than a record that is extremely limited in the quality of what is perceived, whether that quality be good or bad. I also initially glance at the distribution of reaction times to the various cards to see if they seem to be fairly consistent or whether there are some particular cards which elicit a very deviant reaction time when compared with the patient's general run of reaction times. The deviant cards come in for closer inspection later.

"Having established in these ways a general context within which to think of the patient's general functioning, I then examine the responses individually and in sequence to look for particular evidences of problem areas and deviations from the normal flow of functioning. In the case of a record that is extremely disrupted throughout, the search for individual problem areas is of less significance than the over-all fact of disruption. In cases where the over-all context is generally satisfactory, the search for focalized disturbance is more likely to be rewarding. In this search there are certain specific things that recur frequently enough to merit special comment. The standard considerations with regard to the handling of colored cards versus achromatic cards is one such thing. It is worth noting whether the presence of color poses problems for handling that the achromatic cards do not pose, or whether the reverse is true. It is also worth noting whether specific cards are especially disrupting in a generally adequate context. In this latter regard Cards IV, VI and VII are likely to be especially revealing. I use the notion that responses to Card IV have to do with attitudes towards the father, Card VII to the mother, and Card VI to the male genital sexuality. The handling of the lower area of Card VII I regard as likely to be significant for the handling of female sexuality. With regard to content, I am interested in responses that have to do with oral, anal, or genital function. Oral responses include all food responses for oral incorporation and all biting and aggressive mouth activity, such as talking or orating for oral intrusiveness and aggression. Responses of dirtiness and smeariness are related to anal level of functioning, and all projecting areas, in the case of males, and hollow areas, in the case of females, are seen as relevant to genital functioning. With regard to these levels I am interested in the presence of more responses than one would ordinarily expect of the particular type, and also the absence of responses where one would ordinarily expect them: the absence is particularly noticeable in cases where projecting areas are consistently omitted from responses. Conflict areas can sometimes be deduced from the sequence of responses. In this regard, for example, the sequence of an extremely aggressive animal, followed by an extremely timid one, such as a lion followed by a rabbit, may reflect a conflict in the area of expression of aggression. Conflict can similarly be reflected in choice of locations. When things are going smoothly, with locations being chosen in a systematic fashion and then suddenly a series of small details are chosen, one can assume that the conflict area has been tapped before the sequence of tiny details has occurred. The nature of the conflict can be deduced not only from the content, but also from the determinants, shading vista, color (and how they are used), and also from the areas of cards that frequently elicit responses relevant to particular problems. For example, on Card VI the phallic projection may be handled adequately but the succeeding responses may reflect disturbance which may then be referred back to the fact that the phallic projection was perceived. In all of these cases the way in which the disturbance is shown does reflect in a small way the manner in which the patient handles such conflicts elsewhere. For example, in the last illustration one would expect that this is a patient who could on the reality level accept phallic needs, but would later feel anxiety about them.

"In general, the sequence of responses to Rorschach stimuli are regarded as analogies to other life situations. In each case the sequence is considered in terms of what sort of real life situation model would fit it. For example, the failure to perceive certain significant areas of the cards would be related to a failure to perceive in other life situations, and therefore to the defense mechanism of denial, or repression, depending on whether there is evidence of the things seen but not admitted or whether it is simply not seen. The alternation of one type of response with its opposite would reflect a similar alternation in life situations, in which the person would appear to be very vacillating, and possibly immobilized in the problem area. The tendency to see colored intrusive parts of the Rorschach cards in an uncontrolled (CF or C) fashion, would be analogous to a real life situation of being inundated by affect rather than being able to cope with it. The failure to perceive color at all would be related to the denial of affect. Fluctuation between these modes of response would relate to similar fluctuation in the handling of affect.

"The movement variable deserves special consideration. In general, it is related to vividness and quality of fantasy. The sex and stature (big or small, real or imaginary) of the figures seen as alive, the kind of action they indulge in, the intensity of the action, and other such variables are seen as related intimately to the nature of the patient's own fantasies and may reflect primary areas of conflict. One of the important features to be considered is recoverability when a disrupting response occurs. When a whole series of responses are poor after a single poor response, this reflects a much more disturbed balance of ego strength than when a single poor response is followed immediately by good ones. The use of shading, and the point in the protocol where shading is used, is thought to reflect specific areas of anxiety (if shading is not an all-pervasive variable) and may reflect focal problems. At the same time, the adequate use of differentiated shading reflects ability for empathy, and acute sensitivity to subtleties of the environment. Whether these features are used effectively or disruptively can be determined only by the context in which they occur.

"It is realized that picking out individual things to interpret from the Rorschach record is a process that can go on indefinitely and can lead to only a vague picture of how a personality statement is arrived at. Rather than go further into the picky details of analysis I shall summarize the general features of what I do.

"First, a general picture of over-all functioning is obtained by examining the total scoring, and the psychogram. This together with the reaction time distributions provides the general picture of whether the patient is in fairly good contact with reality or not, whether perceptions are rigid or flexible, and whether or not anxiety is all-pervasive and disruptive or not. This establishes a context within which focal problems can be delineated. In general, I look for specific spikes in the midst of the general level of performance, either better or worse responses than are usually given by this patient, unusual reaction times, unusual context, locations or determinants. Specific comparisons in this regard have to do with color versus achromatic cards, comparison of handling of Cards IV, VI and VII to the rest of the cards, and specific deviations with regard to the use of color, movement, and shading, as well as form quality. Conflict areas are isolated, in terms of psychosexual levels of development, and isolation of conflict is also possible in terms of vacillations in the kind of content used, or in the kind of activity or use of color, for example, reported. The general personality picture is described in terms of the over-all context and level of functioning, the statement of specific areas of difficulty, the isolation of focal conflicts, the nature and effectiveness of defenses used. These things are arrived at largely through analogies having to do with relating the performance on the Rorschach to model situations elsewhere. In general, the Rorschach performance is seen as a small scale map from which one can extrapolate to significant samples of behavior and fantasy outside of this particular situation. In general, I attempt to arrive at an over-all hypothesis with regard to functioning in terms of my first impressions from the over-all record and from the sequence and item analysis, and then to search the record for contraindications of the original hypothesis, and arrive by a series of approximations in this way at my final formulation of the dynamics and of the specific problem areas."

XVII : SOME SIGNIFICANT ASPECTS
OF CHILDREN'S RORSCHACHS

CONTRARY TO WHAT MANY clinicians believed a decade or more ago, the Rorschach test has proven to be a useful tool in the psychological examination of children, even the very young; and the possibility of adequately administering, scoring and interpreting the Rorschach protocols of children of all ages is no longer in doubt. As soon as a child is able to verbalize his reactions to the cards, he can give a record that reflects his stage of personality development. At two years of age a bright, verbal child is capable of giving quite satisfactory responses, as was seen in the case of Amy in Chapter XIV. However, the average child of this age, provided his attention can be directed to the blots, usually gives whole, undifferentiated, and frequently perseverated responses. For example, a two-year-old may call the blot on Card I "a tree." He seems to feel he has found the solution to this experience and continues to give the same response to the other nine cards. The average two-year-old is able to respond only to the whole blot on each card, and his concept is frequently incompatible with the form of the blot. Such a performance suggests that he is unable in most situations to differentiate reality from unreality and that he does not have any ability as yet to recognize the practical or more detailed aspects of his environment. His responses, in fact, are sometimes reminiscent of those given by deteriorated and/or psychotic adults who are out of contact with reality.

As a child matures, he begins to differentiate between the blots, and gives a different response to each card. He may continue to use the whole blot for his responses, despite the fact that only a part of the blot may fit the concept he is using at the time. Such responses are similar to the confabulatory responses of disturbed adults, whose reality testing is very tenuous. For example, the blot on Card VI may be "a cat." The child points out first the head and whiskers in

319

the upper D area; and then, if questioned, vaguely refers to the remainder of the blot as the rest of the animal. Such a response is found in the records of three and four year olds. As a child grows older he may still use confabulatory responses but he makes a greater effort to justify all the parts of the blot as parts of his concept. The cat of Card VI is given legs and may be "sitting" or "spread out on the floor." While such justification is not always as realistic as this example, the attempt shows the child's movement toward better reality testing.

By six years of age, the average child is usually able to give adequate form responses to most of his blots, and has begun to use some of the more obvious details for his concepts. For example, the blot on Card I, in addition to being a winged creature of some kind, may be broken down into the three large D's and seen as "two bears dragging somebody away." This attention to details suggests the emergence of an ability to deal with the practical aspects of his environment. The reader will find an interesting and much more detailed discussion of the psychological significance of these preschool age patterns in the *Developments in the Rorschach Technique,* Volume II, Chapter IV, by Klopfer and others.

Concomitant with this development of better form responses through the preschool years and the attempt to use the details of the blot, we see a gradual appearance of other determinants. Sometimes simultaneously, but usually one after another, movement, color and shading appear in the child's responses, suggesting a growing awareness of stimulation from within himself and an attempt to respond to the world and the people about him. In the case of movement responses, animal movement is the first type to appear. When "the bat" of Card I is "flying," or the "bears" on Card VIII are "climbing," we see the beginning of an awareness on the child's part of his instinctual drives. This type of response is common during the preschool years. By six years of age we can expect to find in addition to FM at least one human movement response in the average child's record. This suggests, as in the case of normal adults, that the child's instinctual forces are becoming ego-controlled and that he can make a more productive use of his fantasies. Inanimate movement responses which are rare in children's records are indicative of inner tension.

In the case of color responses, pure color is often found in the records of very young children, such as "sky" to blue areas or "fire" to the red areas, and indicate uncontrolled responses to environmental stimuli. As a child grows older vague form may be attached to the color response, as "a spot of blood" or "flowers" which suggest an attempt at control. The more mature use of form-determined color responses, like "red bow tie" to the center D of Card II, appears in the records of older or more mature children, who show a more conforming and controlled type of behavior than at the preschool level.

In this emergence of movement and/or color, we see the beginnings of the frame of reference in which the child's personality is developing. If color responses are the first to emerge or if the color areas of the cards are dealt with first and/or without regard to the rest of the blot, it would appear that his personality traits are developing in an extroversive, outgoing frame of reference. If, on the other hand, there are movement responses with no color used and/or the child is obviously avoiding the color areas, as was the case with Amy's early Rorschachs, the child would appear to be developing in an introversive, withdrawn frame of reference. The infrequent appearance of shading responses in the records of children suggests that there are a few children with an unusual sensitivity to their environment. Such records may warrant special investigation. If, however, a child by the age of five or six continues to give only whole responses and those determined by form alone, he is presenting a picture of immaturity and/or constriction with the possibility of emotional disturbance, especially if the form quality is unusually poor. We must then look to the content of the responses or to other information about the child, such as psychometric or historical data, to help explain the situation.

Getting a Rorschach record from a young child frequently involves considerable flexibility in administration. Much patience and ingenuity may be needed, but the rewards are more than worth the effort involved. One of the most frustrating aspects of the testing of young children is trying to get them to locate their responses. It is less exasperating to both child and tester if the inquiry follows each response in a preschool record. Even then there may be difficulty, since the child may think his concept is being challenged and react to this by changing his response, denying it, or becoming outright negativistic. Any of these reactions, however, may be of diagnostic value. As maturation continues and the child's responses, therefore, are more easily justified and located by him, he becomes increasingly better able to conform to the standardized procedure of administration. In fact, by the time he has made a good school adjustment, whether in kindergarten, first grade or later, there is rarely any need for more flexibility than with an adult in a similar testing situation.

In the scoring of a child's record, as in the administration of the test, one is sometimes tempted to be more flexible than with an adult record. This is not advisable, as it tends to give a distorted picture of the child's stage of development. For example, if the form quality of a response is poor it should be scored F minus, regardless of the tender age of the subject; and, if there is a confabulated or contaminated response, it should be recognized as such. These and other similar evaluations tell us a great deal about the thinking of a child and help us to estimate his maturity.

After the administration and scoring of the Rorschach, comes the intriguing task of interpretation. Here again, it is important to adhere to the standardized procedure, at the same time recognizing the fact that the record is that of a child of a given age. Before attempting to discuss this important aspect of the Rorschach test, I want to point out some of the more striking differences and likenesses between the Rorschach records of children and those of adults. The following observations are derived from the report of the normative findings of the original study * and indicate what can be expected in the Rorschach records of children at different ages, and how these expectations differ from adult records.

Rejections

The younger the child the more apt he is to reject at least one, if not more of the cards; and such a reaction can be used to estimate his degree of maturation. Around the age of seven years, however, rejections are so uncommon that they appear to have the same significance as adult rejections, and should be evaluated accordingly. For example, one might raise such questions as: Does the rejection suggest general negativism on the part of the child? Is it related to the stimulus from the card itself? or, Is the rejection a function of the general immaturity of the child?

Reaction Time

Significant discrepancies between the reaction times to color versus achromatic color cards, or an exaggerated reaction time to a specific

* *Rorschach Responses of Elementary School Children*, Nettie H. Ledwith, University of Pittsburgh Press, 1959.

card, may reflect some sort of affective disturbance that should be investigated further. Children, on the average, regardless of age, tend to respond to each of the Rorschach cards within approximately ten seconds after it is presented. Any significant increase in this reaction time should be evaluated in terms of the card or cards which elicited the delayed response. For example, an exaggerated reaction time to Card IV might suggest some problem in relation to authority figures; a significantly longer average reaction time to color cards, in contrast to achromatic color cards, would pose the problem of difficulty or hesitancy in handling interpersonal or environmental situations. A significantly short reaction time can be thought of in terms of impulsivity and/or other interpretative ideas applicable to adult records.

Number of Responses

There is a variation between the number of responses given by children and that given by adults. Very young children rarely give more than one response to a card. This number gradually increases with age so that, before twelve years of age, the number of responses in a child's record approximates the thirty responses considered optimal in an adult record. The standard interpretation in regard to the productivity of the child seems relevant here, as in the case of adult records. For example, overproductivity on the Rorschach cards suggests an attempt to appear more adequate than one really is, and is usually connected with anxious feelings of inadequacy or insecurity. Underproductivity, on the other hand, may stem from withdrawn, depressed, or even negativistic attitudes on the part of the child. Not only the quantity but the quality of the responses should be considered in making any interpretation in regard to the number of responses given.

Location Areas

The percentages of the different location areas, W, D, d + Dd + S, tend to differ in the children's records as compared to those of adults. The younger and less mature the child, the greater the tendency to give whole responses of an undifferentiated, perseverative quality. Detail responses, large and small, are uncommon among the very young children, but begin to appear in the records of the older preschoolers, increasing in quantity to the point of adult expectancy around eight or nine years of age. Unusual detail and space responses are rarely given by young children, and occur in the records of only a small percentage of children up to twelve years of age. When integration of the parts of the blots is attempted in a response, this is usually poorly achieved during the early years, but an adequate achievement of such integrated responses develops with age and maturity. The proportions of W, D, and d + Dd + S in a child's record can be expected to approximate the proportions expected in a normal adult record shortly before twelve years of age.

This gradual shift in the locations of a child's responses through the years, from 100% W at three and four years of age to a proportion that approximates an adult record of 25% W, 60% D, 15% d + Dd + S at the twelve year level, indicates a growth and maturity on the child's part in viewing the world about him and in handling the concrete problems which face him. From a diffused undifferentiated view of the world at three, when the child is still unable at times to tell reality from unreality, he gradually matures into a person who is able to face his practical problems without getting bogged down in details, and he also learns to profit from his experiences without having to make the same mistake twice.

Determinants

The variation between children and adults in the use of determinants—form, movement, shading and color—differs according to the determinant in question. As for *form* responses, it is important to note both the quantity and the quality in relation to the age of the child. Young children are apt to use form as a determinant for most of their responses, but the quality of the form is frequently poor. The quantity of form responses decreases and the quality increases through the preschool years so that by six years of age, we can expect to find about half of the child's responses determined by form —most of which is of average quality. As the child matures, this percentage, which approximates adult expectations, remains fairly stable; but the quality of the form improves with age. When, as is usually the case by twelve years of age, the good form responses thus approximate 50%, we see the reflection of healthy ego functioning, in which the demands of society and the needs of the child are being reconciled. When form is used in excess of this amount we see the same sort of stifling control noted in adult records high in F%. The cause for such constriction may be multidetermined, and can usually be found by studying other aspects of the record. It goes without saying that the high F% of the preschool child is due to the fact that he is in the process of ego construction and still lacks the ability to integrate the stimuli from his inner and outer worlds. Older children are reflecting in their high F% one or more such personality factors as repression, rigid compulsive defenses, severe or crippling anxiety, a lack of integration powers due to brain damage and the like.

The quality of the form reflects the quality of the intellectual control or adaptation to society. The higher the F+, the greater the reliance on ego control. F— responses, on the other hand, suggest poor ego control and indicate, particularly in a constricted record, breaks in reality contact. Form, when combined with other determinants, should also be evaluated in relation to its ego factors. The quality of the form in the F dominated responses indicates the quality of the control. For example an FC— response suggests that control has been attempted in the emotional area but it is defective. In a response where the F is subordinate, as in a CF response, lack of control is indicated.

The *movement* responses, M, FM and m in children's records, differ in quantity from those found in adult records, but appear to have the same general meaning. *Human movement* responses, which rarely appear in the records of preschoolers, begin to emerge at six years of age, at which time one such response can be expected. The use of this determinant gradually increases with the age of the child. An average of 3M at the twelve year level, seems to indicate that the instinctual forces, as in the case of normal adult records, are ego-controlled in such a way as to allow and encourage a productive use of the child's fantasies. If the form of such a response is minus in quality, there is the implication that fantasy has broken with reality, and bizarre behavior can be expected. If the human movement is ascribed to less than a whole human being or to an animal, there is indication of immature fantasy activity. In adult records, M in large quantities and of superior quality, is thought to mean superior ideational ability and productivity. It is important to evaluate the quality and location of such responses before making any interpretation. There have been a number of instances in my experience in which children of mediocre ability gave a large number of M's, which, carefully evaluated, seemed to be suggestive of a pseudomaturity relating to the child's attempt to identify with one or both parents in a conflictual marital situation.

Animal movement responses represent a less mature emotional level of functioning than human movement, and indicate that the instinctual promptings from within the individual are only partially controlled. These responses occur in the records of very young children, and they have a tendency to increase throughout the preadolescent period. The predominance of M over FM, as is the optimal ratio in an adult's record, is found only infrequently in the record of a child under twelve.

The use of *inanimate movement* is uncommon among children and, when such responses do occur in a child's record, they seem to be indicative of anxiety over some deep conflict that the child is trying to repress, but which keeps coming to the surface in a discomforting way.

Shading responses, K, c, C', are less common in the records of children than in adult records. KF, an indicator of confusion and diffuse anxiety, is used by many children around six years of age in such responses as "clouds," and "smoke," but tends to decrease in frequency after that age. FK and Fk, with implications of a mature introspective or intellectual approach to understanding one's inner feelings, is not used by young children, but can be expected in the records of a few older children. *Texture,* or c responses, which are associated with one's sensitivity to environmental and social situations, are seldom found in the records of children of six years or younger. Such responses become increasingly more common with age, but are not used by all children at any age. When such a response is dominated by form, this is an indication of tact in dealing with the environment. When form is subordinate, as in *cF* or *c,* there appears to be an awareness of emotional deprivation, and a desire to be loved and protected. An excessive use of the determinant suggests an emphasis on sensuality and its satisfaction at a more or less direct level.

Achromatic color responses, *C',* can be expected in the records of a few six-year-olds, but seem, in contrast to texture responses, to decrease from that age on through the years. Such responses in a child's record seem to reflect feelings of rejection or emotional deprivation, which frequently result in a depressive attitude of moodiness or sulking behavior.

Color responses, *C, CF,* and *FC,* are considered, as in the case of adult records, to be reflections of the child's emotional reactions to the environment. *Pure color,* or *C* responses, which represent the egocentric, impulsive reactions to environmental stimulation and thus indicate a lack in ego control, are more common in the records of very young children and gradually disappear by twelve years of age.

Such responses of "blood," "fire," "paint," and so forth have less pathological implications in the records of very young children than when found in adult records, in which case they indicate affect inappropriate and immature. Such affect is certainly more age-appropriate for the preschooler.

Color-form or *CF* responses are common in the records of children at all ages. They indicate a certain amount of the narcissism and aggression noted in the *C* responses, but this is controlled just enough for the child to cover up these feelings with more socially-acceptable behavior. *Form-color* responses, *FC,* appear in the records of certain children at all ages but do not show the increase with age that would be expected from the literature. This type of response suggests that emotionality, the aggression and egocentricity noted in the less controlled responses, *CF* and *C,* have been so controlled as to result in the child's thinking of the needs and desires of others, as well as of those of himself, and is thus an indicator of mature interpersonal relationships. A large amount of *FC,* without other less controlled color responses, however, can mean a complete lack of aggression, and/or an excessively passive child.

Rorschach Ratios

No attempt will be made to include here a discussion of all the ratios that can be used in evaluating an adult's record, since many of them seem to have little meaning in children's records. That the two ratios, $M < FM$ and $FC < CF + C$, found in the records of children under twelve years of age, are the reverse of adult expectancy is not surprising, since both of these ratios point to levels of adjustment in regard to an individual's inner and outer worlds that can be expected to be less adequate in children than in adults. Only the more mature children, like Amy, are able to harness their fantasy at high productive levels (and thus approximate the $M > FM$ ratio of adults) or to make their emotionality subservient to the needs of others, as shown in an $FC > CF + C$ ratio of a normal adult.

The *percentage of responses to the last three cards* is a ratio in children's records which shows consistency with adult expectancy—around 35%. Significantly lower or higher percentages suggest a variation in the strength of the emotional impact which the individual experiences from his environment.

Shock Reactions

Children show the same kinds of shock reactions to color and shading that are found among adults. A shock reaction to the color cards suggests a neurotic conflict, the source of which can usually be determined in other areas of the record. It is thought by some to indicate a disturbance of psychosexual development at the oedipal level, and such seemed to be the case with a number of children in my study. Shading shock, which appears to be a sign of discomfort and fear of one's own basic anxiety, the source of which is not always easy to pinpoint, seems to occur less frequently among children than does color shock.

Content

The kind and diversity of the content categories are, as with adults, indications on the one hand of the stereotypy of a child's thinking, as evidenced by a preponderance of *animal* content and little else; and on the other hand, his flexibility, as seen in a diversification of content categories. Pathognomic responses like "fire," "blood," "smoke," "paint," which seem to indicate blunted or inappropriate affect in an adult, are fairly common among very young children who have not yet learned to control their emotions. Before six years of age, such responses are not uncommon, but this kind of content is gradually replaced by animal content so that, around seven years of age, one can expect about 50% of the child's responses to be animal in content. This percentage remains fairly stable through the pre-adolescent years. As a general rule, one can expect more *animal* and less *human* content in a child's record than in that of an adult. The appearance and diversity of other content categories reflect, as in adult records, the extent or limits of the child's interests.

Popular Responses

A few responses other than those listed by Klopfer as adult populars, meet the criterion of one in three responses given by children. These "children's populars" change with increasing age, gradually approaching the adult populars. These adult populars are also seen by children, even the very young; and the number increases likewise with the age of the child. By twelve years of age, it is not uncommon for a child to give as many as five such responses. The absence or excess of popular responses reflects the degree of ease with which a child can adapt to the thinking of those about him. A detailed discussion of children's populars may be found in the author's *Rorschach Responses of Elementary School Children.*

Judging from the foregoing discussion of the more formal aspects of the Rorschach records of children, we need not be surprised at finding any or all of the Rorschach scoring categories and determinants in a child's record from eight years of age on. Although the locations, determinants, and content categories in children's records may be similar to those used by adults, the quantity and quality differ not only from that of adults but also differ among the children themselves according to maturity level, as well as other characteristics of each child.

Individuality as Expressed by the Rorschach Responses

While it is important to know what can be expected in the way of Rorschach responses from children as they mature from year to year, it is equally important to be aware of the fact that no child follows the norms as outlined above. Instead, he reflects in his records his own particular pattern of development, since each individual develops at his own speed, showing acceleration in one area, regression in another and even standing still at another point. When these differences in development are noted in a child and reflected in his Rorschach, he should be considered *not* as "deviant" but as an individual showing his individuality. This last statement cannot be emphasized too strongly, especially with the "norm-bound" beginning Rorschacher.

It is in this concept of the child as an individual unlike all other individuals that the more subjective aspects of the Rorschach come into play. Even though these subjective characteristics of the test responses are less definable and more elusive than the formal aspects described above, they, none the less, play a very important part in the interpretation of a record. For example, many facets of the testing situation itself seem to defy objective evaluation, but at the same time appear to influence the child's responses to the Rorschach cards. One such important factor in the testing situation is the person who administers the test. While it is a generally accepted fact that such characteristics of the examiner as sex, age, personality factors and attitude toward the child can influence the amount and kind of responses which the child gives, no way has been found to "standardize" examiners. Just as it is thus impossible to "standardize" the examiner, so it is with the child taking the test. His attitude toward being tested, some recent emotional trauma, even his current condition of physical health are among the many variables that may account in part for his performance on the test. Some of these elusive influences were partially offset in the longitudinal study of normally functioning children from which much of my knowledge of children's Rorschachs was acquired. Since each set of six yearly Rorschach protocols obtained from each of a large sample of normally functioning children was obtained by the same examiner under similar testing conditions, the resulting records tend to give a less distorted picture of each child's development than might have been the case under less standardized conditions. Even so, there were many extenuating circumstances that had to be evaluated as these records were interpreted. It is, therefore, extremely important that the clinician who interprets a Rorschach be aware of the variety of these and other more subtle variables that can influence a child's responses.

Knowledge of the importance of these subtle influences may frequently lead the examiner to vary his administration technique. A recent clinical experience well illustrates this point. A seven-year-old boy of superior intelligence whose mother, herself a disturbed person, had looked for signs of mental disturbance in the boy since his birth, had been exhibiting some bizarre behavior which was of great concern to mother. His initial reaction to the Rorschach cards was atypical to say the least; but, at the same time, seemed to have the flavor of pretense or superficiality. After the first card was responded to with bizarre concepts involving much verbal nonsense, he was given the following instructions: "Now tell me what you *really* see on this card." This was repeated with each card. The normal responses which usually followed such a request, when compared with much more bizarre and what seemed to be "superficial" responses given initially, provided further diagnostic meaning to this child's problem. It was obvious from this and other confirming evidence that the child was behaving as his mother expected him to behave; but, underneath this superficiality of emotional disturbance, lay a core of healthy reactions. That the reverse seems to occur occasionally is suggested by the seemingly healthy Rorschach protocols that are sometimes given by children with histories of emotional maladjustment. The clinician must be aware of such discrepancies and be prepared to account for them. Cues and clues for the explanation of such situations can be found sometimes in the Rorschach and sometimes in the additional psychological tests or historical data about the child. One must be constantly alert to such nuances, and make the Rorschach interpretation with the whole situation in mind.

Once the Rorschach has been administered and scored, with the clinician as alert as possible to the ways in which a variety of factors may have affected the protocol, how does he best proceed with the next step, that of interpretation? What does the interpreter look for in the Rorschach protocol, and how does he go about his search? A primary consideration in the interpretation of a Rorschach record is that of relating to the specific theory of personality to be used in integrating the Rorschach findings. The interpreters in this study, like the majority of clinicians who use the Rorschach in the field of child guidance, have made their interpretation in terms of the Freudian theory. They are primarily interested in the child's ego functioning—his ability to deal with anxiety, an evaluation of his reality testing, and the way in which he can integrate his experiences. On the other hand, there are many other clinicians whose interpretations may be based on one or more of the non-Freudian personality theories. If one is to give the most effective and meaningful interpretation to a record, however, the first important step is to choose some definite theoretical framework in which to operate. Of equal importance is the consistency with which the interpreter relates to the framework he has chosen. A review of the interpretation techniques described by each of five psychologists in the preceding chapter suggests that there is much agreement among these and other workers in the field as to what the Rorschach responses can be expected to yield. Any disagreement that may be present seems to be related to whether the Rorschach findings be considered absolute or relative, i.e., should the "blind" interpretation of the Rorschach be considered the final word on the personality evaluation of the child? It is my opinion that the Rorschach interpretation should be based primarily on the response to the Rorschach cards, but made in relation to the findings of the other psychological tests, with as much reference as possible to the behavior and background of the individual giving the responses.

One of the primary values of the Rorschach test is the variety of clues it offers for determining the dynamics of personality structure and development. The most obvious of these, or rather the clue usually sought initially, is information about the child's level of intellectual functioning. For example, we immediately look for answers in the Rorschach to such questions as: Is this a dull child striving to appear more adequate? Is this an intellectually average or even bright child bogged down in the mire of emotional maladjustment? Or is this a well-adjusted child approximating his potential level of functioning? Not only are the answers to these and other such questions frequently found in the Rorschach records, but there are oftentimes clues as to the whys and wherefores.

Such clues frequently lead to the emotional area of the child's life: to indicators of the anxiety level of the individual, to the sources of his anxiety, and to the way in which he is defending or trying to defend himself against these anxious feelings. No attempt will be made here to review the Rorschach sources of such indications, since they are well documented in Rorschach literature and referred to in the chapter on "Interpretation Techniques" in this book. Among the many other Rorschach clues already referred to in the same chapter are those that suggest the identification struggle of the child, his concept of himself as a person, and how he relates to other people in his environment.

Another important diagnostic factor of the Rorschach is the way in which the response reflects the behavioral and interpersonal dynamics of the individual. This has been demonstrated repeatedly in the personality pictures in the preceding chapters. Within the framework of these Rorschach reflections of personality development, the psychometric and historical data frequently acquire a sort of third dimension. This depth perceptive quality of the Rorschach tends to place in proper perspective the various bits of information about each child and, as a result, the reasons for the child's specific behavior are frequently better understood. For example, Amy's early and continued application of the "brakes" to her academic achievement appears in the Rorschach reflection to be related to her identification struggle between the two mother figures whom she saw as rivals. She sensed the difference in their values, and, because of a need to get along with the natural mother, Amy adopted her mother's values in regard to academic ambitions. Another example of this depth of perception is in relationship to Danny's struggle against feminine identification. With mother's obvious attempts to feminize him, and father's determination that this be averted, Danny's Rorschach protocols reflect his confused struggle against mother and his increasing warm relationship toward the father figure. Another instance in which the Rorschach gives a clearer picture of what is happening occurred when, in Patty's case, we saw through her overtly bland acceptance of parents' marital difficulties to the deep concern that this situation

held for her. Many similar examples of insight into the child's behavior could be cited among the Rorschach pictures that these and
other children present.

Pitfalls in Rorschach Interpretations

The Rorschach interpretations found in this book are made up
of inferences drawn from the clues discussed above, as well as from
many other clues inherent in the objective and subjective aspects of
individual records, without access to behavioral or historical data.
The fact that these interpretations were thus "blind," while giving
an added note of conviction in regard to the validity of such interpretative phenomena, also points up areas in which the clinician
might go astray in his interpretations. As was noted in the comments
of some of the "blind" interpretations, clinicians must constantly be
aware of certain pitfalls in interpretation, and allow leeway, particularly in predicting actual behavioral expectations for the children. An
example of the way in which a clinician can thus be led astray was
seen in Larry's Rorschachs, in which there appeared a number of
anatomical responses as he approached adolescence. That anatomical responses suggest bodily preoccupation and from that is deduced
psychosomatic symptoms is frequently an apt interpretation. In Larry's case, however, historical data and human figure drawings indicated that the bodily preoccupation was an attempt to cover up
a sexual preoccupation that was evidently related to his feelings
about women, and was also a factor in his inability to progress into
a heterosexual stage of development.

Other pitfalls obvious to the experienced clinician are the face
value or atomistic evaluations of the objective aspects of the Rorschach responses. For example, a significant increase in the number
of responses does not always mean an increase in productivity. An
evaluation of the responses can point to such changes as an increase
in anxiety reflected in this pseudo-productivity. As a result of the
anxiety factor, this increase in responses could mean an actual decrease in the individual's constructive use of his resources. For this
reason, the interpreter must continually keep in mind the global approach to the evaluation of a Rorschach record. One or even more
seemingly pathological responses do *not* make a schizophrenic, nor
do a few healthy responses counter-indicate a disturbed personality.
Before any interpretation is made, therefore, there should be several
lines of inference leading to this interpretation; and these lines should

start from a variety of sources, such as content, scores, test attitudes and behavior, as well as from their interrelationships. As a last cautionary measure, it is always well if the final interpretation of the Rorschach is based on the combined results of many threads of inference, drawn from each of a battery of tests, as well as from historical material.

Values in Serial Rorschachs

Just as the Rorschach responses of a child add depth to the understanding of his personality traits, so does the series of yearly Rorschachs add breadth to this understanding. For example, to the clinician oriented in the psychoanalytic theory of personality development, these serial Rorschachs are especially rewarding in the study of psychosexual development. The various stages—oral, anal, genital and oedipal—encountered among the children in the longitudinal study were illustrated among the records presented in the previous chapters. In such a study, involving a large number of children over a long period of time, there was the added confirmation that the residuals of early stages of psychosexual development are normally carried over to some extent to the next stage, and even appear with some frequency at a much later stage in the child's development. This is illustrated in the behavior of a child who, under stress, may suddenly regress to a psychosexual level far below his normal functioning. For example, there is Anna who, at six years of age, gave responses that showed considerable regression, with a schizoid trend. This record might have been considered the product of a dull or very disturbed child. However, there were reflections in this record of the cause for this regression—a traumatic incident involving mother's tragic death. It is important to note also that later Rorschachs revealed the potentials for better functioning that were not so clear in the first record; and, still more important, there were definite signs of Anna's ability to recover and to approximate her potential level of functioning.

Another real value of serial Rorschachs is the fact that, in this way, one can see how from year to year transient impacts from the environment, whether benign or traumatic, work certain changes in a child's behavior and attitudes; and how, in most instances, the child in question seems to return eventually to his more or less basic personality pattern of functioning observed in the very first record. In fact, throughout the six records of each child in the study, one not only notes these personality traits growing deeper, but also observes them spreading out into different areas of the child's behavior.

This phenomenon is particularly apparent in the consecutive records of Amy, whose insight into her own basic introversive personality pattern causes her to attempt to change it. This has been done only to the extent that she has developed an overlay of extroversiveness, which makes it easier for her to function socially, but which has not changed her basic personality pattern.

It should be pointed out that these basic personality patterns do not in themselves constitute the normal, neurotic, or psychotic reaction which the child eventually develops in relation to his life situations. Above and below this basic pattern, there are many overtones and undertones or variations of the theme which seem to embellish the child's growth process. In many children these variations are normal reactions to life situations; in some they may take on a neurotic tone; and, in a few, they may conceivably produce the discord of psychosis.

Such an observation raises certain questions that seem pertinent to therapeutic intervention when applied to emotionally disturbed children. It seems reasonable to assume that therapy can alter the neurotic and even psychotic variations to the extent that they are more harmonious; but what about the basic personality theme? Is the answer to this question inherent in determining the time at which the child's personality pattern is set? The Rorschach findings of this study suggest that the personality pattern is rather clearly formed by age six. In other words, the main theme has been determined by the time the child starts to school. Is it possible that such a pattern or theme has been established at an earlier stage of the child's life? Answers to this and similar questions help to determine the part that therapy can play in the developing of a more harmonious personality symphony in the lives of disturbed children.

Such answers have implications for the time of initiation, the quality, the quantity and the duration of any therapeutic intervention that may be needed in effecting a permanent change in a child's basic personality structure. The results of the study from which these impressions have been formed suggest that the earlier, the stronger, and the more continuous the therapeutic impact, the more effective such an intervention can be in working the desired change. An opportunity for validating such subjective impressions concerning the outcome of therapy is offered in settings like a child guidance clinic. It has been frequently noted in such settings that the changes in a child's functioning effected by therapy, are reflected in the periodic changes in the Rorschach records of these children. Unfortunately, there have been no studies to determine what part maturation plays in these changes or how permanent these effects of therapy may be. The need for such an investigation in regard to the lasting effects of therapy is only one of the many avenues of further research that have become increasingly clear to me in my search for more knowledge about children's Rorschachs—a sort of confirmation of the fact that the more one learns about a subject the more one is aware of the additional information that is necessary for a fuller understanding of that subject.

There are many inviting research paths other than the one just referred to that offer fascinating possibilities for using the Rorschach as a tool in learning more about the personality development of children. This is neither the time nor the place to attempt to describe such research possibilities, but the reader no doubt has begun to formulate many ideas of his own as he followed the personality development of the different types of children in the early pages of the book. In addition to the ideas that seem so obviously to need the clarification that can come only through research, and perhaps as an emphasis upon some of these ideas, I would like to stress the need for more knowledge about the healthy aspects of the personality of children. Let us search for the strengths that help children overcome what at times appear to be unsurmountable obstacles; find out how these strengths can be used to the best advantages in child rearing; and determine how, in the case of an emotionally disturbed child, such strengths as he may have, can be best used in helping him to deal with this disturbance. In this way, the healthy factors of personality development can be given a proper emphasis without ignoring the pathological, but certainly without the morbid preoccupation with such factors that sometimes occur among workers in the mental health field. The Rorschach test can be an effective tool in such a study.